The artist painted this picture to show his ideas about
the future of the earth. Read this book; then paint
a picture of what you think the earth will be like

From a painting by Herbert Paus

PATHWAYS · IN · SCIENCE · VI
A COURSE FOR ELEMENTARY SCHOOLS

Our Earth and Its Story

By GERALD S. CRAIG

Assistant Professor of Natural Sciences
Teachers College, Columbia University

and GOLDIE M. JOHNSON

Supervisor of Elementary Science
Montclair, New Jersey

GINN AND COMPANY

BOSTON · NEW YORK · CHICAGO · LONDON · ATLANTA · DALLAS · COLUMBUS · SAN FRANCISCO

𝕿𝖍𝖊 𝕬𝖙𝖍𝖊𝖓𝖆𝖚𝖒 𝕻𝖗𝖊𝖘𝖘

GINN AND COMPANY · PRO-
PRIETORS · BOSTON · U.S.A.

Preface

If we are to apply the scientific attitudes and methods of science to our social, economic, and political problems of tomorrow, we must develop, in the elementary school, a generation conversant with these scientific attitudes and methods. We shall fall short of our possibilities if we do not give children an opportunity to understand the fundamental concepts and principles of science. It is through the children in our elementary schools that we shall be able to apply the scientific attitudes and methods to the gigantic problems of civilization. In this direction the elementary school has an opportunity to make a contribution to education and to society.

With these problems in mind, "Our Earth and Its Story" has been designed to assist the child in orienting himself intelligently with respect to the universe about him and to give him an acquaintance with certain of the basic principles and concepts of science. Thus, the book is intended for the children who will have opportunity to extend their study of science, as well as those who are forced to withdraw from school at an early age.

The child is given an opportunity to relate himself to both time and space through a series of problems portraying some of the principal events in the earth's history. He gains an appreciation of the antiquity of the earth, the endless grind of universal forces, and man's own struggle with physical and biological environment, with the subsequent defeats and triumphs.

The story begins with the formation of the earth, develops throughout the long past, and closes with the present day. The book aims to make boys and girls conscious of their own part in the future of the world and challenges them to an appreciation of scientific attitudes. It may be considered as basic to the study of both the natural and the social sciences of the secondary and collegiate levels.

"Our Earth and Its Story" is the last book in the series of Pathways in Science. The unit utilizes the concepts and meanings developed in previous books and gives them further development. The content and plan of all the books are based upon intensive studies of elementary science made by the authors. These studies [1] involved an analysis of children's interests in science, educated laymen's needs in science, and present practices in the elementary schools, and an exploration of the various fields of science in search of challenging themes appropriate to the elementary school. The authors were able to have their material tried out in various schools; the activities and experiences of the teachers and of the boys and girls coöperating are reflected helpfully in the resulting book.

The vocabulary of the text has been checked throughout by the use of the Buckingham-Dolch Word List.

[1] Certain Techniques Used in Developing a Course of Study in Science for the Horace Mann Elementary School. Bureau of Publications, Teachers College, Columbia University, New York City, 1927.

Whenever over-grade words are needed for the enrichment of the science vocabulary of the children, they are carefully explained.

The text conforms to the recommendations and the spirit of the Thirty-first Yearbook, Part I, of the National Society for the Study of Education and the requirements of recent state and city courses of study in elementary science.

A manual for teachers accompanies this text. It will be found most valuable in guiding teachers in the presentation of the units. Additional activities are provided to enrich the content, and a bibliography is available to assist the teacher in building up a professional background in science.

The authors wish to acknowledge their indebtedness to Dr. B. R. Buckingham and the members of the editorial and art departments of Ginn and Company for their coöperation in the preparation of this book.

They wish also to express their appreciation of help received from the following sources in securing illustrations:

Field Museum of Natural History for the privilege of reproducing a number of fine paintings of prehistoric times, by Charles R. Knight, which were donated to the museum by Ernest R. Graham.

The Director of the Science Museum in London for the series of illustrations on the development of transportation.

Metropolitan Museum of Art, American Museum of Natural History, Los Angeles Museum of History, Science, and Art, Detroit Institute of Art, Walker Museum, Amherst College, Mount Wilson Observatory, Lick Observatory, Harvard College Observatory, Lowell Observatory, New York Central Railroad, United States National Museum, United States Biological Survey, United States Geological Survey, United States Weather Bureau, United States Forest Service, United States Bureau of Mines, United States Army Air Corps.

G. S. C.
G. M. J.

Contents

Contents

OUR EARTH AND ITS STORY

You have read many times about the lives of great men and women. You have learned where and when they were born, what they did when they were children, and something about the adventures they had when they grew up.

The earth too has a story. There was a time when there was no earth. When it was born, it was probably smaller than it is now. As it became older, it had many adventures and changed a great deal. Great rivers and oceans appeared on it, and great wrinkles called mountains. It shook and quaked. It spouted forth streams of melted rock.

Perhaps the greatest event was the coming of life, and especially of man. No story of the earth is complete without an account of man. Man alone of all the living things of the earth is interested in studying about things on the earth and in the sky and in finding their secrets.

This book will tell you about the earth and its story. The story of your favorite hero began with his birth and ended with his death. Perhaps he lived to be sixty, seventy, or a hundred years old. But the story of the earth covers millions of years. Millions of creatures have lived and died, races of men have come and gone, even mountain systems have been made and worn down to level plains. The story of these things is the story of the earth. We hope you will find pleasure in reading it.

UNIT I
Wonders of the Sky

1. What the Ancient People thought about the Stars
2. What is beyond Our Solar System

Have you ever watched the stars on a clear night? Have you ever thought that boys and girls watched those same stars one, two, or even three thousand years ago?

The ancient people were so much interested in the stars that they studied them as well as they could, even though they had no instruments. The stars told them many things that they needed to know. By watching the stars they knew when the seasons would change. The Egyptians learned from the stars when the Nile would overflow its banks. People used the sun to tell the time of day and the stars to guide them in their travels at night.

Since the stars could help them in so many ways, men began to believe that the stars could do many other things for them. They even thought that the stars could foretell wars, the rise and fall of nations, and the deaths of emperors and kings. If a certain event took place again and again when the stars were in a certain position, the ancient people believed that the event was influenced by the stars. In this way many stories, or legends, grew up about the stars.

And then, years afterwards, the telescope was invented. Man's ideas about the stars began to change. Read Unit I to find out the difference between what the ancient people thought about the stars and what we think about them now.

Problem 1 · What the Ancient People thought about the Stars

1. The Study of Stars began Long Ago

Many years ago the ancient people looked up into the sky and saw wonderful things. These early people saw the sun as it "came up" in the east in the morning. They watched it as it seemed to travel across the sky during the day. The day grew hotter when the sun was overhead. In the evening the sun disappeared below the horizon in the west, and the daylight faded as the blue of the sky changed to crimson, purple, and gold. Shepherds and priests watched the stars as they came out slowly, one by one. They watched and wondered.

What were these tiny jewels that flickered in the sky? What was the moon that it could not outshine the sun? What made either of them shine? And the biggest question of all was Where did they go when they could no longer be seen? Did they really sink into the ocean?

Alone on the hillsides the early shepherds watched their flocks during nights that were usually clear and cloudless. There was no one with whom they could talk. There was nothing but blackness all around; only the stars sent down a friendly greeting.

The days were so hot in most of the desert countries that traveling in the daytime was almost impossible. People traveled during the evening and the night be-

During the long nights while they were protecting their sheep, the shepherds watched the stars

cause it was cooler. Great caravans of Arabs passed slowly and silently over the desert. During the long hours of the night these ancients watched the ever-present stars; as they traveled onward, the stars seemed to move along beside them; when they rested, the stars seemed to stop and shine over them.

At a very early date travelers learned to use the

stars as guides. The moon and the stars gave them their only light. Certain stars, such as the North Star, pointed out their way. Is it any wonder that these people were so interested in the tiny lights coming to them from so far away?

None of these people really knew much about the stars, and no one could tell them because there was no one who knew. They could not find out either by talking to other people or by reading books, because no one at that time knew any more about the stars than they did. They had no telescopes or other instruments to help them. There was no place where they could find the answers to their questions. Therefore they made up their own answers.

2. Some of the Stories Ancient People Told

With the sky as a ceiling these ancient people imagined pictures in the sky. Arabs, Greeks, and American Indians saw there animals, giants, and heroes. They liked to lie and watch a group of stars and fancy that they saw a giant with arms and legs and a sword. Then, when they had made a whole picture, they thought there really should be a story about this new hero, and they made up a story about him. That is how we got many of our legends.

Isn't it interesting to know that the shepherds and the Indians, with oceans and lands between them, had the same name for one group of stars? This was the Great Bear, in the north. It is the group that we think looks most like a big dipper, and that is what we call it. It may be seen on any clear night.

There are many stories about the Great Bear. Almost every group of early peoples had such a story. In those times people worshiped many gods, who, they believed, ruled the heavens, the sea, and the earth. The Romans told a story to explain why they could see two bears in the sky.

Callisto was such a beautiful woman that the goddess Juno became jealous of her. To get rid of Callisto, Juno changed her into a bear. One day a young man who was out hunting saw her. She recognized him as her son, Arcas. Callisto forgot that she was a bear and that her own son would not know her. She went toward him, and in his fright he raised his spear; but Jupiter, the ruler of the gods, stopped him and changed him into a bear. Then he hurled both bears by their tails up into the sky, where nothing could harm them. But when he threw them into the sky, their tails were stretched, and that is why the Great Bear and the Little Bear have long tails.

The Indians tell another story. A number of Iroquois Indian hunters were chasing a bear. They were just ready to kill him when three huge giants appeared. The giants began fighting the Indians and killed all but three. They would probably have killed all the Indians, but suddenly these three hunters and the bear were picked up and thrown into the sky. They can be seen in the north now, where the Indians say the three stars in the bear's tail are the three hunters still chasing the bear.

This picture shows how the Greeks thought Apollo looked as he drove his sun chariot across the sky

There is a myth that tells us what the early Greeks thought about the sun. This story says that the sun was a chariot of fire drawn by very swift horses. The Greek god Apollo drove this chariot of fire through the sky each day from east to west. When Apollo drove the horses too close to the earth, there were very hot days. But sometimes he did not come very near, and then the days were cold.

Other groups of people were puzzled about the Milky Way. The Chinese thought it was a river. Certain tribes of Indians said that it was the dust kicked up by a buffalo and a horse as they raced across the sky.

E

Grandparents probably told these stories to their grandchildren as they all sat around the fires at night. They were interesting stories, and as these children grew up, they in turn told the stories to their grandchildren.

These myths, or stories, were told over and over again. Each time a story was told it was changed a little. The people who repeated the story could not remember it just as it was told to them, and so they told it a little differently. After a while, when these stories had been told over and over again, people began to believe that they were true. Later, when these ancient people learned to write, they wrote about some of these myths in books. In this way these myths have been kept until the present time, and although we do not believe them, we enjoy reading stories that were told by people who lived thousands of years ago.

There were men who were not satisfied with these fables. They could not believe that they were true, and they began to search for the facts. These were men who were willing to give up their old ideas and accept new ones. They had to watch and talk and experiment, just as we do today. These men had very few things to help them. Often they made mistakes and had to correct them. But people have never given up, and they are still searching for the truths about the world.

At one time people thought that a giant called Atlas held up the earth. They thought that the earth was larger than the sun. Then, again, they decided that the earth was the center of the universe and that the sun, moon, and all the stars revolved around it.

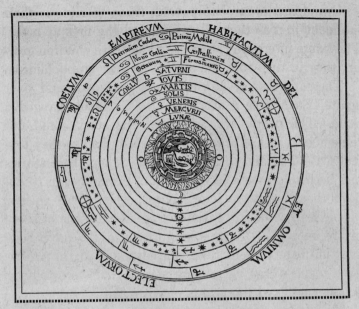

Many, many years ago this drawing was made to show how people thought the sun, planets, and stars revolved about the earth. Can you find which words mean Mercury, Venus, Sun, and Saturn?

Even at the time of Columbus most people were positive that the earth was flat, and that if anyone dared to sail very far into the ocean, he would come to the edge and fall off the earth. They were not convinced that they were wrong, even when Columbus succeeded in his voyages to America. Later, men sailed around the globe, and gradually people began to believe that the earth was round. All this time men were making mistakes, but they were learning and discovering new facts. They have changed their beliefs many, many times.

Men watched the stars with simple instruments that

Galileo was a great discoverer. With his little telescope
he discovered that the planet Jupiter had moons and
that our moon was covered by mountains and valleys

they had made. Galileo, in 1609, was one of the first
to use the telescope in discovering new facts about objects in the sky. As time went on, better instruments
were developed, and men began making careful studies
of the stars.

Scientists have had special instruments for observing
objects in the sky only a few hundred years, yet they

With great telescopes, men who study the stars today are able to
see distant groups of stars which Galileo probably never dreamed of

Courtesy of Mt. Wilson Observatory

have learned many interesting facts. Their explanations have not always proved as satisfactory as they
hoped them to be, but they have continued to work
until they have discovered many things that are true
and satisfactory. They know that the planets with their
moons revolve about the sun and make our solar system.
They have also looked far out beyond this solar system.

think it is very hot. At the seashore it is sometimes 125° F. on the sand, and the sand burns us. Boiling water has a temperature of 212° F., and nobody wants to put his hands in boiling water. But none of these temperatures are anywhere near the temperatures of the stars.

There are higher temperatures that you know about. Has the oven of your gas stove at home a regulator? On some stoves you can move the regulator until it points to 550. That means that the oven would then be heated until its temperature was about 550° F. A gas flame in the stove could have a temperature of about 1000° F., yet that is not hot in comparison with some of the temperatures of the stars.

The sun is a yellow star, and the temperature at its surface is about 11,000° F. That is very hot. Most substances would melt before they became that hot. But the inside of the sun is still hotter. Its temperature is many millions of degrees at the center. Yet the sun is only an average star in temperature and size.

Some stars are larger and some are smaller than the sun. The sun is hotter than some stars and not so hot as others. It gives off heat and shines by its own light.

Stars give off heat and light in all directions. They send much of their light and heat out into space. Some of it reaches the earth, some of it reaches other planets and other stars, and a great part of it never reaches any object. On our very hottest days we think that most of the light and heat of the sun must be reaching the earth, but really we receive only a very small amount of it.

This photograph of part of the sun shows streamers of hot gases shooting out thousands of miles from the sun's surface

Photograph by the Lick Observatory

The sun is a million times larger than the earth. If you could put a thousand times a thousand earths together, they would equal the size of the sun. And yet we learned that the sun was only an average star in size. That means that many stars are larger than it is. One of the stars that we sometimes see in the sky is 27 million times as large as our star, the sun. Let us see: if we should put 27, times a thousand, times a thousand of our suns together, we should have a star the size of this star.

The sun looks much larger than the other stars because it is so much closer to the earth. Stars look small because they are very far away. Some of the largest stars appear to be the smallest because of their great distance from us. As you look at some boy or girl near you, he looks large. Watch him as he goes down the street. Doesn't he seem to become smaller? Have you ever looked down a street at night and seen the electric lights? Which ones looked the dimmest? Those farthest away seem to give off less light because of their distance from you. At night a candle held in your hand would give more light around you than an electric light a block away. Now light a candle in a room with an electric light and compare them. The electric light by which you read is many times as bright as the candle. Some very large and bright stars seem dim because they are millions and millions of times farther from us than the sun.

Light coming to us travels very rapidly. It travels about 186,000 miles a second. That means that light travels almost as far as seven and one half times around the earth while you wink an eye. Our fastest way of traveling is by airplane. Suppose that an airplane travels 150 miles an hour, that it can refuel in space, and that it does not need to stop for repairs; it would take this airplane almost two months to travel as far as light travels while you snap your fingers. Light travels millions and millions of miles in one year. The distance which light travels in a year is called a light year.

Light comes from the sun to the earth in about eight minutes. It takes light four years to come from the next nearest star. Four years is a long time when com-

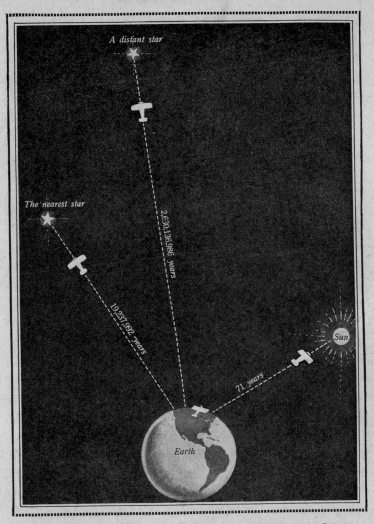

A distant star

The nearest star

2,630,136,986 years

19,237,992 years

Sun

71 years

Earth

This drawing shows how long it would take an airplane, flying at 150 miles an hour, to travel to the sun and some of the stars

pared with the eight minutes that it takes light to come from the sun. When you remember that the sun is 93,000,000 miles away from the earth, you can begin to realize how far away the next star is. Can you find out how far that star is from us if it takes its light four years to reach the earth?

The light that we see coming from some of our stars left those stars about the time that Columbus came to America. Other light that we see started from other stars thousands of years ago, possibly when the cave men lived on the earth. Other stars are so far away that it takes their light millions of years to reach the earth.

It is thought that there are thousands of millions of stars in the sky. Astronomers, who study the stars, are unable to see all of them even with their telescopes. We can see only about two thousand with our unaided eye. Some of these stars, like our sun, may have planets.

There are some objects that we can see in the sky that are not stars. These are the planets belonging to our sun. They look somewhat like stars. Many people see them and think that they are stars. They are really very different. They do not seem to twinkle as the stars do, and they do not stay in a group. They seem to move from one group of stars to another. You have to watch them for several weeks before you can notice that they have moved. They travel in fixed paths. They all go around the sun.

Stars shine by their own light. Planets do not shine by their own light; but they shine because the sun

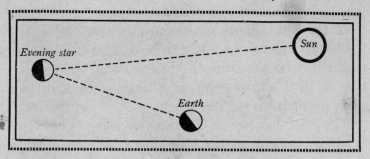

How the sun's light is reflected from certain planets so
that we can see them from the night side of the earth

shines on them, and they reflect the light of the
sun. You have seen light reflected by lakes and mir-
rors. Light is reflected from the planets in much the
same way.

Often in the evening we say we see a bright star in
the west after sunset. Usually it is a planet. We cannot
see all the planets with the unaided eye. Some are so
far away that we need telescopes to see them.

For a long time scientists have said that there are
eight planets. Recently a ninth planet has been discovered. Scientists think that there may even be other
planets that have not yet been discovered. Some
planets have moons that revolve around them. The sun,
the planets, and their moons are all part of the solar
system. It is the "sun" system. The sun is the center
of the solar system, and the planets with their moons
revolve around the sun. There are many things to
learn about the solar system. There may be many other
solar systems beyond ours.

This is a part of the Milky Way. The white streak is made of many stars, so close together that you cannot see through them. Our solar system is a part of the Milky Way galaxy

Photograph by Harvard College Observatory

2. The Milky Way

We have always been thrilled by that broad, white streak across the sky that we call the Milky Way. We have heard the story that a milkmaid spilled her bucket of milk across the sky, but of course we know that is not true. Scientists tell us now that the Milky Way is a part of a system of stars which is called a galaxy.

This galaxy is about the shape of a watch or a gingersnap (round and nearly flat). It is so large that it contains millions and millions of stars. These stars are many light years away from one another. We cannot see all of the stars that form our galaxy. When a telescope is used, millions more can be seen, and there is every reason to believe that there are millions of stars too dim to be seen even with a telescope.

Our sun is one of the stars in this galaxy. All the planets of the solar system travel around the sun without ever getting near the outside of the Milky Way. Our solar system is thought to be about one third of the distance from the center to the outside of the galaxy. When we look up at the Milky Way, we are looking through the thickest part of the cooky. It is so thick, and we see so many stars, that they form a white streak. When we look out through the sides, we are looking through the thinnest part, and we see fewer stars. They are not thick enough to make that part of the sky look white.

A few of the objects that we see when we look out through the side of this gingersnap mass are not in the galaxy at all. They are not even single stars, but are great systems of stars far beyond our galaxy. They are so far away that whole groups of stars look like one star.

The Milky Way is only a part of our galaxy, or system of stars. There are clusters of stars within our system. These have many different shapes and forms. If we look through a telescope, we can see one cluster in the group of stars called Hercules. Without a telescope this cluster looks just like a star.

There are certain groups of stars in the sky which are called constellations. Almost all the stars in these groups are also in our galaxy. It happens that when we look at certain parts of the sky without the telescope, there are stars which appear to be close together. They are really millions and millions of miles apart, but they are so far away from *us* that we cannot see how far away they are from one another. Constellations of stars are the groups which the ancient people knew and studied. Great clusters of stars have been known only since astronomers have been using telescopes.

There are certain constellations that we can see on any clear night during the year. These constellations are the ones that are near the North Star. Since the north pole of the earth points to the North Star, that star and the stars around it may always be seen on clear nights by people north of the equator. There is another group of stars that can be seen only by people living south of the equator. Can you find the North Star? Now can you find the Big Dipper? The Big Dipper is one of the constellations that we can see the whole year round. The two stars on the side of the Dipper opposite the handle are called the pointers. If a straight line is drawn through the pointers, it points to the North Star or polestar. That is an easy way to find the polestar.

The Dipper does not look very large, does it? But if you could start to travel across the Dipper in a very fast train, you could not live long enough to reach the opposite side. It is too far to cross in one lifetime. There was a story once told of a giant that was large

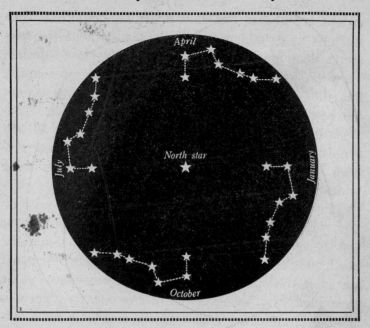

If you watch the Big Dipper at the same time every night for a year, you will find that it seems to change its position in the sky

enough to drink out of the Big Dipper. He was so large that the soles of his shoes were over twenty miles thick.

When the earth moves around the sun during the year, the Big Dipper seems to move around the North Star, but it does not really do this. It seems to because of the movement of the earth, which causes us to see the Dipper from different angles. Therefore in the four seasons of the year we see the Dipper in different parts of the sky if we look at it at the same time each night.

E

Cassiopeia's Chair is another constellation that may be seen during the entire year. Do you know the Greek myth about Cassiopeia? Can you find Cassiopeia's Chair on the side of the North Star that is opposite the Big Dipper? It looks like a big W or M in the sky.

As the earth moves about the sun, different parts of the sky can be seen. Only the stars near the North Star can be seen all the time, and even they are not always in the same position.

You have learned about the constellation of the mighty hunter Orion, which is in the southern part of the sky during the winter months. Sirius, Orion's greater dog, seems to be the largest star in the sky. Procyon, the smaller dog, follows closely at the heels of Orion.

A little to the west of Orion you may find a small group of six stars very close together. This group is called the Pleiades or the Seven Sisters. One of the sisters cannot now be seen without a telescope. There are several myths that tell what has become of the "lost" star.

All these last groups of stars, or constellations, that we have been learning about may first be seen in late autumn in the southeast, then they are seen gradually farther and farther in the west, until in the late spring you cannot see them in the early part of the evening.

In April the Sickle has taken Orion's place in the east. Cygnus, often called the Swan or Northern Cross, is in the north. As the earth revolves, other constellations may be seen.

Things to Think About

1. When an object passes in front of a shining body, it throws a shadow. You have watched your own shadow as you walked away from an electric light. You have seen many other shadows. Now, as the sun shines upon the moon and the earth, it causes these two bodies to throw shadows all the time. Once in a while, as the moon revolves about the earth and the earth revolves about the sun, the moon gets into the earth's shadow or the earth gets into the moon's shadow. This causes an eclipse.

As the moon moves into the earth's shadow, the light from the sun cannot reach the moon because the earth shuts off the light. The moon can be seen only when it reflects light from the sun. Therefore it does not give a reflection when it is in the earth's shadow. At this time you cannot see the moon, and there is a total eclipse of the moon. This is called a total lunar eclipse. Once in a while the moon goes only partly into the earth's shadow. Then there is a partial lunar eclipse. The moon does not follow the same path around the earth in each revolution, and it seldom gets into the earth's shadow. Sometimes it is just above it; at other times it is just below it. Therefore there is not a lunar eclipse every month.

The earth, at times, passes into the moon's shadow, which shuts out the light of the sun. Then you cannot see the sun, and there is an eclipse which is called a solar eclipse. The moon's shadow is so small that a total eclipse of the sun is seen over only a small part of the earth. A total solar eclipse does not occur very often.

See if you can find out when the last solar eclipse occurred. When will the next solar eclipse occur? When will there be a lunar eclipse?

2. Why can you see certain constellations on a summer evening and others on a winter evening?

3. Why can you see the Big Dipper the year round?

4. What would happen to everything on the earth if we received all the light and heat that radiates from the sun?

 *Things to Do*

1. If it takes 1000 years for the light of a star to reach the earth, can you find out how far away it is?

2. Make a chart showing how long it would take an aviator, making a nonstop flight, to go to some of the nearest stars.

3. Make a star map and use it to see how many constellations you can find in the sky.

4. Drop a hundred peas or marbles, one at a time, just a second apart, into a pan. How long did it take you? If you dropped a million peas into the pan in this way, it would take you 11.5 days. If you dropped a thousand million peas, it would take you nearly 32 years. How long would it take if you dropped a pea for every star?

UNIT II

Birth of the Solar System

1. What may have happened to the Sun
2. How the Solar System came to Be

Men have always wondered how the earth was made. Since no man was present at that time, they have enjoyed imagining how it was formed. Perhaps you have read how the Indians, Greeks, and Chinese made stories of the earth. Some of these are very interesting, but we know they are not true.

By studying the earth and the stars, what they are made of and how they move, some scientists attempt to explain how the solar system, of which the earth is a part, was made. Sometimes an explanation seems to be all right for a time, but later scientists may find it is not entirely satisfactory. They are always willing to accept a new explanation when it proves to be a better one.

In Problem 1 you will read about some recent explanations. Perhaps sometime you will read about explanations or theories that may be developed in years to come, which may prove to be better than those given in this book. In Problem 2 you will read how planets and other bodies have been formed.

Problem 1 · What may have happened to the Sun

1. A Strange Star passed Our Sun

All stars are moving. They are moving very rapidly ; some in one direction, some in another. We cannot see them move because they are so far away. Our sun is a star, and it is moving through space as all the other stars are moving. These stars have probably moved in this way for millions of years.

Some scientists think that once, millions and millions of years ago, while all the stars were moving along, two of them were drawing closer and closer to each other. One of these stars was our sun. Both the other star and our sun were moving rapidly. In the beginning they were far apart. As thousands and thousands of years passed, our sun and the other star drew nearer together.

At first the star did not have much effect upon our sun. But as they moved rapidly toward each other, century after century, the force of gravitation became greater and greater. It was like a huge tug of war between our sun and the star. While this great pull was going on between them, each was rotating rapidly on its own axis. Great quantities of the sun's fiery-looking gases began rolling and tumbling. Tides of gases were formed which moved like mountains across its surface.

Had you been somewhere near, looking on at this unusual event, you would probably have seen two suns

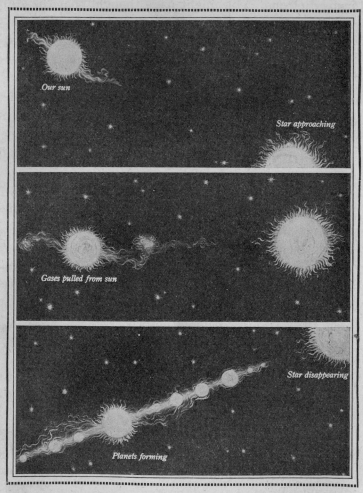

According to one theory a star passed our sun, millions of years ago

instead of one. You might have thought that the stars would crash together, but scientists tell us that they only came very near each other. As the two stars approached, one pulled with such force upon the other (our sun) that it is thought our sun became almost pear-shaped. Great quantities of gases were pulled from it. Then as both stars continued on their ways, some of these gases were pulled back into our sun. Other quantities of gases were left whirling on in new paths of their own.

We see the star that is our sun nearly every day. The other star went on its way. It is probably somewhere in the universe today, but we should not recognize it even if we saw it. This is not the only theory to explain how these gases came from the sun. We shall now learn about another one. Problem 2 will then tell you how these gases changed into planets.

2. A Star Exploded

Some scientists have not been satisfied with the first explanation, or theory, of the way in which the solar system was formed. These scientists think that it did not happen in that way. They believe that a star exploded. This theory may explain many things that all other theories do not, and may prove to be the best explanation.

This theory begins with a star, part of which later became our sun. This star was a glowing mass of gases. Like other stars, it had a temperature of many thou-

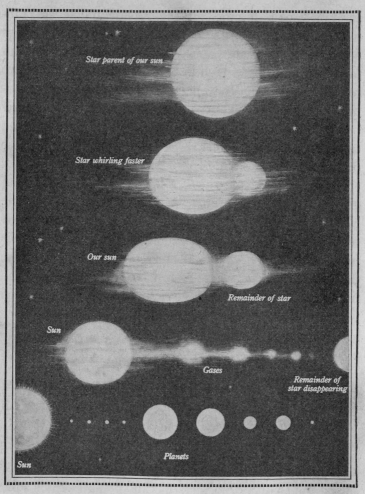

Star parent of our sun

Star whirling faster

Our sun

Remainder of star

Sun

Gases

Remainder of star disappearing

Sun

Planets

According to a second theory the sun was at one time much larger than it is now. Read how a part of the sun was lost and how the earth and other planets were formed

sand degrees Fahrenheit on the outside and several million degrees toward its center. Certain electrical forces acted within the star, and it began to spin faster and faster until it began to bulge. It finally broke into two unequal parts. As they parted, energy from the blinding light pushed each part away from the other. Their power to attract each other was as nothing compared to this other tremendous force. The larger part became our sun, and the smaller part was lost in space.

When the star exploded, a host of smaller masses of gas were hurled off. Some of these masses of glowing gas became the planets. The young planets continued to rotate with the same speed as the sun, and in their turn they hurled off small bits which became their satellites. All this exploding action slowed down the rotation of the young sun and its planets. Our own planet, the earth, slowed down until now it rotates once in twenty-four hours, and its satellite, the moon, rotates once in twenty-seven days.

 Things to Think About

1. The earth was a part of the sun millions and millions of years ago.

2. Other planets may have been formed from other suns in much the same way that the planets of our solar system were formed.

3. The same materials are known to be in the sun that are in the earth. Would this seem to be in favor of the theory that the earth came from the sun?

 *Things to Do*

1. Start a scrapbook called "The Story of the Earth." You can paste in newspaper clippings, pictures from magazines, and drawings which you make yourself. You can continue to make this scrapbook throughout the year. Make a series of drawings to show "The Birth of the Solar System," and place them at the beginning of the book.

2. Perhaps all the members of the class will want to make a motion-picture show of "The Story of the Earth." Plan to show this to the entire school. To do this you will make a series of pictures on a long strip of wrapping paper. These pictures should show the various events in the earth's story which you will read about. Be sure that your pictures are large enough to be easily seen. Make a frame for your motion picture by using a large box with a roller on each side.

3. Watch for stories and articles in newspapers, magazines, and books that tell more about how the earth was formed.

Problem 2 · How the Solar System came to Be

1. The Planets Grew

The gases that were pulled out of the sun may have been in long whirling streams. Probably the streams were the shape of torpedoes, thick near the middle and thinner at the ends. They were streaks of small objects, millions of miles long, extending out between the sun and the star. They may have looked like smoke rolling and curling around after it has left an engine or a chimney. Each stream was a big lumpy mass, thick in some places that were like knots and thin in other places. No one would imagine lumps like those forming balls or spheres, but that is exactly what they did. They broke up into spheres of different sizes.

The most important things that were formed were the spheres which we already know as planets. We do not know exactly how this came about, but there are several theories which help us to understand some things about it.

Many scientists think this is the best theory. As soon as the gases left the sun, they had a great amount of space around them. They had more space around them than when they were a part of the sun; so they expanded. As they did this, the thinner parts of the streams cooled rapidly and soon became small, solid particles of dust. The knots began to separate from one another and to form spheres. There were big clouds of dust surrounding the materials that had collected

37

into spheres. Some of the smaller particles joined and traveled with the larger knots, or spheres.

Some of the small pieces, near the outside of the large stream, were moving so fast that they flew off and were lost. Some moving rapidly bumped into slower ones. If they bumped and bounced off, some of them went so far that they could not come back. Some bumped and stuck together, making one piece instead of two.

Then the thickest knots pulled small pieces to them. As they passed through the clouds of dust, these knots grew and grew by pulling some pieces to them and colliding with others. As centuries went by, the knots became still larger, and at the same time they continued to travel around the sun. The more pieces these central masses pulled to them, the larger they became, until they were small planets.

The spheres had become planets. Some of the original knots were larger than others. The larger the knot, the more it could attract particles to itself. Therefore the largest knots became the largest planets. The largest one became Jupiter, and the next largest was Saturn. Mercury, Venus, Earth, Mars, and Pluto were the smallest ones. Thus planets were formed from these knots. We know of nine planets which were formed in this way. There may be others, which we do not, as yet, know about. It is thought that the planets are still adding dust from different sources. Later these planets collected gases which formed their atmospheres. We shall find out in Unit III how this was done.

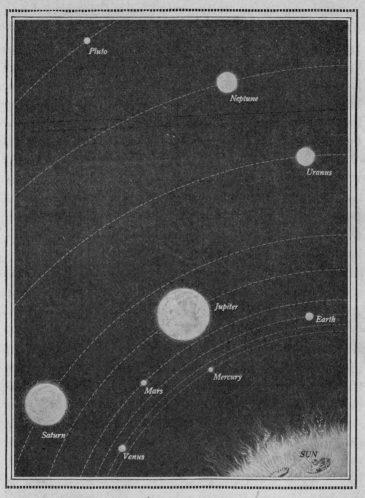

The planets and their paths around the sun

2. The Origin of Comets and Meteors

There are other things that have been formed from
the sun besides planets. Some of them are called comets.
Comets are made up of dust and gases and very fine
particles, or pieces, of rock, which are held loosely together and stay there because of their attraction for
one another. The pull of gravity of each piece attracts
all the others to it. They pull toward the center of the
group and move as one body.

The small bits of rock and the dust and gases which
make up the comets probably came from the sun. Some
of them may have come from the sun in the same way
in which the planets came. Perhaps they came at the
same time. As the long streams of gases were pulled
from the sun, there were some gases that were lost immediately. These hot gases from the sun cooled and
became small bits of rock and dust. And then, as the
knots which formed planets were collecting some of the
gases, dust, and small rocks, there were other particles
so far outside of their pull of gravity that they too were
lost. These lost particles began traveling in space by
themselves. Because of their attraction for one another,
many of these pieces of rock and dust, going in the
same direction and at the same speed, formed groups.
Some of these groups may have been the beginning of
comets.

Other comets are thought to have been made of materials shot out from the sun at different times, in much
the same way that lava, gases, and steam are shot out

This is a picture showing how a comet passes around the sun

from volcanoes. Astronomers see great arms of gases, sometimes hundreds of thousands of miles long, shot out from the sun and then pulled back into it. Sometimes not all the material is again gathered into the sun. This material is lost in space. Perhaps years ago similar streamers were thrown out to a greater distance, and even more of the gases were lost. These may have formed other comets.

The path in which a comet travels around the sun is usually long and narrow. At one end of its path a comet is very near the sun, and at the other end it is extremely far away. When a comet is passing directly around the sun, it travels rapidly. As it goes farther and farther away, its speed becomes less and less because it is being pulled back by the sun. When it has

E

nearly reached the other end of its path, it is scarcely moving at all. It is at this time that the pull of the sun overcomes the force of the comet's speed away from the sun; then the comet begins its journey back toward the sun again.

After it turns on its path, the comet still travels very slowly but gradually gains speed as it approaches the sun. When it is back near the sun, its speed is enormous. This tremendous speed usually makes it possible for the comet to pass the sun without being pulled into it. The pull of the sun is so great, however, that the comet does not continue on a straight course but is forced to turn, and it again starts on its outward journey.

A comet looks rather strange with a head and a long tail. It looks like a ball of fire with flames for a tail. But comets are not fire. We can see them because the light from the sun shines on them and is reflected to us. They shine brightest when they come nearest to us in their travels about the sun. At this time they reflect more light; then, too, the tail is longest when the comet is near the sun.

When the comet is farthest from the sun, the tail, if there is any at all, is very small. Some people think that the material for the tail is gathered to the comet as it is traveling far out in space. There are always quantities of gases, dust, and small rocks that have drifted far into space. As the comets pass close to these lost particles, the pull of gravity of the comets is greater than the pull of any other body upon them, and the lost particles are gathered into the comets.

This is the way a comet looks to someone on the earth at night

Photograph by Lowell Observatory

The particles in the head of the comet are about the size of ordinary marbles or a little smaller. The particles which form the tail are very small and are far apart. The tail is so thin that stars may sometimes be seen through it. You have just learned that the tail is longest when the comet is nearest the sun. It is thought that the sun attracts the head of the comet, but pushes away the tail. Since the materials in the head are larger than those in the tail, they are large enough to be pulled by the sun. But the light from the sun pushes the dust and gases away from the head and makes the tail. The dust and gases in the tail are probably the same that the comet collected when it was far out in space. But with the great force of the light of the sun pushing them away, there is not enough force of attraction in the comets to hold them. Therefore they are again lost in space. The tail is pushed away from the head of the comet much as the tail of a kite is blown away from the kite; so the tail is always on the side of the comet opposite the sun. Therefore, as the comet approaches the sun, the tail is following the head; but as it swings around the sun, the tail is slowly pushed away from the sun until finally the head is following the tail. As some of the gases and dust in the tail are bit by bit pushed out and lost in space, other gases and dust are pushed out of the head and take their place. Therefore the tail that follows the head when the comet is approaching the sun is not the same tail that the head follows as the comet leaves the sun.

There are seen on an average about six comets a

year. These can usually be seen only for a short time,
and then with a telescope. Halley's comet can easily
be seen without a telescope. It is very beautiful and
brilliant. Halley's comet does not come very often; it
may be seen only once every seventy-six years. That
means that it takes this comet over seventy-six years
to complete one journey around the sun. It is thought
that some comets take a much longer time and travel
far out beyond Pluto. Some of the very small comets
come every ten or twelve years. It takes them only a
short time to go around the sun.

Sometimes when a comet comes too near the sun, its
speed is not great enough to resist the pull of gravity
of the sun. When that happens, the comet breaks up
and scatters into millions of pieces and disappears.

Do you remember when you first saw what you
thought was a star shooting across the sky? You asked
about it, and you were told that it was a "shooting
star." Then did you wonder where it came from and
where it went when it fell? You already know that a
"shooting star" is truly not a star at all. A star is so
far away that, if it were falling right toward us, you
could not see it move, and it would take millions of
years to reach the earth. The correct name for "shooting stars," as you know, is meteors.

Meteors are often about the size of a pinhead. Sometimes they are as fine as dust, but once in a while there
is a larger one about the size of a walnut, and sometimes, but not often, there is an extremely large one
that weighs several tons.

There are always little pieces of dust or bits of rock moving about in space in all directions. You remember that at the time that the planets were formed there were many gases and small pieces of rock that were also thrown off and never gathered in by the planets. Some of these began moving about the sun in their own orbits. It is also thought that there are bits of rock traveling about the sun that really have come from comets which at one time went too near the sun and were broken up. Groups of these rocks are known to travel around the sun in nearly the same orbits as some of the comets did before they were broken up. Still other small rocks and bits of dust have been thrown off from the sun in some of the long streamers that we know are always being pushed out from the sun. Other pieces may have drifted in from outside the solar system.

As the earth moves around the sun, either it runs into some of the meteors, or it comes so near them that the earth's gravity pulls them toward it. If this happens, they plunge into our atmosphere and continue to fall rapidly toward the earth's surface. At certain times of the year the earth may move into great swarms of meteors. Some of these swarms are those which have come from a broken comet. At such times we have meteor showers.

When these pieces of rock are traveling around out in space, they are very cold. They are even colder than the air was at the south pole when Admiral Byrd was there. They are colder than anything you can think of.

The largest meteorite that has been discovered
Photograph by W. J. Luyten, Harvard College Observatory

When two objects rub together, the friction makes them very hot. The meteors fall so swiftly that they rush through the air many times faster than the hardest winds. As the cold meteors rush through the air, the friction makes the outsides of them become so hot that they change into gases. This continues until the smaller bits of rock completely change into gases, and there is no solid rock left. They change very rapidly, and, as the gases are scattered in the air, the meteors disappear.

The gases that are given off by the meteors are so hot that they shine. They give off a brilliant light and may seem to us large and dangerous.

Many of the ashes of the meteors fall to the earth during the day and night. Little by little, they add to the weight of the earth.

This huge crater in Arizona was probably formed by a very large meteorite

Photograph by D. M. Barringer

Some meteors are very large. They are too large for
all the rocky material to change to gases before they
strike the earth. The outsides of the meteors change to
gases, but the insides remain solid. It is this solid part
that falls to the earth. When meteors of this kind come
to the earth, they are called meteorites.

Many different-sized meteorites are found. Some of
them are no larger than an egg. Others may be several
feet across. These large meteorites are very unusual.
The largest one that has been found weighs between
fifty and seventy tons and is still in Africa where it fell.
Another meteorite weighs thirty-six and a half tons.
It was discovered by Peary in Greenland. One fell in
Siberia in 1908 which must have been large, for the
forests were destroyed for many miles around. There

is a huge crater in Arizona which scientists believe was formed by a meteorite which fell not more than five thousand years ago.

Most meteorites are made of iron with some nickel and cobalt. There are a few called stone meteorites which are composed of other minerals. They are very heavy for their size. Scientists have examined meteorites in order to learn as much as possible about them.

 Things to Think About

1. Why do some people think that there may be planets revolving about other stars, forming many other solar systems?

2. How many kinds of bodies may be found in the solar system?

3. Why does a comet travel more rapidly as it approaches the sun?

4. Why do the bits of rock out in space not change to gases before they reach the earth's atmosphere?

5. There were many more materials falling upon the earth when it was young than there are now. Why?

 *Things to Do*

1. Visit a museum and look at some of the meteorites that have been found.

2. Write a story about all the things that might have happened to a meteorite. You might name your story "A Meteorite and Its Travels."

3. Rule a sheet of paper into columns. Head the columns "Constellations," "Stars," "Planets," "Satellites," "Comets," "Meteorites." Make a list of as many of each of these kinds of heavenly bodies as you can.

4. Tell into which planet the largest knot grew.

5. Make a chart showing which planets were formed from the largest knots. Make spheres from clay or paraffin to show the sizes of the planets and paint each a different color. On a board or cardboard draw the orbit of each planet and place the sun in its correct position. Place the planets which you have made on their correct orbits and you will have a chart of the solar system.

6. Draw a chart on black paper, using colored pencils, to show the sizes of the planets and their orbits.

UNIT III

Our Changing Earth

1. The Earth has Changed its Appearance Many Times
2. The Age of Volcanoes
3. Mountain Formation and Earthquakes
4. The Coming of an Atmosphere and Oceans

How did the earth get its atmosphere? How were its great mountain systems formed? Have the mountains always been where they are now? Were there times when there were more volcanoes than there are now? What causes geysers and hot springs? These are some of the questions that many have wondered about. Unit III will help you to know something about these questions. You will learn that we are living on a changing earth.

Problem 1 · The Earth has Changed its Appearance Many Times

If you could go back for a minute and take a peep at the earth when it was first forming, millions and millions of years ago, you might think you were dreaming. It did not look then as it does today. At that time the earth may have looked very much as the moon does now, when you look at it through a telescope. Like the moon, it had no oceans, lakes, or seas; it had nothing but mountains and valleys of rocks. We are not sure whether or not the earth had craters like the moon, but we do know that there was nothing living on it. Indeed, there was not even any soil; there was nothing but bare rocks.

The earth has changed its looks many times in the millions of years since it left the sun. Many times the bottom of a sea has become the top of a mountain, and mountains have sunk into or have been carried to the sea. Some rivers have come and gone; others have changed their courses. And some that at one time flowed north now flow south.

It is difficult for us to believe that places which are now thick with plant and animal life were once covered with ice. But many ages ago a great sheet of ice covered part of the United States, Canada, and Europe. As we look at the plants and animals growing in these places today, we should never guess that once ice had been there.

On the contrary, in the very coldest regions of the
world, where there is nothing now but layers and layers of ice, plants once grew in such great quantities that
the sunlight could scarcely find its way through the
leaves and branches. It was like a jungle. Many of
these plants changed to coal, some of which has been
discovered. Prints of fern leaves have been found in
this coal, and these prints show us what plants of that
time were like. They form one proof that such plants
did live there in the past. We know about the ancient
plants and animals only through finding their shells or
bones, or their imprints left in coal, earth, or rocks.
Only a few of these early kinds of living things may be
found alive today, for most of them were not able to
protect themselves from the weather and their enemies
and have long since become extinct.

The kinds of plants and animals living in the world
today have so changed that they little resemble their
ancient ancestors.

Men have flown as many as ten miles out from the
earth, but they have not gone more than a mile and a
half down into the earth. Therefore nothing is known
about the center of the earth from actually seeing and
touching it, but much has been learned about it from
studying the vibrations caused by movements of the
rocks and from other motions of the earth itself.

One group of scientists think that the center of the
earth is liquid; another group believe it is solid. The
latter group believe that the earth is made up of very
heavy material which is probably iron and nickel.

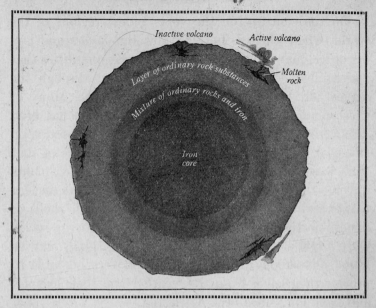

Inactive volcano   Active volcano

Layer of ordinary rock substances

Molten rock

Mixture of ordinary rocks and iron

Iron core

This is the way the earth might look if we were to cut it in halves

The whole earth seems very hard and solid to us. In fact, some scientists believe that its center is firmer than steel. Yet the earth is elastic; the materials of which it is made are able to move under certain conditions. But we are so used to most of these movements that we do not notice them. All scientists agree that the outer parts of the earth are always changing. Even our continents and ocean beds may have been formed in the dim and distant past by these very slow movements of the earth's crust. The lighter rocks came to the surface and bunched together to form continents, much as soap bubbles gather together on the top of

water.   The heavier rocks sank to form ocean beds.
Even now parts of the coast in different places are

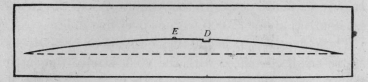

This shows that Mt. Everest, the highest mountain
(*E*), and the deepest part of the ocean (*D*) are small
when compared with the great size of the earth[1]

sinking into the ocean, and other parts are being constantly, but very slowly, pushed up. In fact, so slowly
do these changes take place that it is only after several
years that any change can be noticed.

The uneven fall of particles upon the earth ages ago
may also help to account for the continents. This much
we know, that the continents are made up of rocks
which weigh much less than do those rocks which form
the ocean bottoms. Because of this difference in weight,
it takes a great amount of the lighter rocks to balance
the heavy ones. At any rate, today the continents rise
to an average height of 2400 feet above sea level. Sprin-
kled over these continents are peaks of different heights.
Mt. Everest, which is the highest of all, rises more than
29,000 feet, or about five and a half miles, above sea level.

On the other hand, the ocean beds have an average
depth of 13,000 feet below sea level. Just as there are
peaks on the continents, there are great depths in the

[1] Reproduced from "A Textbook of Geology," by Louis V. Pirsson.
John Wiley & Sons, Inc.

oceans. There is one place in the Pacific Ocean, north of Mindanao, Philippine Islands, which is 32,088 feet, or over six miles, deep. In the Atlantic Ocean the greatest depth is about 27,000 feet, or over five miles.

These depths and heights which seem so great to us are so small compared with the great size of the earth that if we could look at the earth from a distance it would appear only slightly wrinkled.

 Things to Think About

1. Are there any places around your home which show that the surface of the earth is still changing?

2. What is the altitude of the place in which you live?

3. How much cork or sponge would it take to weigh as much as a rock or piece of coal the size of your fist?

 *Things to Do*

1. Find out about the place where you live. Was it once under water? How can you tell?

2. Locate on a map the great mountains of the world; locate the great depths of the ocean.

3. Can you tell of any changes that have taken place in the earth during your lifetime?

E

Problem 2 · The Age of Volcanoes

When the earth was first pulled out from the sun, it was very much smaller than it is now. Some scientists think that it was about one tenth of its present size.

Not all the gases that had been pulled out from the sun by the star which passed so near it ages ago had yet been pulled into the knots which formed the planets. When the gases had cooled, they became bits, or particles, of rock of different sizes. These particles fell to the earth in great numbers, and century after century have added to its size, until it is now nearly 8000 miles in diameter.

The earth has not yet stopped growing. Meteorites still fall upon our earth, although there are only a few compared with the numbers of them which fell ages ago. During those nights you might have seen a meteor every second. Now you may look for hours before you see one, although many enter our atmosphere that we do not see. The greater number of these particles have now been pulled into the planets, for they fell upon the other planets as well as upon our earth. The number of particles which now fall upon our earth is not great enough to make it grow rapidly.

As the meteorites and particles pounded down centuries ago, they added weight as well as size to the earth. This additional weight pressed upon the rock beneath the surface of the earth. As the small particles piled up, layer upon layer, they became so heavy that

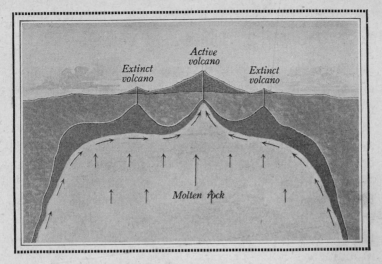

This will give you an idea of the way a
volcano would look if it were cut in halves[1]

the rocks below were squeezed by the pressure and began
to grow warmer. As the years passed, this great pressure from above helped to make the rocks extremely hot.

You have heard of a substance named radium, and
you know that it gives out heat. The rocks of the
earth have always contained radium and other substances which have slowly given out heat through the
ages. This heat, as well as the heat caused by the pressure from above, was stored up in the rocks in great
quantities.

Some substances become hot quickly and carry the
heat away, but rocks become hot slowly and then hold

[1] After diagram in " Our Mobile Earth," by Daly. By permission
of Charles Scribner's Sons.

the heat for a long time. Because of this, they finally
became so hot that some of them melted. There are
certain rocks that melt more easily than others, and it
was these that melted; the others remained as solids.

The rocks that melted formed little pockets in between solid rocks. Needing more space in which to expand, this molten rock pushed up through weak places
in the rocks that were near, and the heavier rocks moved
downwards. The molten rock slowly oozed, or pushed,
its way up to the surface of the earth, often finding a
weak layer of rock through which it burst, pouring over
the land.

At times this molten rock, or lava, found a way out
through the tops or sides of certain mountains. From
time to time not only lava but ashes, pieces of solid
rock, and gases burst forth. Such mountains are called
volcanoes. They may be of any size and shape — from
one or two hundred feet high to the height of some of
our highest peaks, and from little flat-topped hills to
those which are steep and high.

Sometimes the eruption, or breaking out, of these
materials took place with such great force that enormous quantities of gases, water vapor, and ashes, along
with parts of the mountain, were thrown out with a roar
that could have been heard more than a hundred miles.
Great clouds of dust and ashes remained in the air for
months, at times shutting off the sunlight.

At other times the eruptions occurred with less force,
and the lava ran down the sides of the volcanoes and
out over the land. The streams of white-hot lava

During the Age of Volcanoes lava, steam, and dust
burst forth from many peaks similar to Mt. Vesu-
vius, which is one of the remaining active volcanoes

slowly cooled to a glowing red, taking days and even months to cool down to solid rock.

In the northwestern part of the United States, around the Columbia and Snake rivers, great beds of lava have been found which are as much as 3000 feet deep in places and which extend over thousands of square miles. Scientists think that these fields of lava may have been formed by the addition of layer after layer of lava as it oozed forth from cracks in the earth's crust, as well as by lava from near-by volcanoes.

Great chains of mountains have been formed by the flow of lava from volcanoes. Through the centuries terrible eruptions took place, each followed by a period of rest when the volcano was apparently as harmless as any other mountain. Then another eruption would take place with the fresh, hot lava pouring over that which had been thrown out at some time in the past. This took place time after time. Finally, mountains of different sizes were formed. Strange as it may seem, volcanoes are not only on the land, but also on the bottom of the ocean. Eruptions took place there as well as upon the land, and chains of mountains have been formed there in just the same way as they were formed on land. The Hawaiian Islands are examples of mountains that have slowly been built up from the bottom of the sea in that way.

During the Age of Volcanoes eruptions were numerous. Scarcely a day passed without some explosion that added to a mountain that was being built or changed the surface of the earth in some other way. At the points on the earth's surface where the crust was the weakest, volcanic action was most frequent.

Since that age many volcanoes that for centuries shot forth great volumes of smoke and lava are no longer active and are now calm and harmless. We call them extinct volcanoes. Though we may think there are many active volcanoes at the present time, there are very few compared with the great number during the early history of the earth. There are not enough of them now to change the surface of the earth in any great way.

Yellowstone National Park occupies 4000 square miles of the great lava beds which lie around the Columbia and Snake rivers. You have already learned how these were formed. Deep underneath the surface still lie masses of hot granite, which make the park one of the greatest known regions of geysers and hot springs. This hot granite is a reminder of the time when lava was spread over this section of our country.

Geysers are really "water volcanoes," some of which throw water hundreds of feet into the air. This action of the geysers is caused by water underground meeting a bed of hot granite.

When you have seen rain beating down upon the pavement or earth, have you ever wondered what happened to all of it? You know that some of it finally finds its way to the oceans, through the creeks and rivers. Some evaporates and thus goes back into the air. But there is some that seeps down into the earth and goes out of sight. The soil holds some of the water as a sponge does, but it cannot hold all the water that soaks into it. Some of the water forms little streams that travel underground. It is the meeting of this underground water with hot granite that causes the geysers and hot springs in our country.

When the water meets the hot granite, it becomes so hot that some of it changes to steam and collects. There are vents, or openings, that extend from the surface of the earth down to the hot granite. It is through these vents that the steam finally bursts forth, bringing with it the water which has collected in the vent. The geysers spout until all the steam in the vent escapes. Some of the water then runs back into the vent; more is added from water underground, and when a certain amount of steam collects, another eruption takes place.

The Giantess is considered one of the most famous geysers in the park. It does not erupt regularly, as Old Faithful does. It erupts at any time from five to forty days. When it does erupt, the stream of boiling water reaches hundreds of feet into the air.

Other geysers vary in size from small springs that spurt only a few inches high every minute to giants that hurl thousands of gallons of water into the air for several hundred feet.

Hot springs are springs in which the water is very hot. If the water supply in these springs becomes low, they become springs of boiling mud, which is often colored white, yellow, red, purple, or black. Such springs are called "paint pots." When eruptions take place and hot mud and water are thrown forth, these springs are called "mud volcanoes."

The Giantess is one of the greatest of many
geysers in the Yellowstone National Park

Deposits of minerals are found around the vents of hot springs and geysers which often take the form of walls from a few inches to several feet high.

Things to Think About

1. Who first learned about radium? Rocks containing radium and similar substances are called radioactive. It was only recently that we learned about them, but their action has been going on for millions of years.

2. Can you name any other islands besides the Hawaiian Islands that have been formed by volcanoes?

3. Can you think of any time during the history of man when volcanoes did much damage on the earth?

4. In what regions of South America are most volcanoes found?

Things to Do

1. Make a chart or a model of a cross section of the United States, showing the altitudes in the mountain and plains regions.

2. Read the story of Pompeii.

3. Are there many active volcanoes in North America? Make a map showing where they are.

4. Are there any extinct volcanoes in North America? If so, locate them on your map.

5. Draw a line on your map connecting the active volcanoes. Notice in what regions they are found.

6. Do the same thing for the other continents.

Problem 3 · Mountain Formation and Earthquakes

Mountains have been formed in many ways. We already know that some great mountain chains were formed by volcanoes.

Many hills and mountains have also been made by the movements of the rocks which form the earth's crust. It would be difficult to imagine any direction in which these rocks have not moved. Great masses of rock were pushed slowly up until a huge wrinkle was made, the size of a hill or a mountain. Sometimes these huge wrinkles broke while forming, and one part was pushed up and the other part either remained where it was or sank. The part which was pushed up became a mountain.

Some mountains were formed when lava filled great cracks in the earth's crust. Through the centuries the softer rocks were worn away, leaving the great mass of hard cold lava exposed. Mountains have been formed not only in one way, but in many combinations of ways.

Erosion, or the breaking up and wearing away of rock and soil by freezing and thawing, wind and rain, has played a great part in mountain formation. The forces of erosion are always at work, slowly wearing down the softer rocks, leaving the harder materials exposed, filling up low places, or carrying soil and rock to the sea.

Mountains formed ages ago have been worn down

This shows how layers of rock have been
bent by movements of the earth's crust

time after time, and in many cases have been re-formed
by the same forces which made them in the first place.

Just as it took periods of time so long that they cannot be imagined for continents to form, so it took long
ages for mountains to form.

As the crust of the earth wrinkled and folded, the
strain suddenly became so great that the layers of rock
snapped (just as a rubber band snaps when stretched
too far), letting one layer slip past or fold over another.
The actual slipping, or movement, of the rocks may
have been only a few inches, yet such sudden breaks
caused a trembling or vibration of the earth which
we call earthquakes. Sometimes these rock movements

This fence was built in a straight line. You can
see what happened to it during an earthquake[1]

were several hundred miles long; more often they covered less than fifty. Earthquakes always occur where
the earth's crust is weakest.

Earthquakes have disturbed the seas and oceans,
causing great waves which dashed over the coast, washing away cities and sometimes even changing the coast
line. At times the vibrations of an earthquake have
been just enough to cause a volcanic eruption. Landslides (the slipping of great masses of earth) have been
started in mountainous regions, and changes have been
made in the amount of water flowing from springs. At

[1] From Bradley's "The Earth and its History." Ginn and Company.

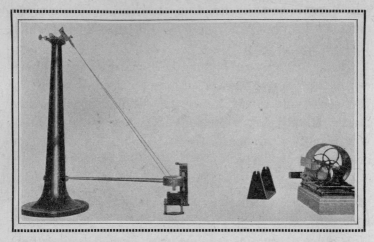

It is possible for a seismograph, such as this one, to record
an earthquake which occurs on the other side of the earth

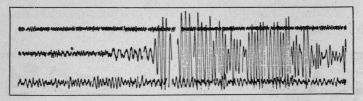

A seismograph made this record during an earthquake

times old springs were stopped and new ones made.
Earthquakes have caused damage of all kinds, and
thousands of lives have been lost. Indeed, the damage
caused by earthquakes has been so great that scientists
have studied them with the greatest care. They have
learned how houses can be built so that few lives are
lost and little damage is done.

An instrument called a seismograph has been made

which can record the direction, the degree of force of the earth's vibrations, and the length of time during which they occur.

Places called earthquake observatories have been established. At these observatories records made by the seismograph are kept and studies of them are made. In this way vibrations in the earth are located, whether they occur in the continents or under the ocean.

 Things to Think About

1. Some mountains are now being formed, while others are wearing away. How many things can you think of which cause mountains or soil to be worn away?

2. What things help to prevent erosion on mountains, hills, and valleys?

 **Things to Do**

1. Learn where some great earthquakes have occurred.

2. Locate these places on the maps which you made showing the volcanoes. Is there much difference between the regions where volcanoes and earthquakes occur?

3. If it is possible, take a trip to see a seismograph, and see one of the records.

Problem 4 · The Coming of an Atmosphere and Oceans

You remember there was a time when the earth was only about one tenth of its present size. Then it was so small that its gravity had much less pull than it has now. If you had been on the earth then, baseball would have been great fun, for the ball would have gone ever so much farther than it does now. A home run would have been easy, for you would have half floated through space with each step. But the truth is you could not have played baseball at all because you would have suffocated. People cannot breathe without air, and scientists think there was little air at that time.

We think that the earth slowly gained in size, and as it did this, it was more and more capable of holding air to it. As its size increased, it gathered an atmosphere.

But where did the air come from for the earth to hold? Did the earth pull it out of space? It could not have done that, for we know of no air out in space between the stars and planets. The earth had to get its atmosphere from somewhere else. Scientists think that the earth collected its atmosphere in several different ways. Many of the gases that are in the air may have been given off during the age of volcanoes. At each volcanic eruption great quantities of steam and other gases poured forth. These gases could not pass off into space because, by that time, the earth had grown to such a size that it could hold them.

There was a second way in which some of the atmosphere may have been gathered. In those days, long, long ago, it is thought that when meteorites smashed into the earth they became so hot that part of them changed to gases. These gases were added to those which had been given off by volcanoes. Some of the gases forming the atmosphere may have been present from the very time that the earth was formed. We believe, however, that gases from many sources have been added together for millions of years and an atmosphere slowly formed.

However, these are only theories, and it remains to be proved just how the atmosphere really was formed.

We know that now the greater amount of the atmosphere is within fifteen miles of the earth, though this blanket of air probably extends as far as two hundred miles or more away. We know too that the air becomes thinner and colder as you leave the earth.

If the earth had no atmosphere, it would be a barren, lonely place. To begin with there could be no living plants or animals; no rain would fall, and no wind would blow. The earth would become extremely hot by day and extremely cold at night. There would be no clouds and no rainbows, and no beautiful colors in the morning and evening skies. The atmosphere makes the earth a place of beauty and a good place in which to live.

With the forming of the atmosphere came the right conditions for condensing water vapor into clouds and rain.

E

As rain poured upon the young earth,
water collected into rivers, seas, and oceans

The surface of the earth was irregular with highlands and lowlands, hills and valleys. There was only a small amount of soil, if any, to soak up the rain as it fell. Hence all the rain went to form little streams that ran down slopes to lower levels. These streams met other little streams headed in the same direction, and they joined, forming rivers.

The rivers emptied into low places, forming ponds, lakes, or oceans, depending upon the size of the low place. And thus running water began to play its part in the story of the earth.

Rains followed rains until, after thousands and thousands of years, the great basins on the earth were filled. We call these great bodies of water oceans.

Today there are millions of gallons of water being poured into the oceans each year, but that is a small amount when we consider the quantity that was added in those ages long ago.

On its way to the oceans the water dissolved very small amounts of certain substances that were in the rocks. These substances, dissolved in the water, were carried through the rivers and lakes and finally to the oceans. Probably the most plentiful substance was salt — the same kind of salt that we use in our food.

There is not enough salt in river water for you to taste it, but in the millions of years that rivers have untiringly brought water to the oceans, they have carried tons and tons of salt with them.

Water is always evaporating from the oceans, but the salt and other substances never have a chance to leave. They must remain in the oceans.

In very dry regions salt and alkali lakes are often found. Some of these lakes were formed when an arm of the sea was cut off from the sea itself, as by an uplifting of the land. Others, such as Great Salt Lake, were formed in valleys or basins which were fed by streams from the melting snows and glaciers of surrounding mountains. If such lakes have no outlets, their waters become very salt.

Ages ago a much larger body of water than the present one occupied the basin in which Great Salt Lake now lies. This large lake has come to be known as Lake

An ancient salt lake dried up, leaving layers of salt

Bonneville. When the rainfall and snowfall were heavier than usual over a long period of time, the basin of Lake Bonneville was full to overflowing. In especially dry periods the evaporation from the surface of the lake was greater than the amount of water brought into it; then the lake shrank in size and probably once or twice dried up entirely, leaving a bed of salt and other mineral substances. Today all that remains of this ancient body of water is Great Salt Lake, which is fed by rivers but has no outlet, so that its waters are very salt.

Great Salt Lake is drying up today. Unless something happens, there will come a time, after many years, when again there will be no lake left, only beds of salt.

Things to Think About

1. Why did not the earth have an atmosphere when it was about one tenth its present size?

2. Why are we interested in the earth's atmosphere?

3. How can atmosphere affect life on a planet?

4. Why couldn't there be rain if there were no atmosphere?

5. How do we get the salt which we use?

6. Great salt beds have been found in different parts of the world. Can you tell how some of them were formed?

 *Things to Do*

1. Draw a picture to show how you think an atmosphere was formed.

2. Draw another picture to show how you think the oceans were formed.

3. Tell why some lakes were formed. Why didn't this water go to the oceans?

4. Locate the oceans of the world and show where the water comes from that empties into them.

UNIT IV

The Layers of the Earth as a Story Book

1. Some Rocks were Broken and Changed to Soil
2. New Rocks were Formed
3. Fossils tell a Story

THE LAYERS OF THE EARTH

Rocks are the pages on which the wonderful story of the earth is written, but it is not easily read because the story is written in signs and we must know what these signs mean before we begin to read. These signs are the pebbles, crystals, and fossils found in the layers of rock which form the surface of our earth. The story begins even before there were living things upon the earth. This unit will tell you what some of these signs mean.

Problem 1 · Some Rocks were Broken and Changed to Soil

A blanket of air covered the earth, and winds blew across a barren land. The sun shone, and the earth rotated. The moon and stars lighted the nights. Water was dashed against rocks by tides and winds, but there was not yet one sign of life.

No plants or animals existed during the first part of the earth's history. When living things finally appeared, they were so small and their bodies so soft that they left no prints or remains of any kind. That is why the early part of the earth's story is difficult to read. The story of the later history of the earth was written more completely because the living things existing during those ages were larger and often had hard shells or bony parts which formed fossils.

During those earliest ages the sun and atmosphere were acting together and changing the surface of the earth. What they did made it possible for plants and animals to live here.

As the sun shone, it heated the air in certain places more than it did in others, just as the sun heats the atmosphere more at the equator than at the poles today. As the air was heated, it expanded, and so weighed less than the cold air. The heavier cold air was pulled down close to the earth and pushed the light warm air upwards. Sometimes this changing about of warm and cold air took place rapidly, causing winds. The more rapidly the exchange took place, the harder the winds blew.

The sun acted in still another way. It shone upon the lakes and oceans and heated their surfaces. This caused the water to evaporate and rise into the air, where it remained for a while as vapor.

Often the warm air was filled with moisture. When the cool winds blew against the warm air, it became cooler and the water vapor condensed and rain fell.

You know that water can dissolve certain substances which are in the rocks. As the rain water trickled over the rocks, it dissolved a small amount of these substances and carried them along to the rivers, which were finally formed. The rivers continued this work as they made their way across the plains or through the mountains to the sea. For hundreds of years some of the rivers continued to flow in the same paths, and as a result the rock was worn away until deep canyons were formed, with the river flowing at the bottom.

These streams of water did more than dissolve materials from the rocks; they also carried small pebbles and sand with them. As these pebbles were carried along, they helped to scrape off other bits of rock by bumping into them and by rubbing against the banks and bottoms of the streams and rivers. In some of the larger and swifter rivers even large rocks, or bowlders, were carried along, which wore away the banks and river bottoms. Much of the sand and soil thus formed was carried to the seas, where it settled to the bottom.

But some of these bowlders and tiny rocks were

© Haynes

Notice how deep this canyon is when compared
with the telephone poles. It has taken thousands
of years for the river to cut through these rocks

Can you see how the trees split the rocks as they grew?

These rocks are being broken up to form soil

broken off in other ways. It was probably the sun that did most of this work in the beginning. As the sun shone upon the rocks in the daytime, it made their surfaces hot, and in the evening, when the sun set, the night winds made them cool. You probably know that other objects expand when they are heated just as air expands when it is heated. As the rocks were heated by the sun, their surfaces became larger, and as they cooled, their surfaces became smaller again. As the heating and cooling of the rocks continued, small bits were gradually cracked away.

Rocks were also broken in another way. The air itself helped to do this. As you know, air is made of

The sun, wind, frost, and rain have carved this Great Stone Face

gases. These gases entered the very tiny openings in the rocks and made certain changes in the rocks themselves. Some of these changes made it possible for water to dissolve some parts of the rock more easily.

Sometimes after a crack or tiny opening appeared, it was filled with water. When it became cold enough, this froze in the crack. What often happens to a glass tumbler or a bottle when water freezes solid in it? The same thing happened to the rocks. The water in the cracks expanded when it froze and caused a larger hole or crack to form.

Have you ever been standing in the hills or mountains and heard rocks tumbling down their sides? Those rocks may have been broken off by the frost. When they went crashing down, they broke other bowlders as they bounced from one to another on their way to the valley below.

The wind blew sand and soil already formed against the rocks. These sharp-cornered bits of sand cut the rocks and helped to wear them away. The wind also carried away freshly loosened bits of rock. This allowed the water and air to work on the solid rock underneath.

The waves of water along the seashore dashed against the rocks and wore them away; in this case the weight of the wave was added to the usual action of the water.

And so this is how it happened that the rocks were broken up and soil was formed. The sun caused expansion; the gases of the atmosphere made changes in the rocks; the freezing of the water in pores and cracks of

In digging their homes animals bring new soil to the top

rocks caused chipping; the wind carried tiny bits of broken rocks away and blew sharp-edged sand against surfaces of rocks; and water carried the rocks and sand along toward the sea, often dropping some of this material in places along the way, until our rocky barren earth is now covered in many places by rich, fertile soil.

All these changes are going on today in addition to the changes which plants and animals are also making. After plants and animals came upon the earth, they also helped in breaking up rocks and in forming soil.

The roots of plants help to break up rocks. Tiny seeds become lodged in cracks. A little soil drifts into the crack also. The seed grows and may at last become a tree or shrub. As it grows, the rock is spread farther apart or may fall entirely apart.

The roots of plants under the ground probably break up more rocks than we should at first imagine.

Animals living under the ground, such as earthworms, gophers, and ants, bring soil up from underground and leave it on the top. In this way air, water, and sunshine reach the soil and break it up into still finer bits.

 Things to Think About

1. Which do you think did the most to make soil, the sun, air, or water? Could only one of these have made soil?

2. What does man do to make soil from rocks?

3. Have you ever felt the wind blowing sand against your face? Then can you understand how it could help to break rocks up into soil?

 ***Things to Do***

1. Find a place near your home where soil has been carried down by streams and deposited.

2. Look for a rock cracked by frost or other means.

3. Find a place near your home where sand or soil forms drifts, or where the banks of a creek or river are being worn away.

4. Look on a map and see if you can tell why rivers flow through the places they do. Why do some flow more swiftly than others? Tell what effect this has upon erosion.

Problem 2 · New Rocks were Formed

1. Sedimentary: Rocks made from Sediment

You have often heard the expression "as solid as a rock." Can you think of anything that is more solid than a rock? And yet you have just learned that even rocks are not so solid that they can remain that way forever. In time they too are changed.

Rocks have been broken and worn into tiny bits, and these bits, in turn, have been used to form new and different kinds of rocks. It took years and years of the united efforts of the sun, wind, and water to crumble the rocks until sand and clay were formed. And during more and more years the rivers and streams carried this sand, clay, and mud and poured them into lakes and oceans. This sediment settled on the floors of the large bodies of water and remained there, while more sand, clay, and mud were being piled on top. There they were to be again changed to rock.

You must not think that the sun, wind, and water stopped their war against the rocks just as soon as they had a certain amount of work done. They have continued that action all through the long ages of the story of the earth, and they are still at work. Rocks that you see today will at some time be crumbled. But the action is too slow, and it will take too long, for you ever to hope to see it happen. As long as there is sun, wind, and water, they will never fail to break the rocks and form more sand and clay. Just so long as there are rivers and streams, they will never fail to carry loose sediment and deposit it on the floors of seas and oceans, and they will continue to heap other sediment on top, forming layer upon layer, at the bottom of the waters. Rocks are always being torn down, while others are being formed.

Did you ever cover yourself or have someone else cover you with sand, as you were lying on the seashore or on a sand pile? Do you remember how heavy that small amount of sand was? You had to push part of it off with your hands before you could get up. How heavy would it be if you had several feet of sand over you? Just imagine, then, how much weight must have been pressing on layers of sand and mud at the bottom of the oceans when they had hundreds of feet of sediment above them. The pressure was extremely great, and the layers of sediment were pressed and cemented together.

Ages afterwards, as the surface of the earth slowly sank in some places and slowly rose in others, some of these layers at the bottom of the seas and oceans appeared above the surface of the water. The layers of sediment that had been cemented by pressure and heat had become rocks. Rocks that were formed in this way from sediments are called sedimentary rocks.

When you look at them, you would never guess that these sedimentary rocks could in any way be related to the rocks from which they were formed. They do not look at all like them.

There are several kinds of sedimentary rocks. One kind is called sandstone. You can guess that this was

A conglomerate rock is made of pebbles cemented together. See if you can find a rock that looks like this

formed by sand that piled into layers. Sandstone may
contain a small amount of lime that has helped to cement the grains of sand together, or it may have some
clay, but most of it is sand. Sandstone is used in building, but it does not wear so long as granite or marble.
It scratches off quite easily. It may be red, gray, or
yellow. The color is caused by minerals, such as iron,
that have been dissolved in the water and been added
to the rock.

When pebbles have been cemented together by sand
and a little lime, the resulting rock is known as a conglomerate rock because it is a mixture. If the pebbles
that formed this conglomerate rock are smooth and

nearly round, the rock is called pudding stone; the pebbles are the "raisins" or "plums" of the pudding.

Shale is another sedimentary rock and has been formed from clay. Under a great amount of pressure the clay, or shale, may become a fairly hard rock that is known as slate. Do you know how slate is used? You can always recognize either shale or slate when you see it because it breaks into scales. When you breathe on it, it has an earthy odor. Have you ever passed through hills or mountains and noticed large red or gray pieces of rock that were splitting off in sheets? That was probably either slate or shale.

If you have played along the seashore, you have collected some of the shells that have been washed up by the waves. Do you remember how many shells were broken or had holes rubbed in them? It was difficult to find complete shells of many different kinds. Shells are broken by the waves as the waves dash them against other shells and against rocks and pebbles while carrying them to shore. These shells found on the seashore are only a few of the shells of the sea; many of them sink to the bottom far from shore and are never washed up.

The shells and bones of animals have a great amount of lime in them. It was this lime that helped to form much of the limestone in the earth. As the animals in the sea died, their shells and bones sank in the water. As more shells and bones were added each year, the layers at the bottom became thicker. Water that ran into the oceans carried some lime that it had dissolved from

U. S. Geological Survey

These shells and the sand may be changed
into rocks millions of years from now

A limestone quarry contains rocks that were once many shells

rocks on the land. This lime was added to the layer of shells on the floor of the ocean. In much the same way that sandstone was formed, this gathering of lime was pressed into limestone. Great mountains are made up almost entirely of limestone that was made under water and later forced up into mountains.

Limestone is quarried and used in buildings. This stone is also used in other ways. It is heated and changed into quicklime, or lime, and it is sold to be used for whitewash, mortar, and plaster.

Limestone and sandstone and other sedimentary rocks may contain fossils. As the sand and lime were put down in layers, bodies of animals and plants were often covered. Sediment forming on top prevented de-

Many animals once lived in these fossil shells. Can you read any more of the story written on this rock?

cay, and fossils were formed. Since these rocks have not been heated greatly, many of the fossils have been preserved.

2. Metamorphic: Rocks made by Heat and Pressure

Sedimentary rocks have not always remained the same. Many of them have been changed into a second kind of rock. It was after some of these rocks had been formed that some of the greatest changes took place on or near the earth's surface. Layers of the earth were twisted and folded into mountains, hills, and valleys.

Place a number of sheets of paper together and bend them. Can you imagine that they are many layers of soil and rocks, and that each layer is many feet thick? As you bend them, see if you can make mountains, hills, and valleys. Some layers of the earth were pushed up as others were forced down, and it took many, many times as much force to bend and twist the layers of rock as it took for you to bend the paper. Some of the layers were forced to a great depth and had tons of pressure above them and often very high degrees of temperature below them. It was this intense pressure and the heat that pressed and baked the sedimentary rocks into other kinds of rocks. When rock is changed in this way, we say that it is metamorphosed, and we call the rock metamorphic rock. Metamorphic means changed.

Layers of limestone that had been formed from the lime of shells and bones of animals were changed by pressure and heat. This limestone was metamorphosed and formed marble. That means that limestone and marble are made of the same things, and that marble was made from the limestone.

Shale was metamorphosed into slate. If there was enough heat and pressure, many kinds of sedimentary and other rocks were changed into a rock called schist. There are many different kinds of schist. One is found often. It contains mica and is called mica schist. Sandstone was pressed and melted and cooled into quartzite. The little grains of sand have been pressed closely together and almost melted, so that you can scarcely see any of the grains.

Melted rock once filled two long cracks in this mountain. The softer rocks have worn away from the sides, leaving the wall of harder rock

3. Igneous: Rocks made by Heat

There are other rocks that have been formed in a third way. These are called igneous rocks, which means that they have been formed from heat. All the rocks that have at one time become so hot that they melted, and then later cooled, are of igneous, or fire, beginning. The very first rocks were igneous.

You already know that some of the rocks and minerals below the surface of the earth have at times melted and formed pockets of hot rock. It was from these pockets of melted rock that the igneous rocks began. Some of it poured out of volcanoes as lava and cooled

Quartz crystals

on the outside of the earth. At other times the movements of the earth's crust and the pressure from below caused a great crack in the surface which extended for miles. These cracks often occurred in the softer layers of sandstone and shale. Lava pushed out of the cracks and formed harder layers. Some of the lava from these cracks and volcanoes cooled very rapidly and formed volcanic glass, which is called obsidian. The lava that cooled slowly formed basalt.

Sometimes the melted rock pushed up only part way through sandstone or other soft rock and cooled under the surface. Years afterwards the soil and softer rocks were washed away, leaving this hard rock as a great wall. Rocks that cooled under the surface in this way are usually called diabase.

Other igneous rocks have cooled on the inside of the earth. Usually, when melted minerals and rocks cool under the surface, they form crystals. Crystals of different rocks have different shapes, and you can recognize different rocks by their crystals, if you examine them carefully. Some rocks are made up of a number of minerals that have formed crystals. Sometimes the crystals are very large. Sometimes they are so small that you will need a magnifying glass to see them.

Granite is a very common igneous rock that is mined in quarries. It is used for buildings and monuments. It is a very hard rock and wears well. It takes years and years before the wind, sun, and water affect it much. Granite was formed deep within the earth, ever so long ago, but in places it is now on top of the earth. Softer rocks and soil have been worn and washed away, leaving the hard granite standing out like a sentinel.

4. Rocks are made of Minerals

All rocks are made of substances which are called minerals. There are many different kinds of minerals in the earth.

A few rocks are made of only one mineral, while others contain several minerals.

Granite is a rock that is made of several minerals. The clear crystals in granite are quartz. The shiny flakes that shine in the sun are bits of mica. The pearly crystals are another important mineral, called feldspar.

Granite   Gneiss

Granite and gneiss contain the same minerals. Read
the text to learn the difference between these rocks

Gneiss is a rock that is made of the same minerals of
which granite is composed, but in gneiss these minerals
form streaks, or layers, in the rock. In granite the minerals are scattered and form no streaks at all. Compare
pictures or pieces of granite and gneiss.

Quartz is the most common mineral on the earth. It
is quartzite pebbles that you find along the seashore, or
quartz crystals that you find in the rocks on hills or
mountains. If you rub quartz on most of the other
rocks, it scratches them because the quartz is harder
than most minerals. It is softer than a few minerals;
it is softer than a diamond, which is the hardest mineral
known. One way to test a piece of rock that you think
is quartz is to rub it on glass. If it scratches the glass,
it is very likely to be quartz.

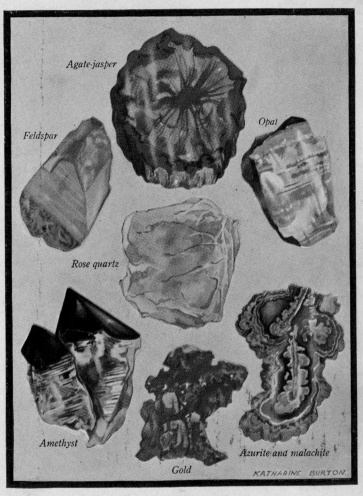

Agate-jasper

Opal

Feldspar

Rose quartz

Amethyst

Gold

Azurite and malachite

KATHARINE BURTON.

Some of the minerals and semiprecious stones which you may see

Quartz may be found in different colors. When it was melted and was being made, certain metals, such as iron and others, were mixed with the quartz. Each substance caused it to have a certain color. Amethysts are quartz crystals that have been colored purple. Amethysts are used in jewelry. There are other kinds of quartz, such as milky quartz, rose quartz, and agate. Agates were formed by quartz that was dissolved in water, and as the water passed through other rocks it left the quartz, which formed in layers. Quartz is found in many rocks. Quartz that is colorless and looks like glass is often called crystal.

Mica is another very common mineral. It is smooth and shiny. It splits into very thin sheets that are brittle and transparent. There are two kinds of mica; one has a very light color, and the other is dark and smoky-colored.

Our precious stones and metals are minerals that are found in the earth and mined from it. Some of them are plentiful, but others are very rare.

 Things to Think About

1. Can you think of any rivers that carry great amounts of sediment which they deposit in lakes, seas, or oceans?

2. Why are sedimentary rocks so called?

3. What happens to the shells at the bottom of the ocean?

4. Is limestone a sedimentary rock? How do you know?

 *Things to Do*

1. Make a list of the most-precious stones and metals.

2. Make a map of the United States, and with colored circles and squares show where the common minerals are found.

3. Should you like to make some crystals and show in what way some of the rock crystals were formed? Fill a test tube or a tumbler about half full of hot water. Make a solution by adding a little common table salt to the water. Keep adding a little at a time until some of it remains at the bottom of the tube and will not dissolve. Tie a string to a match or a pencil placed across the top of the glass or tube. Let the string drop into the solution, and set the solution aside to cool. As it cools, crystals of salt form on the string. Other crystals may be formed in the same way by using solutions of boric acid or copper sulfate. Look at your crystals through a magnifying glass. Do they look alike? Do they look like any of the crystals in your rocks?

4. Make a rock collection and label the pieces.

5. Visit a quarry and see if you can tell how the rocks in the quarry were formed. Can you find rocks that are in layers?

6. Paint pictures of scenes that show rock formations or unusual formations on the earth's surface.

7. Have you ever visited a cave? Tell how the cave was formed. What kinds of rocks are found in caves? Collect pictures of caves, showing different formations.

Problem 3 · Fossils tell a Story

1. How Fossils were Found

Have you ever wondered how scientists learned so much about plants and animals that lived many ages ago? Many kinds of those plants and animals have not existed for thousands of years, and yet scientists know their size and shape; they know whether animals had feathers or tough skins, and they know the kind of food they ate. But how do they know? They have learned these and many other things from fossils.

A long time after the earth was pulled away from the sun, and yet millions and millions of years ago, the history of the earth was being written in stones and fossils.

Fossils may be the remains of plants or animals, or they may be only prints; but they are things that show something about plants and animals.

When you step in the mud, you leave a print. The print dries and becomes hard. Now if by chance that mud with your footprint in it could be preserved from harm and possibly hardened into rock, it would be a fossil. People finding it thousands and thousands of years from now would be able to tell many things about you.

Long ago animals died, and some of their bodies became fossils. Some may have died on the prairies and have been quickly covered over by sand. Others may have sunk in quicksand or asphalt lakes or may have been caught in floods and so quickly covered by water

103

Men have learned many things about extinct animals by studying fossils

and sediment that their bodies were preserved. Some fossils have been discovered in places where the soil is now always frozen, and the bodies were preserved by the intense cold. At other times animals were suddenly covered by great landslides or by lava, dust, and ashes from volcanoes.

Water animals died, and the remains of some of them

were quickly covered by sediment. Sometimes pressure from the layer of sediment covering the animals, heat from the earth, and minerals in the soil and water, acting together for thousands or perhaps millions of years, turned some of the bodies to stone.

Plants were covered in the same way, and their shapes, or imprints, have been found in the rocks and in coal. Birds made tracks along the muddy banks of rivers and lakes. Footprints of other animals living long years ago have also been found. In times long past such tracks were covered, and through the ages some have slowly turned to stone. Of course not all the prints made by plants and animals in the past have become fossils. But enough of them were preserved in different ways so that many may now be found.

Through the centuries soil collected on top of the tracks of animals and on their bodies and on plants, and buried them. Some of this soil became rock, and then as mountains and valleys were gradually formed, the rock containing the fossils was pushed up in places and exposed. The rain, snow, wind, and freezing and thawing weather have all helped to wear away the rock and soil covering the fossils.

Scientists believe that there are still many fossils buried in the earth.

Have you ever lived in a place where you could find rocks that contained shells or bones or prints of animals? Have you ever found the print of a fern leaf in a piece of coal? Many fossils are found in limestone and sandstone. People living in the central part of the United

E

Notice how the parts of a flower and a leaf are shown in these fossils

States often find fossil shells in these stones. This proves that the place where they live was once under water and that sea animals lived there.

2. Logs turned to Stone

Would it not seem strange to see a log of a tree that had no wood in it? That is what you can see in parts of Arizona. There is one place where great trunks of trees are lying on the ground, but there is no wood to be found anywhere. The trees have turned to stone. Beautifully colored minerals have taken the place of the wood, and the trees have become petrified.

Petrified wood can be found in other places, but the Petrified Forest in Arizona is one of the great wonders of the world. This forest is not standing. Great stone trees lie scattered on the ground. They have been preserved for centuries.

We do not know exactly what happened, but we read a story from the rocks and petrified trees. This desert country of the Petrified Forest must once have been under water. The trees did not grow where they are now found. They grew higher up on the hills and plateaus.

For many years rivers and streams washed the mountains and carried mud, sand, and pebbles to the sea. This erosion continued, year after year, until the mouth of the river became filled with materials that the river had emptied into it. This sediment slowed up the speed of the water. Again, there were times when hard rains fell. Streams rushed into the rivers and filled them to the tops of their banks. Often they were filled to overflowing, and water rushed out upon the land. Trees were uprooted and washed out. They were hurled into the stream of swiftly flowing water and carried to lakes and seas. The great trees growing on the plateaus were no exceptions. In time they too were washed out and floated down stream. They were carried farther down until they came to an eddy, a place where the water turned around and around and flowed very slowly. The trees were caught in this whirlpool and floated no farther. In time they became water-soaked and sank to the bottom.

Through the following ages the river continued to wash sediment over the logs. The logs lay there buried in the mud, and protected from the air, which would cause decay. The water dissolved mineral matter from the rocks and carried it along. Gradually, in some way that is not quite understood, the water exchanged the wood of the tree for the mineral that it held dissolved. For centuries and centuries wood was taken from the cells of the tree and minerals were deposited in its place. The minerals so gradually and completely replaced the wood that the forms of the cells were not destroyed. When scientists examine a thin piece of petrified wood under the microscope they can see the forms of the cells. They can recognize, or identify, the kind of trees that they were.

These trees were buried under the water and mud for countless ages. Then the land slowly rose, and the water dried up. The bottom of the river became dry and hard, completely hiding the buried trees. Later the softer stone and soil above the trees were worn away. Erosion continued for many years until parts of the forest came to light. Some of the trees are still underground. Some are just cropping out from hillsides. Many give color to the desert. Many pieces of this petrified wood were used for arrowheads and knives by the natives. Later, carloads of it were shipped out and made into ornaments. To preserve these trees a large part of the forest has been set aside as a national park. Thousands of tourists each year make a trip through the forest to enjoy the beauty of the logs of stone.

Things to Think About

1. Fossils are not found in igneous rocks. Can you explain why?

2. In some fossils of shells there is nothing left except the print of the shell. What has happened to the shell?

Things to Do

1. What kinds of fossils can you find where you are living?

2. Try to find a fossil in a piece of coal.

3. Make a print of a leaf in plaster of Paris to show how a fossil may have been made in mud.

UNIT V
Early Life

1. Life Started on the Earth
2. Life Stays on the Earth

You have been reading about the early history of the earth. You have learned something about how its continents, oceans, and atmosphere have been formed. You have learned also about the great forces which have been working on the earth.

But during all that time, although it was millions of years long, there was no life on the earth. Could we have visited the earth at that time, it would have seemed strange to us to have seen no plants and animals. It would have been a lonely place.

How did life get started? Did all the living creatures come at one time? What dangers did they face? Did they all succeed in living?

In Unit V you are going to read about the first plants and animals, which were tiny and weak. Then you will read about other forms of life, which developed and covered almost all the earth. You will see that climates changed and that life had come to stay on the earth for millions and millions of years.

Problem 1 · Life Started on the Earth

1. The First Life

After millions of years of restlessness, of volcanoes and earthquakes, of rising and falling of land, there came a time when things could live on the earth. The gases had collected to form an atmosphere about the earth. There was water in the air, and rain had fallen. Rivers flowed down into the oceans.

All the conditions that plants and animals need in order to live could then be found on the earth. There was air, moisture, heat, and light.

No one knows just how life first started. It is one of the many things that we do not know at the present time, but we are sure that life began a very long time ago, millions of years ago. We are also sure that the first living thing was very tiny. There are some reasons for thinking that the first things which lived and grew upon the earth were more like plants than animals.

Perhaps in some pool or a part of the ocean where it was just warm enough, a little plant started to live. It may have been so small that we could not have seen it with a microscope. Of course that first tiny plant did not look at all like our great plants today.

After millions of years some of those forms of early life no doubt developed into tiny one-celled plants and animals. It is thought that from these forms came the many-celled plants and animals whose forms or prints have been found in the rocks.

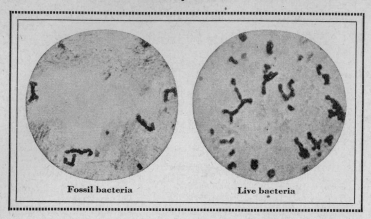

Fossil bacteria　　　　　Live bacteria

A comparison of bacteria which lived many
years ago with bacteria which are alive today[1]

Many things are known about one-celled plants and
animals because some of these forms are living today.
There are immense numbers of them, although we cannot see them with the eye alone. We must use a microscope to see them. They eat and grow, and when they
become a certain size, each divides in half and makes
two instead of one. Then each of these two grows and
divides in half, and there are four. Each of the four
divides after a while, and there are then eight. You can
easily see that it would not take long until there would
be millions of these tiny living things.

No two living things are exactly alike, although they
may be of the same kind. You may have seen a great
many dogs. But how different they look! Even dogs
of the same kind do not look alike. One collie dog does

[1] From " Origin and Evolution of Life," by H. F. Osborn. Charles
Scribner's Sons.

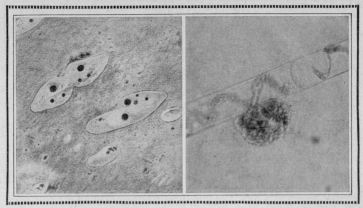

These are one-celled animals as they appear when one
looks at them through a microscope. The one on the
left is dividing and making two animals. The round
figure on the right is an animal feeding on a tiny plant

Photograph by Professor Francis E. Lloyd

not look exactly like other collie dogs. He may be a
little different in the shape of his head, the color of his
hair, or the length of his legs. You may have owned
several cats. Did they all look exactly alike? If you
will take a number of leaves from the same tree, you will
see that they are not exactly alike. This has been true
of all living things, probably from the beginning.

None of these tiny plants was exactly like the others.
Perhaps after a time one of these small living things
could not make its food; so it started to live on the
others. This one may have been the first animal. Today we have many small animals, so small that we need
a microscope to see them. They cannot make their
own food, as green plants can; therefore they must use
plants for food in order to live.

That first animal may have been able to circle around a plant and use it for food. Then after a while it divided into two, and there were two tiny animals instead of one. Then these two divided, and so on, until there were thousands of these tiny animals.

During all that time the plants and animals were very small. If we had been watching, we should have thought that huge plants, such as our trees, and animals, such as elephants, could never live on the earth.

But after a long time a number of cells began living together. They gradually began to act as if they were one living thing instead of many. Of course you can see an advantage in their living together. Each could have a special work to do. Some could act as a mouth and take in the food, while others could digest it.

These little cells did not plan to work together. It may have happened that some of them lived so close together that they could not do otherwise. Later when the water became so crowded that it was difficult to get enough to eat, the many-celled plants and animals may have been better able to secure food than many of the smaller, weaker ones. At any rate, more many-celled plants and animals developed. But not all living things became many-celled, for we have many one-celled plants and animals living today.

After a long time some plants and animals began to live on land. It is needless to say that they did not suddenly march out and go on to the land. It may have been that certain of these living things lived near the shore. Sometimes the tides caused them to be out of the water for many hours. Some of them finally became able to grow on the dry land, perhaps at first only around wet rocks. But later some differed enough from the others so that they were able to live on land all the time.

2. Jellyfishes

It is not easy to read the chapters in the earth's history that deal with the first life. The first animals were so small that they left no record of their story. They could make no footprints, and even when they died their bodies were too soft to leave any fossils.

Just as you have seen that living things of the same kind today are not exactly alike, so in the past the young plants and animals were not always exactly like their parents. Some of them may have differed a great deal, and after thousands of years a new kind of living thing sometimes developed. At times this new kind of living thing was more successful in finding food and in protecting itself against the cold, heat, and enemies than its great-great-grandparents.

Thus new kinds of living things developed. One of these early kinds of animals was the jellyfish. It was very much like the jellyfishes we see along the seashore when the waves wash them in. It was soft and had no shell. It was too soft to leave many prints in the rocks.

While the jellyfishes were floating around getting their food from the water, some little animals began forming shells on the outside of themselves. These shells were hard, and they protected the little animals from their enemies, for by this time animals were eating one another and using one another for food.

3. Trilobites

As yet the earth was almost barren, but the sea was full of queer little forms of life. One kind of animal that was living then and succeeded in protecting itself against its enemies for a long, long time was the trilobite. The trilobites were animals that had a tough outer covering on top and a soft skin underneath. This hard top saved them from many an enemy that tried to attack them from above.

There were many kinds of trilobites. Some of them lived by eating other animals that were not so well protected. Some lived entirely upon plant life that they found in the water. Others preferred a well-balanced diet and ate both plants and animals. They liked both meat and vegetables.

These animals were numerous in early times. They were found in many different parts of the bodies of water. Some lived on the bottom of the shallow seas, some floated around in the water, and others lived out in the deepest places.

Most of the trilobites were strong, but some of them were poor swimmers. Since these poor swimmers had other ways of catching their food, they did not always need to swim after it.

Usually these little animals lived on the bottom of

These trilobites lived in ancient seas

Courtesy of the United States National Museum

the seas, which was often soft. They darted and plowed their way through the soft bottom of the seas in search of food. Others burrowed into the mud with only their eyes sticking up out of the mud. There they lay ready to grab any plant or animal that happened to be passing their way. Usually the trilobites were very flat. Their big eyes extended out on top of their heads.

When enemies of the trilobites became very numerous, the trilobites had to protect themselves in better ways. Before this time they had depended upon their tough skin for protection. But this did not protect the soft parts underneath. Some of them learned the trick of

These shellfishes and trilobites were left
on the shore when the tide went out

rolling up in a ball, which enabled the hard surface on
top to protect the soft part inside. Many of these grew
spines that stuck out like porcupine quills.

The only trilobites that continued to live were the
ones that developed this trick of coiling up. The others
were killed. Soon, then, the only living trilobites were
those that rolled up.

But even this trick did not always protect them.
Larger animals had a way of killing them. The enemies
had claws and pincers with which they grabbed the
trilobites. Possibly, if the trilobites had had pincers
like crawfishes and lobsters, they might have protected
themselves and continued to live.

By the time of the Coal Age, which is a later age, the trilobites were rapidly disappearing. All of them are extinct now. We shall never see one alive, but we know what they looked like from their fossils.

Many times while the trilobites were plowing around in the mud or were swimming about, great loads of mud were piled on top of them. Rivers carried sediment down into the seas, and the sediment covered the animals, or great landslides slipped down upon them before they could escape. There they remained while the mud was being changed into stone. As they lay there, they were making a record of themselves. Any print like this of an animal that shows us how the animal looked millions of years ago helps to tell the story. It is fossils like these that have played an important part in showing us what the earth was like long, long ago.

Many fossils of simple types of seaweed have been found on the same pieces of stone with trilobite fossils, which shows that they lived in the seas at the same time that the trilobites were so numerous.

 *Things to Think About*

1. Bacteria, which are one-celled plants, are so small that more bacteria than there are people in New York City can find plenty of room to live in one drop of milk.

2. Why do we think the first living thing was a plant?

3. Why did life not appear on the earth as soon as the earth was first formed?

E

 *Things to Do*

1. Collect a number of leaves from a tree. Are they exactly alike? What differences do you find?

2. Look at a number of trees of the same kind. Do you find them exactly alike?

3. If you have a chance to look at a large number of animals, such as a flock of sheep or a herd of cattle, see what differences you can find.

Problem 2 · Life Stays on the Earth

1. The Age of Fishes

Millions of years passed during which the animal and plant life of the world was composed mostly of simple forms. Then there came a time when life that was not as simple as the earlier forms began to develop. In some of the later layers of rocks, fossils are found which show that fish-like animals and true fishes began to inhabit the water. Because of the number of these fossils this age is sometimes called the Age of Fishes.

The development of fishes was a very important one. All the animals which you have been studying thus far had no backbones. Either they had no hard parts to their bodies at all, or they simply had a hard covering or shell. None, up to this time, had backbones. But during this age they began to develop bony skeletons. Animals, such as jellyfishes and trilobites, which have no backbones, are called invertebrates, and animals with backbones are called vertebrates. Fish-like animals were the first known vertebrates.

One of these early fish-like animals was very small, perhaps one or two inches long. It had no fins on the sides of its body with which it could swim. However, it had a tail that was somewhat like a fin and which it used for moving about in the water. This animal was somewhat like an eel. It had no real jaws with which to bite or chew, but it had a circular mouth with little suckers on it. Since it could not bite or chew, it had to

123

Notice how the tails of these early fishes differ from those of today. Some of the first fishes had armor

Some of the early fishes grew to be giants. This one was eight feet long. His name is *Arthrodira*

suck its food. This animal was probably the first vertebrate.

The shark that is found in our oceans today belongs to one of the oldest groups of living fishes. Sharks were one of the very first of the true fishes. They were about five feet long. These true fishes had fins on each side, and their bodies were covered with scales. All the early fishes were simple in form and were protected by their covering of scales and by a backbone.

Fossils show that during this age large seaweeds were numerous in the seas and oceans. They were tall and had many shapes, and they furnished food for many of the sea animals. Smaller animals depended upon these plants to protect them from their larger enemies. When they were hidden in the seaweed, their enemies could hardly see them.

Trilobites were rapidly growing fewer during the Age of Fishes. Their fossils are not so numerous as they were in the previous age. They may not have been able to protect themselves against their enemies. Other animals were taking their place. Corals and sponges of various kinds that had hard coverings were becoming more common. They were very much like the corals and sponges that live in our oceans today. They fastened themselves to rocks and seaweed, where they remained and formed great colonies.

Other animals were also developing. Horseshoe crabs which looked somewhat like our common kind had appeared just before this age. Scorpions, which were probably the first animals to leave the water and

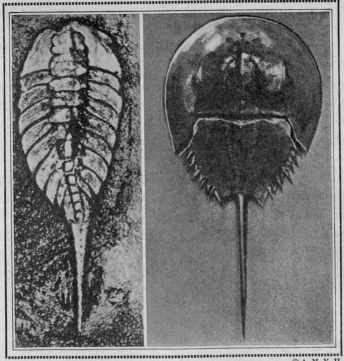

On the left is a fossil of a horseshoe crab which lived millions of years ago; on the right is a horseshoe crab of today

to go upon the land, lived at this time. Their bodies had several joints in them, and to a few of these joints were fastened several pairs of legs. The first scorpions had lived under the water, where they grew to be about three feet long. Smaller scorpions, about two or three inches long, learned to live on land as well as in the water. Some of these kinds have lived through hundreds of millions of years and today look very much as they did then. A sting at the end of their tails has possibly protected the scorpions and enabled their kind to live up into the present age, although they are not so common now as they were then.

Fossils indicate that the climate during this age was probably mild over almost all the earth. Many parts of what is now North America were covered with water, and some of what was then land is now under the ocean. For the first time in the history of the earth there was rich vegetation, which means that the land was covered with plants of many kinds. There were many large forests, but the trees in them were not at all like our well-known oaks and maples. You will read about some of these trees a little later.

2. Early Plant Life

During the ages when different kinds of animals were becoming extinct, and when others were developing, many changes were taking place upon the earth. Climates changed, and land rose and fell. This was probably one cause of the extinction of some plants and the development of others. During the Coal Age, which followed the Age of Fishes, there was a great deal of rainfall over many parts of the earth. The climate was mild and warm all the year round; it was summer all the time, even as far as Greenland, a country which is now almost covered with ice. Great forests of large ferns and tropical plants grew rapidly in the warm, moist atmosphere about the many swamp lands. They could

A fossil fern leaf
Courtesy of the Walker Museum

grow a little each day of their lives. They grew upon a land that knew no winter and that was always green.

But the giant forests that were so numerous were filled with trees that would seem strange to us. The great fern trees were among the giants of the age. Some of them grew to be sixty feet high, or about the height of our common trees, while others grew to an even greater height. None of them had strong woody stems; their trunks were soft and spongy.

Most of these ferns reproduced by spores and had no flowers. But there was one kind that did produce seeds.

As you walk through the woods sometime, notice the small ferns which you may happen to pass. Can you imagine a fern like them as tall as an elm tree? You could never find one as large as that now, and even the smaller ones are becoming scarce.

However, not all the ferns in the Coal Age were of giant size. Some of them grew to be only twenty or thirty feet high, while others were no taller than our own small ferns. In those forests of so long ago the

Ferns are no longer giants of the forests

smaller ferns crowded beneath the larger trees. These, with the giants of the forest, were all so close together that a strong wind never broke through. It was nearly always calm in the center of a large Coal Age forest.

But the ferns were not the only giants, nor were they the greatest of them. Certain plants called horsetails filled the swamps, and many of these grew to be eighty or ninety feet high. The stems were jointed, and at these joints leaves grew in a circle about the stem.

Horsetails grow in our meadows and swamps of to-day, but they are only small humble plants, nothing more than weeds, often lost to sight among the grasses. The stems of these weeds are jointed and pull apart easily. Some children are familiar with these plants, which they pull apart and make into "whistles." When there are leaves on the plant, they are just little scales that are somewhat like tiny needles. They grow around the joint of the stem, which does the work that the leaves of most plants do.

Horsetails do not have flowers like those we find on flowering plants. A cluster of cases that looks like a cone grows on top of the stem or on a separate stalk. These cases contain spores, which grow into new plants.

Club moss is another kind of primitive plant that is found today. It is often called ground pine. It is not really a moss, neither is it a real pine, though it somewhat resembles a pine. During the Coal Age it was the largest and most noticeable of all the trees in the forests. It often grew to be one hundred feet high and three or four feet in diameter. It had stiff needle-shaped leaves which were from four inches to nearly a yard in length. These grew on branches that stretched out from near the top of the tree. Today the descendants of this giant are all small herbs trailing along the ground, where they are seldom noticed and are almost lost among the higher plants.

The *Cordaites* were other great forest trees. They were probably the most important in the forests, but they have long since become extinct. Nowhere in all the world can *Cordaites* be found. The giant redwoods in California are their nearest relatives that we know. But you will read about the redwoods later.

Cordaites were huge trees, over a hundred feet high, with crowns of sword-shaped leaves. Like some of the ferns, they reproduced by real seeds. They were among the first of the cone-bearing trees like our pines, hemlocks, and spruces. These trees had wood that was a little more like the wood of our modern trees. It was less soft and spongy than the trunks of ferns. The tallest plants of the earth were becoming more like our modern trees.

But many of the plants that lived millions of years ago in the Coal Age either have become entirely extinct or are now very rare. As the plants lived and grew and produced seeds which grew into more plants, the climates began to change again. Near the close of the Coal Age the seasons changed. The climate was no longer warm and moist all the year round, but it slowly began to be cold and dry. As many years passed, some of the plants could not become used to living in the cold and dry climates, and many became extinct. Others managed to live, but they became dwarfs. The only ferns and horsetails that succeeded in living are now small and inconspicuous. Not one exists as a tree. *Cordaites* could not continue to live under the new conditions. So it is that many kinds of plants which grew then do not live today.

3. The Coal Age

What happened during the Coal Age

During the Coal Age there were times when the surface of the earth was wrinkling; some of the land was sinking, and some of it was rising. Several times the land that had been sinking began to rise, and some land that had risen began to sink. As the land sank lower and lower, it became lower than the sea, which slowly

A swamp in the Coal Age

came up over it until swamps were gradually formed. At first the water was not deep enough to kill or drown immediately the trees, ferns, and other plants. They continued to grow as they stood in the water.

Twigs and leaves fell from the trees into the water. Animals died, and their bodies were buried under the water. Later, as the water crept farther and farther over the sinking land, the trees began to die. Some continued to grow, while others fell at their feet, their trunks adding to the increasing supply of plant and animal matter in the bottom of the swamp. The land sank lower, and all these materials were covered with water. This went on until all the plants of a once large forest were covered with water.

Sand, mud, and clay were washed down on top of the plants, and little by little more was added. Great storms caused water to rush in, bringing more soil. This mud and water kept the air away from the fallen trees and prevented their complete decay. Then, as years passed, more and more sand and mud were washed in from the higher country around until all the old plant life was far below the surface. The sand and mud were heavy and pressed upon the plant and animal matter, which was now far down in the earth where it was much hotter than on the surface. This heat and pressure began to change the plant and animal matter.

Many years afterwards this land beneath the swamp began rising. It rose very slowly, only a few inches in a century. After many centuries it was again above sea level, and plants could again grow. The mud and sand that had washed down into the swamp made a good place for plants to grow. Then, as in the past, a great forest sprang up, which grew throughout the year, during all the seasons. Smaller plants, ferns, trees, and animals began to grow rapidly. They grew for many years, and some grew to be very large. Then, again, after many centuries the land was once more lowered, and swamps covered much of the land that is now the United States and Europe.

This rising and falling of the land continued for thousands of years. Each time the land rose, a new forest grew; each time the land fell, a forest was drowned, until there were many layers in the earth of trunks of trees, stumps, and plant materials covered with mud,

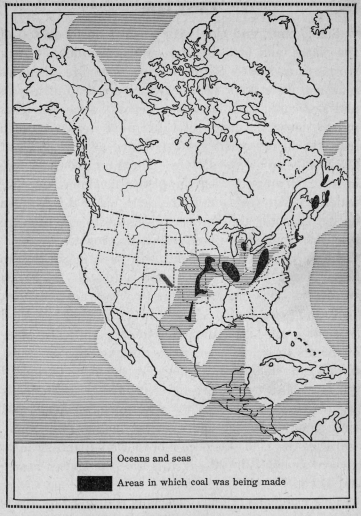

Oceans and seas

Areas in which coal was being made

The white part of the map shows how large North America was at one time. Notice that a great inland sea extended up through what is now the central part of the United States[1]

[1] Based by permission on a map in "Historical Geology," by Pirsson and Schuchert, published by John Wiley & Sons, Inc.

sand, and clay. Each time a forest grew on top and land was washed in, the pressure on the lower layers was increased, and they became hotter.

The plants that were covered on the bottom of the swamp began to change, as they were pressed harder and harder from above. The heat and pressure, after years of time, pressed out much of the water and changed the animal and vegetable matter into muck and peat. These are materials that have only partly changed to coal.

Ages ago, during the time that forests were growing above it, this peat was gradually undergoing more changes. It was being pressed and heated, and heated and pressed, until almost all the water and other impurities had disappeared. Black carbon remained, in the form of coal.

In this way great fields of coal were formed. Most of the coal that is now known was formed in this period in the United States, Europe, and China. There are many fields, however, in other countries. Coal fields have been found even in the Antarctic country. It is from these old forests and swamps that we receive the coal that heats our homes and keeps us warm in winter.

Several different kinds of coal were formed. We have said that peat was first formed. When pressure and heat were added, the peat was changed to lignite, which is a brown coal with many impurities in it, and then to bituminous, or soft, coal. A great amount of the coal that is mined now is in this stage of development. When the vegetable matter was under the greatest heat

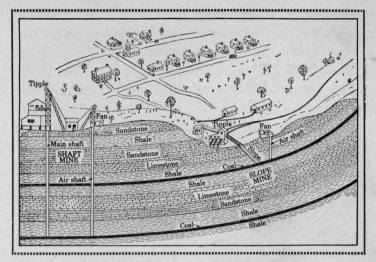

This coal was once a living forest. Today men must go underground to mine it

Courtesy of the United States Bureau of Mines

and pressure, anthracite, or hard, coal was formed.
Get as many of these kinds of coal as possible and
compare them.

Not all coal was made in the past. There is coal
that is being made today. Peat may be found in different parts of the world. In the swamps in Florida,
Virginia, and North Carolina, peat is being made at
the present time. It is being formed very, very slowly.
Do you think that men who are living now will ever
burn it?

Coal was not formed in as short a time as it takes to
read about it or in as short a time as it seems in reading.
Under the most favorable conditions it takes vegetable

E

Swamps like this may be found in many places today.
These trees may be changed into coal, centuries from now

matter, if none of the material is lost, about three
hundred years to produce a coal bed one foot thick.

The rate of plant growth during the Coal Age is not
known, and a great amount of material must have been
lost in the making. Therefore it is estimated that it
probably took almost ten thousand years for plants to
grow and then be changed into a layer of coal one foot
thick.

Some of the coal beds in Pennsylvania are two hundred and fifty feet thick. If one foot of coal was formed
every ten thousand years, imagine how long it took to
form one of these thick coal beds.

Then, later in the Coal Age, mountains rose up far

above the swamps, and the water drained into seas and oceans. During the last of the age much of the land had again come up above the water.

The Age of Amphibians

The Age of Amphibians was a part of the Coal Age. It is thought that up until that time most animals lived in the water, but now several kinds began to explore the land. They could not walk right out of the water and begin living on land. It took centuries for them to become adapted, or accustomed, to living out of water. In the meantime many of them died because they could not adapt themselves to the new conditions.

We do not know exactly why they began their life on land. Perhaps some of them had been in a lake that was formed by the rising of the land. As it dried up, the lake became smaller. It was crowded with many animals. Some of the smaller animals found that they were more protected in shallow water than in deep water, where many of their largest enemies lived. Perhaps as the lake became dry, many of the animals were left on the mud flats. Only those animals succeeded in living that differed from the rest in such a way as to be able to breathe in the air. Many millions of animals died because they could not change their way of living.

If you remember, many water animals have gills like fish. They use these gills for breathing, to take air into their bodies. They take water in through their mouths, and it passes along the gills, which take air out of the water and then allow the water to pass out.

Although frogs and toads did not live in those days long ago, it was their ancestors that were among the first animals that succeeded in living on land. These ancestors were animals that lived part of their life on land and part in the water; such animals are called amphibians.

Amphibians lay their eggs in the water, where the eggs remain until they are hatched. The young animals spend the first part of their life in the water. They breathe through gills and have no legs.

Gradually legs grow out of their sides. Their gills are replaced by lungs, and they are then prepared to live on land as adults. Often they stay close to the water, sometimes using the water as a place to hide for protection.

The earliest amphibians had two ways of breathing. They could use their gills in the water and could breathe through their lungs on the land. This was a very important change from earlier animals. They had legs to walk on the land and a kind of tail that they used in swimming.

At first they had small heads and long slender bodies. They were somewhat like the common salamanders, or newts, which are found under rocks in streams. Some of the later amphibians were large with large heads and short heavy bodies.

Since some of these later amphibians were large and awkward, they are thought to have been rather lazy, slow-moving creatures. Some were seven or eight feet long. Probably these big lazy animals lay half on the land and half in the water, waiting for some animal

This is how the earth may have looked during the Age of Amphibians

After a drawing by S. W. Williston

to pass by. They enjoyed the sun, rested, and ate their meals whenever food chanced to come their way.

Some of these creatures were protected by a heavy outside armor. These were the animals that were slow, awkward, and lazy. They had little need for other kinds of protection. However, some amphibians did not have this heavy outside covering for protection. This kind developed legs for fast running, and they were able to flee from their enemies.

This period is called the Age of Amphibians, but there were other animals living at the same time. Snakes and lizard-like creatures were also found then, but the Age of Reptiles came later. Many of the other animals at this time had shells or hard skins to protect them, but the majority had not as yet developed a backbone.

Other animals of the Coal Age

If we could go back and walk around during a day in the Coal Age, we should see several kinds of animals that would look quite familiar. There were many insects which were the ancestors of our dragon flies, grasshoppers, crickets, beetles, and cockroaches. Many of them were very large. Fossils of cockroaches show that they were very much larger than they are now, some of them being about four inches long. There were about five hundred different kinds, and all of them were meat-eaters. They lived upon smaller invertebrates and upon one another, and the scorpions and spiders lived upon the cockroaches.

The cockroaches, however, were not the greatest giants of the day; they were just the giants of the cockroach family. Beetles of several kinds were present in great numbers. The true giants of the meadows and swamps were the dragon flies. We think that we are seeing large ones when we see some that measure four inches across their wings. We are told that in the time that the amphibians were walking around in great numbers, some of the dragon flies would have measured two feet across their wings. How should you have liked to meet a large group of them? They were perfectly harmless and would not have hurt you at all. There were thousands of insects, but there were no bees or ants. Can you guess why?

Animals of any age depend upon the kinds of plants which furnish them with food. Since there were no flowering plants, it would have been impossible for the bees to find honey. Bees did not develop until there were flowers. Most of the insects lived upon other animals instead of upon flowers and plants. Some of them lived by eating the leaves of the plants.

It is thought that there were no insects at this time that could make a noise. We know that there were no birds, and the world was without their songs. Probably the only noise would have been the croaking of frogs. Wouldn't that have been queer?

 Things to Think About

1. If your room is fifteen feet high, how many times as high was a ninety-foot horsetail?

2. Club mosses that once grew to be one hundred feet high in the Coal Age forests are about six inches high in our own forests.

3. Why is coal sometimes found in hills and mountains, when it was formed in swamps?

4. Is coal being made as rapidly as it is being used?

5. When you put a shovelful of coal into the furnace, think about where it might have been formed. Does it take as long for it to burn as it did for it to form?

6. Is man a vertebrate or an invertebrate?

7. Can you think of any reasons for animals' becoming extinct?

Things to Do

1. Make a list of animals that are now living which are vertebrates.

2. Make a list of animals that are now living which are invertebrates.

3. Name the different kinds of coal and tell how each was formed.

4. If one foot of coal was formed every ten thousand years, how long did it take a coal bed to form which is two hundred feet thick?

5. Build a coal mine showing layers of plants and animal matter.

6. Tell how coal is mined.

7. Write the history of a piece of coal.

8. Write a story telling what you think the life of an amphibian would have been like in the swamps.

9. Make a series of drawings to show how you think the earth looked in the different ages about which you have been studying. Add these to your scrapbook of "The Story of the Earth."

UNIT VI

Life Continues to Develop

1. The Age of Reptiles
2. The Earliest Known Birds and Mammals

Great numbers of fishes and amphibians had lived during the past ages, but their kinds and numbers were growing less. Many of the primitive ones were becoming extinct; there were fewer giants and more that resembled our common types.

At the same time that these animals were disappearing, new kinds were developing. This was the age when scaly, backboned animals with great bony skeletons began to live. They were the first reptiles, and this period of time is named for them the Age of Reptiles.

The earliest of these animals were very different from their descendants the snakes, alligators, and turtles of our fields, forests, and swamps. Among them were the dinosaurs. It was during this time that the earliest birds and mammals began to develop. You will read about these in Unit VI. This unit, like the other units of the earth's story, covers millions of years.

Problem 1 · The Age of Reptiles

This was an age when reptiles were everywhere. Huge reptiles walked on land; others with wings that were similar to those of the bats skimmed over land and sea in search of food; still others lazily swam or half floated through the water, looking for something to eat. Can you imagine what a day in the Age of Reptiles might have been like?

A grassy plain on the edge of a river or swamp that was bordered on the other side by a forest was a delightful and favorite spot for these prehistoric monsters. Many of them fed on near-by trees and came down to the water to drink.

Dinosaurs varied in size, shape, and habits. Many of these creatures were very small and swift-running. They ran on their hind legs and stood almost erect. Others were tremendously large and continued to grow all their lives. They never reached a full-grown stage, but continued getting larger as long as they lived. They were the giants of all the ages.

The dinosaurs were strange beasts, but they were not clever. Their brains were so small and poorly developed that they could not depend upon getting out of danger by using their intelligence. They had to depend upon their great size or upon scales and horns to protect them.

There were two chief classes of the giant dinosaurs. Some were huge animals that fed upon leaves of

© F. M. N. H.

Fin-backed reptiles which were probably meat-eaters

trees, or ate plants that grew along the banks of the rivers or on the bottoms of swamps. The others were great flesh-eating animals with saw-edged teeth six inches long. They were cannibals and ate the less fortunate vegetable-eating reptiles that came near them.

Diplodocus was one of the vegetable-eating dinosaurs that walked on all four legs. Sometimes he reached a length of eighty feet if measured from the nose to the tip of the tail. How many times as long as your room is that? How many children could have sat on an animal like that? Had you tried to ride this animal, you would have had to be very careful. If he had switched his tail to one side, he could have knocked down rows of children. When he was walking, he would scarcely have seen anything so small as a child.

These are some of the early reptiles that lived before the dinosaurs

This dinosaur, *Diplodocus*, had a very long neck and tail, and by standing on his hind legs and by stretching out his neck he could have looked over a three-story or four-story building. But of course there was no building of any kind for him to look over. However, he did look over the tops of trees and eat their branches. When he stood up on his hind legs this way he braced himself with his tail.

Brontosaurus, which means "Thunder-Lizard," was a close relative of *Diplodocus*, but he was probably a little smaller. The longest one known was about seventy feet long and fifteen feet high at the hips. The body was large and stout, with a long neck and tail and great, heavy legs. His foot made a print that covered nearly

This armored dinosaur was well protected

a square yard. He weighed from eighteen to forty tons, but his head was only about as large as a horse's head, and his brain was very small. A favorite pastime of this beast was to wade lazily through a swamp, eating plants from the bottom of the water. Every once in a while he may have stretched his neck to look around to be sure that no enemy was slipping up on him unawares. What huge animal of today do you know that walks on the bottom of rivers for protection? Do you know an animal that is said to stay in the water because he is very heavy? Perhaps the *Brontosaurus* stayed in the water because he was buoyed up by it. By this we mean that the water helped to hold him up so that there wasn't so much weight on his feet.

The Plated Lizard, or *Stegosaurus*, also ate no meat. If you could have seen one of these animals, you would have thought him the funniest-looking creature that you had ever seen. He had two rows of bony plates, which were about two feet across and ran up and down his back from head to tail. On his tail he had bony spines that were three feet long. If he had swung his tail to one side when you were laughing at him, it would not have seemed so funny.

This reptile was smaller than some of the others. He was about twenty feet long and ten feet high at the hips. Yet he would seem large to us. His hind legs were very much longer and heavier than his front ones. His neck was so short and stout that he could not reach his head up very far; it was held down near the ground. His neck was as short as the neck of *Diplodocus* was long.

There was a three-horned dinosaur that looked somewhat like a rhinoceros. His name was *Triceratops*, which means "Three-Horned Face." He had one horn over each eye and one on his nose, and a peculiar skull reached back off his face. He used his horns in fighting other animals, and also in protecting himself against his enemies. Imagine two *Triceratops* fighting together.

All four of these animals — *Diplodocus*, *Brontosaurus*, *Triceratops*, *Stegosaurus* — and some others were plant-eaters. They were harmless to all animals except those that got in their way when they were walking and were stepped on. Other dinosaurs were not so harmless. Since the fossils of the *Allosaurus* show him to have

© A. M. N. H.

Allosaurus was an enemy of other dinosaurs

had powerful jaws that contained long, sharp teeth, scientists have called him a flesh-eating dinosaur. He was very swift-running and could catch other animals for food. These dinosaurs had sharp claws with which they held the animals they had caught, while they tore off the flesh with their great teeth. Teeth of the *Allosaurus* have been found with fossils of vegetable-eating dinosaurs. An *Allosaurus* may have knocked out a tooth in a battle with an animal that it later used as food. Its skin was somewhat like leather.

The largest of these dinosaurs were over thirty feet long and about eight feet high. There was a smaller, bird-catching *Allosaurus* that was only seven feet long. Its feet were similar to birds' feet. Some of the fossils that men first thought were bird tracks are now believed to be fossils of small dinosaurs. Many of these reptiles may have lived on dead animals, as crows and buzzards do now.

No animal living today is as dangerous as that fearful beast of long ago named *Tyrannosaurus*. He was not so large as *Diplodocus* or *Brontosaurus*, but he was larger than *Allosaurus* and was the tyrant of the dinosaurs. He was over forty feet long and twenty feet tall. If three men stood, one on the shoulders of another, they wouldn't reach the height of this animal. Just think how Thunder-Lizard or Plated Lizard must have felt to have this monster chasing him with outstretched front feet and claws and with a mouth wide open, showing long, sharp teeth. These large animals could take very large steps, but *Tyrannosaurus* could run faster and usually caught up with the more clumsy animal.

Some of the reptiles lived in the water. *Ichthyosaurus* was a fish-like reptile. His head was made in such a way that he could catch fish very easily. He lived on the fish he caught. His paddle-like limbs made it easy for him to go through the water.

The pterodactyl, which is sometimes called Finger-Wing, was a flesh-eating reptile that could fly. It is sometimes also called the dragon of the air. It had no feathers, but there were membranes, or skin, stretched over its arms, and these membranes were fastened to one finger that was very long. Some pterodactyls had long tails; others had very short ones. It was a long time after the first reptiles appeared before any of them started to develop wings. The wings did not just

E

These pterodactyls were flying reptiles

suddenly appear. It may have been that as certain reptiles used their back legs a great deal for walking, their front legs became wider, and by flapping them they were able to help themselves move about. But of course we do not know just how it happened.

Some of these flying dragons were small; others were large. They varied from the size of one of our common sparrows or swallows to a size larger than any birds that we know. When these largest ones stretched their wings, they measured thirty feet from tip to tip. That is larger than some of our small airplanes.

The pterodactyls, or Finger-Wings, flew long distances from shore and probably fished as they glided over the water. They may have chased insects too. None of these animals exist now, and the only way we know anything about them is by the fossils we have found. Landslides which covered these animals, or sediment that washed over them, kept the air away from them, and their bones were left as fossils.

Fossils of dinosaurs have been found all over the earth, on every continent and on New Zealand. Many have been discovered in the western parts of the United States. The dinosaurs lived there before the Rocky Mountains were formed, at a time when that country was level and covered with lakes and tropical plants. In the western part of the United States eighty acres of land has been set aside as the Dinosaur National Monument. This park has many fine fossils of dinosaurs, and from them men will probably learn other things about these animals. Some of the very finest skeletons have been found in this park.

Problem 2 · The Earliest Known Birds and Mammals

The earliest known birds and mammals developed during the latter part of the age of terrifying lizards and flying reptiles. They were the beginning of a new group of animals. Until this time all the animals — the trilobites, fishes, amphibians, and reptiles — were cold-blooded. But in this new group were the first warm-blooded animals that had ever lived upon the earth. However, many other warm-blooded animals developed later.

Fossil skeletons of the first kind of bird are found in the same layers of rocks in which fossils of the early reptiles are found. While dinosaurs were numerous on the land and water the first birds were struggling to live.

This first kind of bird is called *Archæopteryx*. Its fossil skeleton shows that it was a small bird, about the size of our common crow or pigeon. It was not nearly so large as most of the flying reptiles that flew and glided through the air during the same time. A bird so small must have had difficulty in living when other flying animals were over ten or fifteen times larger.

Archæopteryx did not look very much as birds do now. It had feathers as our birds do, but the entire body was not covered. The wings and tail had many feathers, and there were some on the back, but there were very few, if any, feathers on the head. Its tail was longer than the rest of the body, and it was covered

156

Can you see how *Archæopteryx* differed from birds of today?

with long feathers. Except for the feathers, the wings looked somewhat like the wings of the flying reptiles. They were short and rounded, and had claws that the bird used for holding on to the branches of trees. Perhaps it used these claws for climbing. The wings were not very strong, and the muscles that birds now use most in flying were absent.

This ancient bird differed in other ways from modern birds. It had jaws that contained many small teeth, and it did not have a beak at all. Its head was small with very large eyes.

The *Archæopteryx*, with its wings for flying and the claws on its wings for climbing, could very easily live in the trees. Any animal that lived in the trees at that dangerous time had a great advantage over some of the other small creatures. It was not very safe for any small animal to walk on the ground, where it was likely to be eaten or stepped on by the great dinosaurs. It was just as dangerous to live in the water because the seas were inhabited by huge monsters. But a bird as small as a crow might easily be safe, hidden carefully among the leaves of the trees. Then, if it were disturbed, it could fly to a near-by tree and again hide itself. The *Archæopteryx* failed to live on through all the ages that followed, but some of its near relatives are living now.

Today there is a bird living in South America which, like the extinct *Archæopteryx*, has claws on its wings that it uses to climb trees. This bird cannot sing; it makes a very harsh, croaking noise. Since it is somewhat similar to the *Archæopteryx*, some people think that the extinct bird made a croaking sound and could not sing.

Other birds soon developed. Only a few fossils of these are found, and they show that the birds soon took on various ways of living. Many were quite different from the *Archæopteryx*.

One kind was a good swimmer. Its feet were partly webbed, which helped it in swimming. It could swim through the water with great speed and could dive very easily. This bird caught most of its food in the water.

Giant birds also developed, some of them being eight or ten feet tall. Their wings could not hold them up in the air, but they did not need to fly, for they had long, strong legs that carried them rapidly over the ground. They had strange heads that were almost two feet long and looked somewhat like a horse's head. One of the largest of these birds was the Elephant Bird.

Although several kinds of birds had developed, there were as yet no birds that could sing as the birds do today.

At the same time that the giant lizards and flying reptiles were numerous on the land, in the sea, and in the air, and the *Archæopteryx* was struggling to live, other animals scarcely as large as rats sped swiftly along the ground. They dodged from one hiding place to another quite unnoticed, as they hunted for food and avoided their enemies. Always keeping as nearly out of sight as possible, these tiny beasts had a hard struggle to keep alive in a land that was inhabited by giants.

Fossils of the teeth of these animals have been found which make scientists believe that these dwarf-like creatures ate juicy grasses and roots which they found along the ground. They also ate worms and insects. They robbed the nests of birds and lizards and ate their eggs or young. It is also believed that most of them climbed trees and ate any seeds, nuts, and fruits which they found there. Sitting among the branches and leaves of the trees, they were quite safe from the land monsters and could eat in peace.

These animals were the first of a group that had never before lived upon the earth. Up to this time no

This duck-billed platypus is probably a descendant of the early egg-laying mammals

mother animal ever had food in her own body with which she could feed her young. The mothers of this group could produce milk in their bodies, and they fed their young until they were old enough to search for their food. Since the animals that feed their young on milk are called mammals, these small animals were the first mammals that ever lived on the earth. The first mammals that developed during the Age of Reptiles were very different from our mammals, such as the cats, dogs, and cattle. But they were also very different from the other animals that lived at the same time.

These early mammals were among the first animals that cared for their young. Before this time animals had laid eggs on the ground or in the water and had left them alone to hatch. When the young crawled out of their shells, they had to care for themselves; they had to find their own food and keep away from enemies. Mothers of the early trilobites, fishes, amphibians, and reptiles probably never knew their young. Fishes met their young and passed them as strangers. Some had probably eaten their own young for food. The early mammals were not like that; they laid eggs, and it is thought that they remained with the eggs until they were hatched. After that the mothers nursed the young and protected and cared for them until they were large and strong enough to care for themselves. Since the mothers fed them and protected them from danger, a larger number of the young succeeded in living. Perhaps that is why these kinds of animals have lived upon the earth for so many years.

These mammals differed in another way from all the animals that had lived before. They were the first fur-bearing animals of which we know. Birds had a covering, too, but it was made of feathers, not fur. Birds had developed feathers and were warm-blooded, but no fur-covered animal had ever lived before that time.

It must have been a strange world to have furry little beasts moving swiftly and quietly along the ground, trembling as they moved lest they be discovered by one of their powerful enemies.

These early egg-laying mammals were so small that if one of them had stood by the side of a great dinosaur it would have looked as small as a cockroach would look standing beside a man. Since they had no weapons of warfare, perhaps their size protected them and allowed them to pass swiftly and unnoticed in the grass, far

The opossum is a marsupial. While these young are on
the mother's back another family may be in her pouch

below the eyes of the terrible monsters. It was probably because of their size, speed, and knowledge of how
to keep away from the giant creatures that they succeeded in living at all.

These kinds of animals lived for many centuries,
but only a few of them were able to protect themselves
enough to live through all the following ages. However, there are two kinds of animals in Australia that
may be descendants of these early creatures. They
are the duck-billed platypus and the spiny anteater.
Both are egg-laying mammals. Out of several hundreds
of different kinds of mammals living on the earth today, these are the only two that lay eggs.

The kangaroo is a marsupial living in Australia. Do you
see the young kangaroo peeping from its mother's pouch?

Later during this same age another class of mammals, called marsupials, appeared. They were animals whose young were born alive, as mammals today are born. But these mammals carried their young about in a little pouch, or bag, that the mother had for that purpose. The young of marsupials were not fully developed when they were born and were carried in the pouch until they were large enough to care for themselves.

The kangaroo of Australia is a marsupial. If the mother kangaroo is being chased by enemies while she is carrying a large young one in her pouch, she has been known to throw it into a bunch of grass or bushes and to run on, in order to lead her enemies away from it.

Besides she can run faster when she has less to carry. Later she comes back for the young. That is one way she has of protecting herself and the baby.

 Things to Think About

1. In how many ways do mammals differ from reptiles? How do they differ from amphibians?

2. Can you think of any reasons for the dinosaurs' becoming extinct?

3. Why do you think the first animals were not warm-blooded ones?

4. Why do the birds and most mammals, which are the only warm-blooded animals, have a covering of feathers or fur?

5. In what ways does a mammal differ from other kinds of animals?

6. Scientists have found dinosaur eggs. Why can these eggs not be hatched?

 ***Things to Do***

1. Model a dinosaur out of clay.

2. In winter make a dinosaur out of ice and snow, just as you would make a snow man.

3. Draw a picture of the flying reptile known as the pterodactyl.

4. Paint a picture of an *Allosaurus* catching another dinosaur.

5. Figure out how many children could have sat on a *Diplodocus* eighty feet long from his head to the tip of his tail.

6. Imagine a day during the Age of Reptiles and write a story about what might have happened on that day. You might imagine the discovery of a country today which was still in the Age of Reptiles.

7. Draw a large picture of a typical scene during the Age of Reptiles. Add it to the other pictures in your "Story of the Earth."

8. Arrange an exhibit of fossils for your school museum.

UNIT VII

The Rise of Plants and Animals

During the ages when mountains gradually rose and fell and when different kinds of animals slowly developed and then became extinct, the kinds of plants growing upon the earth also changed. By the time that the reptiles had developed, the giant plants of the Coal Age—the ferns, horsetails, club mosses, and *Cordaites*—had become either extinct or dwarfs. Horsetails, once the size of trees, were now small plants over which the animals tramped. Ferns that produced seeds were now fast becoming extinct; those that had been giants of the plant kingdom were probably more like our common fern.

Reptiles had inhabited the land for a long, long time, during which the mammals were small and weak. As reptiles then grew fewer in numbers, the mammals became the next group of powerful animals.

Then the world gradually grew colder, and a covering of ice formed which again caused the death of many groups of animals. This was not the first time that much of the earth had been covered by snow and ice. You will read in Unit VII about all these things and about how the world began to be as it is today.

Problem 1 · The Rise of Modern Plants

Plants that seem very strange to us now were beginning to be common in the early part of the Age of Reptiles, and later in that age they became so numerous that it is sometimes called the Age of Cycads, after the plants by that name. The cycads were more numerous during this period than at any other time before or since. But enough of them have lived up into the present age to give us an idea of what they were like. A few cycads are somewhat like palms or ferns, but usually they have woody trunks that grow straight up without branching. Leaves come out at the top of the tree and form a crown. Some cycads have a stem or trunk that grows entirely under the ground, and the leaves spread out aboveground just like those of a radish, turnip, or carrot. Other cycads have trunks that grow to be from twenty to fifty feet high. These are a foot or more in diameter, and at the top of these trees grows a cluster of large leaves that are cut into narrow leaflets.

Cycads do not drop their leaves in the autumn. Like the evergreens, as the leaves grow old they fall off one by one during any season. As the cycad leaf falls, it leaves the base of the stem, where it was fastened to the trunk. These bases collect and form a protection for the trunk of the tree.

These plants live to be very old. One cycad that is six feet high is believed to be a thousand years old, and it is still living.

Some cycads have cones that contain seeds. The cones are often of very bright colors, orange or yellow, and they stand straight up in the middle of the top of the tree.

The cycads that are living today are found mostly in the Southern Hemisphere. There are only two kinds found in the United States. These grow in Florida. They belong to the group that has its stems underground and a crown of leaves with many narrow, sharp, pointed leaflets sticking out above the ground.

One kind of cycad lives today in Mexico and grows to be five or six feet tall. This variety has large seeds that are somewhat like chestnuts. People boil or roast them to eat. A valuable food that is known as sago is produced from this cycad. It is therefore sometimes called a sago palm, although it is not related to true palms.

These cycads are only a few descendants of the many kinds that were so important during the middle of the Age of Reptiles. During that time cycads grew in almost all parts of the world. Their fossils are found over several continents from the Arctic to the Antarctic regions. Some of them were very much like our modern varieties, while others were quite different. Fossils of leaves show that some were very large — three or four feet long and from sixteen to twenty inches wide. Fossils found in the Black Hills in South Dakota show that there the cycad trees had short barrel-like trunks, usually from a foot to four feet high. Some of them were thicker than they were tall.

A cycad living today in Florida. At one
time some cycads were much larger

At this time there was an increasing number of cone-bearing trees which were similar to some of our ever-greens. There were certain trees which were early relatives of the big sequoias that grow in California at present. They are the "big trees" that you hear so much about. They are all that remain of great forests which grew from Canada to California.

In the latter part of the Age of Reptiles, the sequoias covered many parts of North America, Europe, and Asia. But with the changing climates and the glaciers that followed, they continued to grow only in one place in the Sierra Nevada.

These trees are probably the oldest living things known. Their annual rings of growth show that some of them are from two thousand to three thousand years old. They are the largest known of the cone-bearing trees. The redwoods, which are one kind of sequoia, are sometimes from 200 to 360 feet tall and about ten or fifteen feet in diameter. One tree has been found that is 308 feet high and twenty feet thick, and its red bark is eleven inches thick. It has been estimated that there is wood enough in that tree to furnish the lumber to build twenty-two houses of ordinary size.

These trees have been able to live through many conditions which would kill other trees. They are most unusual because insects do little injury to them and they will not burn easily. The wood contains a good deal of moisture, and it does not contain pitch, which burns readily. Perhaps it is these advantages which have enabled them to live so long.

Some of these redwoods began growing hundreds
of years before Columbus discovered America

Photograph by United States Forest Service

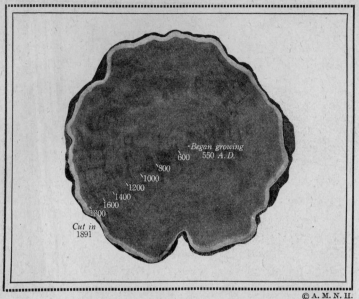

Began growing
550 A.D.
600
800
1000
1200
1400
1600
1800
Cut in
1891

We tell the age of a tree by counting
the rings. How old was this redwood?

The worst enemy of the redwoods has been man, who at an early date cut down hundreds of trees for lumber. Since that time the forest has been made a national park, and the trees are protected. They will probably live for many more centuries.

There is another tree that appeared during the Age of Reptiles that has a great deal of interest for us. This is the ginkgo tree. It is often called the maidenhair tree because it has very peculiar wedge-shaped leaves which resemble the leaves of the maidenhair fern. Today it is the only living kind, or species, of a large family of trees that grew in many parts of the world.

Ginkgo trees are living today because they
were used by the Chinese as sacred trees

It has had a very unusual history. In Japan and
China it has long been held as a sacred tree. The people
planted ginkgoes around their temples and cared for
them. In this way this species has been saved. From
China and Japan it has been taken to many other coun-

tries, where it is used as an ornamental and shade tree. It has lately been reported that wild species of ginkgoes have been found in some of the mountains of China, but it is doubtful that they are found wild in any other place.

The ginkgo trees of the present are probably direct descendants of those trees that lived during the Age of Reptiles. They are probably the oldest species of living trees that have come down to us without many changes. Perhaps for ten million years ginkgo trees have looked almost exactly like their ancestors of so long ago. It would be almost impossible to tell the difference between the prints of the ancient leaves and prints of the leaves of today.

Since this tree is used about the temples of the Chinese and is planted in parks as an ornamental tree in different countries of the world, it is protected and will probably not become extinct for some time, although all the other members of the ginkgo family have long since died out.

The logs of stone in Arizona, which you read about earlier in this book, were a living forest during the Age of Reptiles. The thousands of fossil logs that are scattered throughout this region tell a great deal about some of the trees that grew millions of years ago. The logs that lie as stones on the desert tell us that many of the trees grew to be from three to four feet in diameter and that they grew to great heights. Many of the logs are from sixty to eighty feet long. One unusually large log is seven feet in diameter and 125 feet long. Just think what a giant of the forest that tree must have been.

This stone log makes a natural bridge in the petrified forest

One great log forms a natural bridge across a ravine that is about thirty feet wide and twenty feet deep. As this log lay on the softer sandstone and clay, the water washed under it and wore away the softer rocks, making the ravine. The hard stone which now forms the log was strong enough to withstand the years of weathering. It is thought that this is the only bridge in the world that is made of a log of stone. The log reaches over each side of the ravine and is 111 feet long. It is four feet thick at one end and eighteen inches at the other, which makes it large and strong enough for people to walk on in crossing the ravine below.

None of these trunks have branches remaining on them. All the branches had been broken off and most of them destroyed, but a few petrified, or stone, branches are found scattered about over the ground. We do not know exactly how these trees looked, but they were some kind of pine-like trees that bore cones. They lived long before our present-day trees began to live. The oaks, elms, and maples would then have been strangers in a strange land. Most of the trees at that time bore cones. These ancient pine-like trees became extinct in North America ages ago.

Fossils have been found of about four hundred kinds of plants that lived a little later in the Age of Reptiles. During the period that plants were developing, each new plant became more like plants that we know. At the time that ferns, cycads, sequoias, and ginkgoes were most numerous, the land was covered with green. There had been no flowers on the earth in the millions of years of the earth's story previous to this time.

Then gradually new kinds of plants developed which added many colors to the earth. These were the flowering plants. The fields became gay with color. These new species of plants were to grow upon the earth throughout the ages to come. Ferns and cycads were crowded into the background, and the world seemed to be bubbling over with flowering plants. The last bright spots had appeared to make this earth we know an earth of birds and the songs of birds and the beauty of flowers.

With the coming of the flowers it was possible for honeybees, moths, and butterflies to develop. They darted from flower to flower, searching for the honey on which they lived. They were the last great group of insects to develop.

Problem 2 · The Fall of Reptiles and the Rise of Mammals

1. Many Reptiles became Extinct

During the Age of Reptiles mammals were very small and unimportant. Their brains were small in comparison with their bodies. If you could have lived then, you could never have imagined that mammals would be the most important animals of the next age. These mammals, during the Age of Reptiles, had a very difficult time trying to protect themselves and to live. They struggled this way for many years, but most of them did not succeed in living into the next age. However, they represented the beginning of the development of the mammals that live today.

Reptiles had lived upon the land for a long, long time, while mammals scarcely counted in the animal world. But there came a time when reptiles were not so great and so strong as they had been. We do not know exactly what happened to the great dinosaurs and other giant reptiles, but their kind began to fail. During the last part of the great Age of Reptiles, and in the beginning of the next age, there were many changes in the surface of the earth that may have affected the dinosaurs.

For ages the surface of the earth had been gradually changing. Soil had washed from the highlands into the seas. Pressure had been collecting in places within the earth, and so again layers of rock slipped upon other

179

These are the reptiles of today

layers, lava flowed out of cracks, and volcanoes poured forth into the air volumes of steam and other gases. Volcanic dust and ashes spread over the surface of the earth. Mountains were gradually pushed up where seas and swamps had been. The water drained from the highlands, and the swamps slowly dried up and disappeared. The swamp-loving dinosaur must have had great difficulty in finding food. All these changes may have helped to cause dinosaurs and many other animals and kinds of plants to disappear from the earth. But while they were disappearing, other groups of plants and animals grew in size and number.

Hence the Age of Reptiles passed, leaving only the turtles, lizards, and crocodiles as the most important reptiles to live on through the ages. However, it was at this time that snakes began to increase in number, although at first they were small, quite rare, and were not poisonous.

It was also at this time that mammals began to develop tremendously, and the age that followed was one in which mammals were the most important animals. They began to grow larger, and as their bodies grew larger, their brains increased in size. They became more numerous. They were not like the egg-laying mammals and marsupials that had lived during the Age of Reptiles. And even though they were curious-looking creatures, they were more highly developed than the first mammals.

These later mammals were beginning to be more like our modern species of animals. Many of them lived only during this age and then became extinct.

The mammals were of many kinds. Some of them grew to be huge beasts, larger than any living elephant. Some of the very largest mammals that we know about lived at this time, but there were also many small mammals.

There were animals that walked on five toes, others walked on two, while some walked on only one. The two toes of some, and the one toe of others, were tough and thick and were called hoofs. The animals that had these were called hoofed animals. They were usually the kind that fed on the thick grass of the plains or on weeds and shrubs or on the leaves of trees. They had the kind of teeth that could chew grass and plants. These hoofed animals were usually harmless;

but they always had to be on the watch for animals that might harm them.

Many of the five-toed mammals did not eat grass and weeds and leaves of young shrubs and trees. Their teeth were formed for eating flesh, and they lived upon the animals that fed upon plants.

The plant-eating mammals were not always protected against their enemies. They had no teeth with which to fight, nor claws with which to scratch, but some of them had other weapons. These were often sharp horns or tusks, which they used in battle against the enemy. Some of these animals could run very swiftly and succeeded in escaping their enemies in that way. Others were clever and knew how to avoid dangers. Animals that could not defend themselves could not live.

Some of the plant-eating animals were the horses, rhinoceroses, camels, cattle, bisons, and deer. Of course these mammals were not just like the modern animals with the same names, but many of them were their ancestors and looked like them in many ways.

2. The Age of Mammals

The first horses

The very earliest kind of horse that scientists know about was not like a modern horse. It had four toes on each front foot and three toes on each hind foot. Its body was long, and its legs were short. It was about as large as a good-sized dog or fox.

This shows skeletons of horses during the different ages. The one on the left is the first horse; the one on the right is the horse of today

From Amherst College Collection

Should you like to know the name that scientists gave the earliest horse? It is *Eohippus*. *Eohippus* first lived in the forests, and he escaped from his enemies by running.

As time went on, horses became larger. Later on they had only one large toe, or hoof, on each foot. The legs of the later horses were more slender and could move with much greater speed than the legs of earlier horses. Perhaps only the horses that had developed more slender legs had escaped their enemies. They escaped their enemies by using this speed. By this time many of the forests had changed to grassy plains, and the horse needed to run rapidly in order to escape. Those animals that could not run rapidly were captured and used as food by their enemies, and their kind soon became extinct.

During the early ages many horses ran wild on the plains of North America, but at some time something happened that caused them to disappear from North America. At that same time, however, there were wild horses in Europe and Asia. It was not until the Span-

This is how horses looked a long time ago

iards brought horses with them into the southern United States and Mexico, and later left them to run loose, that wild horses again trampled our plains. They increased in number. Then they were caught, tamed, and used by men until at present there is only one kind of truly wild horse in the world. That is the small Asiatic wild horse. There are not many of them to be found.

Rhinoceroses

The word *rhinoceros* means "nose-horn," which is a very good name for the rhinoceros we know today. But it did not fit some of the earliest of these animals.

Although there were some that had horns with which they protected themselves, most of them were hornless. They had to protect themselves by other means.

The rhinoceros is a relative of the horse. At first it was small and slender and much more like a horse than the rhinoceros we know. But later its legs became shorter, and its body clumsy and awkward. One of the early rhinoceroses was about the size of a fox or a little larger. It was light and slender and could run from its enemies. Another kind was tall enough to eat twigs sixteen feet above the ground. Rhinoceroses roamed over North America in the latter part of the Age of Mammals and in the beginning of the Ice Age.

Elephants

The elephants were not at all like the giants of the jungle that we know. They were small, with very short trunks and tusks. In the Age of Mammals they were not so heavy as elephants are today and could reach the ground with their mouths; so they did not need long trunks. Later the trunk became so long that now elephants eat from the ground without bending their heads, and tusks have become so large that some weigh 200 pounds apiece.

The earliest elephants are thought to have first lived in northern Africa. They were about the size of a pig and lived near the swamps. Later they lived in North America, and in the Ice Age that follows this age some of the largest elephants ever known lived in the ice and snow. These were the mammoths and mastodons.

E

© F. M. N. H.

The giant sloth, which is now extinct

Sloths

A peculiar animal of this Age of Mammals was the sloth. The largest of the sloths was the giant sloth, which was nearly as large as an elephant and had a heavy tail. The back part of its body was very large and heavy; the front part and legs were much lighter, and it lifted its front legs much as the bear does. In this position the animal fed upon the leaves of trees. When branches were a little high, it pulled them down with its claws so that it could reach the leaves. It also grazed in the open country. The sloths were very awkward and walked on the outer edges of their feet.

These animals were among those which have become extinct. Out in the open country the sloths were easily seen by their enemies, the wolves and tigers. Although they had strong front limbs and stout claws which they

This sloth, which lives today in South America, is very much smaller than the giant sloth. It lives in the trees, where it hangs upside down

used in fighting, they probably did not succeed in many battles against their enemies. This may have been the cause of their becoming extinct.

Even though the ground sloth disappeared, its smaller relative, the tree sloth, has succeeded in living and may now be found in the dense forests of Central and South America. These sloths do not find their food on the ground, but live on the leaves of trees. They hang upside down by their feet on branches of trees and have been known to sleep in this position. Sloths have a shaggy coat of hair. Unlike their giant ancestors these sloths have almost no tail at all. Some have two toes on each foot and are called two-toed sloths, and others have three toes on each foot and are called three-toed sloths.

were so long in one kind of animal that it was called the saber-toothed tiger. When the mouth was closed, these teeth extended down over the lower jaw and were one of this animal's chief weapons.

It is thought that the saber-toothed tiger was not a swift-moving animal. It was about the size of the African lion and depended upon killing large slow-moving mammals. With its strong front legs and claws it attacked and held an animal, cutting it with the great dagger-like teeth. Fossils of the teeth of this beast show that sometimes a tooth was broken in battle. The tiger continued to use the tooth, and after a time it became rounded. The saber-toothed tiger began living in the Age of Mammals, but has been extinct for many years.

Seals, sea lions, and walruses lived by feeding upon the fishes and shellfishes which they found in the sea.

Anteaters tore open the hills made by ants and fed upon them. These anteaters were ancestors of the ones which live today. There were armadillos, whose heads and bodies were protected by an armor of small, bony plates. They were so well protected that they have lived on through the years to the present day.

3. Fossils of Animals in the La Brea Pits

In a small area in California, pits have been found that are filled with tar and oil. As you look at these pits, you see nothing but a dirty, black surface with bubbles of gases coming up through the tar. But down underneath the surface the pits hold a wonderful story.

© F. M. N. H.

The saber-toothed tiger and vultures gathered
around the pits to feed upon victims of the tar

If a small stick or stone rolls onto the mass, it makes a dent in the tar. As you watch, you notice that the stone is sinking slowly into the quiet black substance. It sinks slowly, but steadily, until the tar folds over it, and it is gone.

The stone was not alive and was not harmed. But living things in times past have been harmed. Asphalt pits in Los Angeles, called the La Brea Pits, tell the following story.

Animals running upon the prairie in ages long ago did not see the pits in time to run around them, or they did not know what great danger the pits held for them. They ran out on top of the tar, and just as a stone sinks, these heavier animals, whose feet were held fast by the tar, began to sink. If you have walked on an asphalt pavement on a hot day, you have felt your heels sink into the tar. Can you imagine, then, how animals might sink through ten or more feet of tar or asphalt? Their feet were stuck in the tar, and they had no means of escape. They sank slowly, but surely.

Animals caught in this tar trap howled or cried in fear. Perhaps these cries brought animals of their own kind to help them. A mother, hurrying to help her young, might easily be caught in the tar, and she herself be unable to get out. When an animal that lived upon other animals heard the cries, the animal trapped in the tar became an easy victim. If the helpless animal was close enough to firm ground, the enemy enjoyed a good meal. Very often, however, the enemy, not realizing the danger, was caught in the tar himself and died with the others, sinking out of sight. For centuries the tar held just such a fate for many animals.

A number of years ago men took tar out of these pits to sell. It was at this time that bones of those animals of long ago were brought to the surface. For a while no one paid much attention to the bones, but scientists later collected many of them and noticed that they were the bones of animal species which are not living today. Plant-eating animals whose bones have been dug out of the pits are horses, tapirs, bisons, elephants, mastodons, and deer. Some of these kinds are now extinct, and those kinds that are still living cannot be found now in North America. There were many

This hall in the museum at Los Angeles contains skeletons dug out of the La Brea Pits

Courtesy of the Los Angeles Museum of History, Science, and Art

more kinds of flesh-eating animals than of those that ate plants. Many skeletons of wolves, lions, bears, and saber-toothed tigers have been found. These animals, which came to attack victims of the tar, likewise sank within its sticky depths. It is in this way that the La Brea Pits tell us many stories.

Problem 3 · The Last Ice Age

The earth was filled with life and beauty. Modern animals and plants grew, birds sang, and flowers blossomed. But again the climate began to change very slowly. The warm, moist air became cooler. At first it probably cooled only a few degrees in hundreds of years. Then, in the Far North, as centuries passed, warm days became chilly, and chilly days became cold. The cold slowly crept down into what is now Canada, the northern part of the United States, and northern Europe and Asia.

On the tops of mountains it was very cold. The rain changed to snow, which covered the sides of the mountains. At first the snow melted and ran down into the valleys and was carried away by the rivers. But as time went on, it became so cold that not all the snow that fell in the winter could melt in the summer. Layers of snow next to the ground were packed hard. Snow that melted froze again, and the whole mass was pressed into ice. Snow fell winter after winter and remained, adding to the growing sheet of ice.

As the snow became packed and frozen near the tops of mountains, it formed glaciers. Then as more snow collected on top of the glaciers, the weight of the snow, added to the weight of the glaciers, caused them to slip down the mountainsides. Gradually it became so cold that snow and ice collected in great ice sheets in the Far North. The ice sheets grew larger and pushed on

A glacier formed in the mountains. Once many parts of
the Northern Hemisphere were covered with glaciers

southward. Snow continued to fall, until one great
ice sheet, in some places nearly two miles deep, covered Canada and the northern part of the United
States.

During the time when the ice was forming, the animals and plants were having a difficult time. As days
grew colder, birds and other animals moved away from
the cold to the south. Farther and farther they were
pushed ahead of the glacier. Animals that could stand
the cold best were those with thick furs. The woolly
mammoth, the reindeer, and the musk ox lived nearest
the glacial border. They grazed upon the moss and
grass in what are now New Jersey, Nebraska, and other
states along the border. Those animals that could not
endure so much cold moved far to the south.

© F. M. N. H.

Woolly mammoths during the Ice Age

Plants could not live in the cold even as well as the animals. They could not accustom themselves to it. They could not journey to the south, as the animals did. Many of them were frozen. The only way in which they were kept for the future was by their seeds. The glaciers advanced slowly enough to allow many generations of trees and plants to grow. Each time a plant made seeds, some were carried or blown to the south. These seeds grew into plants, which in turn made more seeds, some of which were blown or carried southward. Thus some plants traveled far enough in this manner to keep their kinds living.

After the Northern Hemisphere had been cold for thousands of years, the climate grew warmer, and the ice melted and retreated as slowly or more slowly than

These rocks were dropped by glaciers as they melted

it had moved forward. As it melted, the edge crept back to the north, and many animals followed it, returning to the old homes of their ancestors. Plants also moved northward as they had traveled to the south.

But the climate did not remain mild. Again and again it cooled, until at least four great glaciers formed. As each glacier formed, plants and animals were driven ahead of it. Some lived through the glacial periods and remained in the north, some were driven into South America, and many became extinct. This formed what we call the Ice Age.

Besides having an influence on the growth of plants and animals, the glaciers changed the country. As they moved down mountains and through valleys, they pushed gravel, rocks, and earth ahead of them. At times they were so thick and heavy that they pushed off the tops of hills and made them round. All this earth and rock they carried with them. Then, as they retreated, they left this soil and rock just where they melted. Many signs of this may be found, which show how far down the great ice sheets came.

. There was also another result. As the glaciers melted, great rivers of water were formed, which collected in some places to form lakes and in other places made routes for themselves to the sea, forming new rivers. The Great Lakes were formed by the great ice sheets.

Not all this ice has melted even today. Ice sheets in the Far North are still unmelted, but our climate in the United States has become quite temperate.

Much of the world had been cold and quiet during the Ice Age. An icy calm had covered a large part of the earth. Although the Ice Age was thousands and thousands of years long, it was only a short time compared with the many millions of years of the early history of the earth. Birds returned from the south and filled the woods with cheering songs. Their feathers brightened the earth with their coloring. The green grasses were dotted with the beauty of the flowers. The earth had grown to be more nearly as we know it.

This was not the only time large parts of the earth had been covered by ice. There have been many times when the climates of the earth grew colder. The earth has had several ice ages during its long history.

The white part of this map shows the part
that was covered with ice during the Ice Age[1]

[1] After map in "Geology," by Thomas C. Chamberlin and Rollin D.
Salisbury. Used by permission of Henry Holt and Company, publishers.

Things to Think About

1. What reason have you for thinking that flowering plants have done well on the earth?

2. Why did many flowering plants develop at the time that certain bees, butterflies, and moths were developing?

3. Why do you think our plants and animals of today are more like those described in this unit than like those of Units IV, V, and VI?

4. Can you see why an animal which once roamed North America in great numbers is no longer here?

5. Why does the northern part of North America have more lakes than the southern part?

6. Why is it that there are scratches which run north and south on the rocks in parts of the United States and Canada?

 *Things to Do*

1. Paint a picture of the earth during the Age of Cycads. Then paint one during the age when flowering plants developed.

2. Write a story about what has happened during the life of one of the oldest living sequoias in California.

3. A tree that is twenty feet in diameter would be about sixty-five feet around. Find out how many boys and girls it would take to reach around such a tree.

4. About how much would a tree be worth if there were enough lumber in it for twenty houses of ordinary size.

5. Write a story about the life of a saber-toothed tiger.

6. Draw a picture showing the earth during the Age of Mammals. Add this to your "Story of the Earth."

7. Imagine yourself an animal during the last Ice Age and write a story about the life then.

8. Find out how long the Ice Age was in comparison with other ages. How long ago was it?

9. Visit a museum, if there is one near you, and see how many skeletons of extinct animals you can find. Where did these animals live?

10. Tell what you think the plants, birds, mammals, insects, amphibians, and other kinds of animals did during the Ice Age.

UNIT VIII

Plants and Animals of Today

You have read how plants and animals have developed through the ages. Some succeeded for a while and became numerous. New kinds kept developing. But always there were those that for one reason or another did not succeed and became extinct.

Today we have hundreds of thousands of different kinds of living things. There seems to be a constant struggle among them. They must have food and a place to live. Many have become extinct within recent years. The struggle to live continues. You will read in Unit VIII about the battle for life, about how living things are protected, and how they depend upon one another.

Problem 1 · The Battle for Life

1. How the Battle is Carried On

All plants and animals on the earth are taking part in a big battle for life. Some of them lose the battle, and their kind dies. In some way or another they fail to protect themselves against their enemies. Perhaps their enemies have learned to break their shells or have discovered them in their hiding places, and have killed all of them.

The dinosaurs and many other ancient animals, the great fern trees and some other plants, have become extinct. Perhaps it was because they were not able to protect themselves against their enemies and their surroundings.

Each living object must have some method of protecting itself. If it cannot protect itself or its young against its enemies, it must produce enough young to keep its kind living, in spite of the many perils that are everywhere around it.

Each year many more seeds begin to grow than can ever become fully grown. Under a large maple tree many small maples begin growing every spring. But they are shaded by the old tree, and nearly all of them die for lack of sunshine. Have you ever noticed in your garden that some plants must be thinned out? If they all grew, they would be very tall, thin, and weak plants. Usually a plant that is a little stronger and larger robs the others of the sunlight and moisture that they must have in order to grow. Why is it important to weed your flower garden?

Plants and animals need to protect themselves against many things. Besides the plants and animals that are their enemies, there are other enemies in nature. Perhaps there comes a time when there is a sudden change in weather. During very hot, dry days in summer many ponds become dry, and plants and animals are left on the bottom of the ponds without moisture. Those that have no special ways of living during such times die. During unusually cold periods animals and plants that are not able to stand such extremes of temperature die. The unusual death of these plants and animals may cause shortage of food for others that live upon them. These then die of starvation. If these creatures do not produce enough young, their numbers may grow less until they become extinct. They die, and their places are filled by plants and animals that can fit themselves to many different living conditions.

Some living things are more fortunate. The climate is just right for them, and there is plenty of food. Their enemies have become extinct or have grown so few that these fortunate animals increase rapidly. At times it seems as though they might completely cover the earth. You will remember that at one time in the earth's history the fishes were so numerous that the period is called the Age of Fishes. At another time the reptiles became so numerous that another age was named for them. Many times this has happened; some plant or animal succeeds just so far, and then no more. Living

In summer many animals hunt a cool place, and the leaves
of some plants become curled to prevent the loss of water

Animals fleeing from a forest fire. Few escape

conditions become unsuited for it, until there may be only a few left, or that kind may become entirely extinct.

Changes in temperature are not the only thing that destroys life on the earth. Storms kill many living things. At times when there are great floods many plants and animals are drowned. During times of migrations many birds are overcome by storms and are drowned, or they are beaten against lighthouses and killed. Nests are blown from trees, and the eggs are broken. In many ways the numbers of plants and animals are lessened.

Perhaps one of the most terrible things that happen to forests and forest plants, as well as animals, are the great forest fires. Thousands of acres are swept yearly by fires that destroy millions of dollars' worth of timber. Flowers are scorched, seeds are burned, and roots are killed. Many birds are killed. Young birds in their nests cannot fly away. During one forest fire an osprey's nest, high up in a tree, had young birds in it. The mother osprey was seen to fly around and around the nest, but the young could not follow her. She remained until the fire was very close, and it must have been extremely hot before she gave up and flew away. Many times every living thing is swept out of existence in the path of a great forest fire.

Parasites are plants or animals that live on other plants and animals, using them for food and sometimes as a place to live, in this way destroying them or making it harder for them to keep alive. All these things, as well as the enemies that use it for food, keep one plant or animal from entirely crowding out other plants or animals.

Have you an aquarium in your schoolroom? Is it a balanced aquarium? If it is balanced, all the plants and animals can live in there without outside help. You need not do much to care for it. You scarcely ever need to change the water. You add a little water now and then and cover the aquarium with a glass to prevent evaporation.

In any balanced aquarium the plants give off oxygen, which the fishes and other animals breathe. The fishes supply the plants with the necessary amount of carbon dioxide. Plants furnish food for the fishes and snails.

An aquarium containing plants and animals

If every little tenant in the aquarium does his part, everything goes right. Of course there are times when a fish or snail dies, or something else happens to upset the balance, but a balance upset in this way is not difficult to build up again.

The whole earth, with the living things in the ocean and on land, works toward a balance. It is seldom an exact balance, however, for often plants and animals lose their enemies for a time. When the balance of living things is upset rather badly, it is usually because of something man has done. Perhaps without meaning to do so, he has carelessly brought in some harmful insect from another country and has separated it from its enemies, which keep it from spreading. This happened

Ladybird beetles are enemies of plant lice

in the case of the Mediterranean fruit fly, which has done so much damage to fruit. Without its natural enemy there was nothing in this country to prevent its rapid growth. There was plenty of food, and it increased in numbers until man discovered some way to keep it from increasing.

The cottony-cushion scale insect, an enemy of fruit trees, was accidentally brought into California. It did a great amount of damage before scientists could discover its natural enemy. Finally, ladybird beetles were imported and placed on the trees. They have destroyed the scale to such a degree that it does very little damage now.

In the early history of America birds were so plentiful that man shot them and used them for food. Many other animals were shot and used for the same purpose. Man increased in numbers and pushed westward. As he cultivated the land, the grazing grounds for buffaloes and deer were destroyed. The freedom of many animals was disturbed; they were killed by the hundreds. Towns and cities have destroyed many of the natural nesting places of birds. Forests have been destroyed, and birds do not have as many places in which to live and raise their young as they once had. They are not well protected in the places that do remain. Swamps have been drained that were once places where birds could get food and find some protection. Millions of birds and other animals have been shot just for sport. In fact, man stands out as almost the only animal that kills for sport.

Man is just as careless in destroying plant life. Dogwood and holly trees are stripped of their branches; shrubs and flowers are picked with no thought given to their future. Forests have been cut down, and no trees have been planted to replace them.

In the early history of our country there were so many trees that no one ever thought of a time when trees might be scarce. But man has been very wasteful in cutting down the forests. He cut and burned great numbers of trees when he cleared the land for farming. Quantities of lumber have been used for building and for making furniture. Trees are used for fuel, telegraph and telephone poles, and in the manufacture of paper.

It has been said that so much paper is made in four years that, if it were made into a strip as wide as a news-

In the early history of the United States heath hens were very common. They will probably soon be extinct

paper, the strip would reach to the sun and back. If it takes sixteen acres of spruce trees to make one edition of a large Sunday newspaper, how many acres must it take to make a newspaper that reaches to the sun and back?

Forest fires, often started by the carelessness of someone in handling fire, have destroyed millions of dollars' worth of trees. It takes years for a tree to grow, and it will be many years before forests can be grown to take the place of those destroyed. Forests are disappearing so rapidly that within fifty years few of the original forests will be found. Most of the forests will be those that have grown up since the original forests were cut down.

Forests help to prevent erosion, by which the good soil is washed away. When forests are cut down, erosion takes place. Therefore quantities of fertile soil are washed into rivers and seas, and many acres of land are made useless for cultivation. We need our forests, and we must save them.

It has become necessary to have laws protecting the lives of some plants and animals from man. Some birds that were once living here in great numbers have become extinct. Some others have become so scarce that there are only a few left. There are now laws which say that some animals shall not be killed at all, and that other animals may be killed only a few at a time. Some kinds of plants are protected in the same way. Areas of land have been set aside by our government as a place where wild plants and animals may live without being disturbed.

2. Living Things threaten to Crowd Out One Another

Some plants and animals reproduce rapidly. By that we mean that they have many plant or animal young, which in a short time raise many other young; these in turn raise many, many more. All these young ones we call the descendants of the first plants or animals. Some plants and animals reproduce so rapidly and have so many descendants that if something did not hold them in check they would soon cover the earth. Then there would be only that one kind of living thing. We know, however, that there are many kinds of plants and animals living in different places and in different ways and eating different kinds of food.

Airplanes are used to spread poison
over fields to kill the harmful insects

But some plants and animals reproduce so rapidly
that they do a great deal of damage. Among these are
some kinds of insects. Most of them are such small
creatures that it does not seem possible that we should
need even to consider them; but it is the numbers, and
not the size, of the enemy that counts this time.

It was the citrus-fruit fly that injured so much fruit
in Florida several years ago. You know how much
damage the boll weevils have done in the South, and
you know how difficult it has been to kill them. Perhaps
in the autumn you have had your automobile stopped
and searched for corn, to be sure that you were not carrying the harmful European corn-borer into another

state. That is one way in which the government tries to prevent the spread of this insect. It has been estimated that insects destroy about one tenth of all the crops grown. Each year the insects eat or destroy about two and a half billion dollars' worth of produce.

The great numbers of insects make them all the more dangerous. There are so many of them that when we undertake to kill them, it is as if we were fighting whole armies. There are more insects than all the other animals put together. In fact, of all the different kinds of animals living, about five sixths of them are insects. Do you see why it is difficult to make war against them?

Insects are found in almost every place on the earth, except perhaps in the salt seas. It seldom gets too hot or too cold for some kind of insect to live. We may go from the tops of the highest mountains to the deepest valleys, from the polar regions of the earth to the equator, from deserts to swamps, and we shall find tiny insect pests all the way. Some of the very worst insect pests live in the coldest and hottest parts of the world, on the snow in the arctic regions and in the torrid zone.

Some insects may lay as many as three thousand eggs a day, and within a couple of weeks these eggs have hatched and grown into adults that are ready to lay more eggs. It takes only from eight to fourteen days for an egg to change into an adult house fly. It has been shown that one pair of flies reproduce so rapidly that at the end of one year they would have over five billion descendants, if they all lived. Think how many that would be, and all of them would be descendants from

In one year one pair of flies could have enough descendants
to make a cloud of flies that would cover a city block

one pair of flies! If they were lined up, one behind the
other, they would make a line about 25,000 miles long,
or as far as around the earth at the equator. That number would be over twice as many flies as there are people in the world. If one pair of flies could have so
many descendants, how many could there be from all
the flies that we see in the springtime? How many flies
might you prevent from reproducing if you killed adult
flies before they laid their eggs? Of course all the five
billion from each pair of flies cannot live, because of their
enemies. Adult insects do not protect their young; so the
young must take care of themselves. They cannot do
this very successfully; yet many of them continue to live.

E

Besides the great numbers of these insects there are other reasons why they are so difficult to get rid of. Most of them are as small as the ant or even smaller, and they can easily hide in very small places. They are so small that they are not easily seen, even when they are not hiding. Their enemies pass by them.

Some insects live on such a small amount of food that anything else would starve on the same amount. They can go for a long time without food. Some insects eat food that other animals could not eat, such as dry wood, woolen goods, feathers, and furs.

Insects have various ways of protecting themselves during the winter. During cold weather flies, beetles, and other tiny insects hide under loose pieces of the bark of trees, in trash heaps, or in cracks of buildings. Those that cannot live over winter have eggs or pupæ hidden away, which will live all winter and hatch out in the spring.

Many insects, such as flies, mosquitoes, and cockroaches, do not do much damage, but the cockroaches are great pests. Lumbermen in the North are often obliged to wear gloves and mufflers to protect themselves from gnats, midges, and mosquitoes. In many countries it is not possible for men to live comfortably without first learning to control the insects there.

There are insects that lay their eggs in the caterpillars of other insects. These eggs hatch into tiny larvæ that feed upon the inside of the caterpillar and kill it. Sometimes the caterpillar spins its cocoon before it dies, but the larvæ feed upon the pupa, which develops from the caterpillar, and it does not change into an adult insect. In this way many harmful insects are killed.

Most other animals do not reproduce so rapidly as insects, but many of them lay hundreds of eggs and have thousands of descendants. Animals that take care of their young do not need to have as many descendants as the animals that do not feed or protect their young. One pair of meadow mice might, in a short time, have thousands of descendants. Mice differ from insects in that they take care of their young, and because of this the young have a better chance to live. Do you wonder why the world is not full of mice? It is lucky for us that only a few of these possible descendants live. What are some of the ways in which they are killed?

Most birds must have insects or seeds for food. All spring and all summer the robin is busy hunting for grubs and worms. You can often see him struggling to pull a worm out of the ground to feed himself and his young. Chickadees and warblers are forever searching the trees for small insects. They may be seen running all over the branches of the trees pecking at little things as they go along; these little things are insects and insect eggs. Early in the morning you can hear the woodpeckers tapping on the trees. They tap and listen for a hollow place that may hide a caterpillar or some other insect. Birds eat eggs and caterpillars of the useful insects, as well as of the harmful ones. Birds are always helping to keep down the number of insects that would soon cover the earth if they were ever left long without enemies.

The downy woodpecker and oriole are useful to men[1]

Some plants reproduce in great numbers. Each flower of many plants has hundreds of seeds that are easily scattered and grow into more plants. You probably have noticed how quickly your lawn becomes covered with dandelions if a few plants have been allowed to make seeds. If millions and millions of weed seeds were not destroyed each year, such plants would soon spread over the world.

Each year seed-eating birds destroy billions of weed seeds which, under the right conditions, might produce billions of weeds. Since weeds take the moisture, food, and sunshine away from some of the plants that man

[1] From Caldwell and Meier, "Open Doors to Science."

uses as food, it is very important that many weed seeds should be killed each year.

In order that they may live, plants and animals cause the death of millions of other plants and animals. Because of this and because many are destroyed in other ways, no plant or animal ever controls any part of the earth for long at a time.

 Things to Think About

1. How many ways can you think of in which man has done something to upset the balance of the living world?

2. Why is it so difficult to destroy harmful insects?

3. What do men do to destroy harmful insects?

4. What would happen if all the birds were killed and the insects were allowed to increase?

5. Why is it necessary to weed your garden?

6. Can you think of any plants or animals that need protection so that they will not become extinct?

 *Things to Do*

1. Make a list of harmful and useful insects. If you can find pictures of any of them, paste them on a chart.

2. Do something to help protect our birds.

3. Pick the seed stalk of a dandelion and count the number of seeds that there are in this one flower. How many new plants might have grown from this one flower?

Now count the number of dandelion blossoms on a lawn. If each blossom produced as many seeds as the one you picked, how many seeds would all the blossoms on your lawn produce?

4. Name some forms of plants and animals that have become extinct in fairly recent times.

5. If you have an aquarium, see if you can tell just how each tenant helps to keep it balanced. If you have no aquarium, try to make one. Can you get it to balance?

6. Tell in how many ways harmful insects may be destroyed. What does the government do to destroy them?

Problem 2 · How Animals are Protected

1. Why Animals Need Protection

Living things are almost everywhere on our earth. In nearly every spot, and every corner there is some kind of life. There are few places that are too hot or too cold, too high or too low, or too dangerous for something to live there.

Living things are found in hot springs. These waters would burn our skin in less than a minute, but in them live several different kinds of small animals. Spider-like animals, worms, and the larvæ of some flies make their homes in these springs.

The waters of the polar seas are filled with living things. Millions of tiny crabs, worms, shellfishes, and great numbers of whales, seals, and fishes live in these icy waters.

Down in the depths of the sea live fishes and other sea animals. No sunlight ever reaches them at these great depths. They live in waters that are always dark and very cold.

Living things live in some of the highest places of the earth as well as in the depths. Some fishes live in high mountain streams. Some kinds of snails live along the snow line of the highest mountains, while others live down in the sea at depths of more than three miles.

In some places where the life of animals is often in great danger, living things exist. Mountain sheep and goats climb steep and slippery cliffs in search of food.

In the Niagara River, just a few yards from the plunging waterfalls, snails are found living on stones.

To one who lives in the city, there does not seem to be a great number of animals. There are the sparrows, the animals we have as pets, and in the summer the insects. Even in the country there do not seem to be so many animals. There are those in the farmyards, the birds that fly about, a few, such as the frogs and the fishes, that live in the water, and the insects. Sometimes one finds animal tracks, but the woods and the fields do not seem to be full of living things. These places seem to be quiet places to us, except when the sun is shining brightly in the summer time, and then the fields are lively with the music of grasshoppers, or in the springtime, when the woods and meadows are ringing with the songs of the birds and the croaking of the frogs. Along the shore of the sea there seem only to be the ocean, the sand, and the sky, except at low tide, when shells and seaweed are scattered along the beach.

Even though we do not see them, animals of all kinds are around us. Some are so small that we do not notice them. Others are hiding in the trees, in the ground, in the sand, in the cracks and in the walls of our houses.

The earth is crowded with living things. Think of all the stars that you can see in the sky on a clear summer night. The sky seems filled with them; yet scientists say you can see only about two thousand of them with the naked eye. There are many more living creatures than there are stars that we can see. There are hundreds of thousands of different kinds of animals.

In most cases there are thousands, in some cases millions and billions, of each kind living.

It is a good thing that many animals are destroyed, for the earth is not large enough to allow all animals to live their full life and die of old age. If no English sparrows ever died except of old age, in a few years the earth would be almost covered with sparrows. A single oyster lays sixteen million eggs each year. In five years its descendants would make a heap of shells eight times the size of the earth. These things do not happen, because there are many other animals fighting for the same space and because there is not food enough to go around.

Few animals ever die of old age, except those that man protects, such as his horses, his dogs, and his cats. In the wilds, animals are living in a world crowded with other animals. In trying to get food, they become the rivals of other animals searching for the same kind of prey, or animal to eat. This prey is trying not to be caught. The animal who is seeking it is trying to avoid those that are hunting him. The struggle is a fierce one, but most animals are prepared in some way to protect themselves.

2. The Weapons which Animals Use

To get food is one of the most important things in the life of an animal. While searching for his food, he battles with most of his enemies. Most animals are prepared for such battles, for they are armed with weapons which they use for protection as well as for obtaining food.

Some wolves hunt in packs and use their teeth as weapons

Dogs, wolves, and foxes use their teeth not only in biting their food but in self-defense. Mice, muskrats, rabbits, squirrels, and all the other members of the rat family have long front teeth. These are good tools to gnaw with and good weapons to fight with. The long jaw of the sawfish is armed with two rows of knife-like teeth. The sawfish can deal terrible blows to enemies with his jaw and is not afraid to attack whatever prey he chooses.

Teeth and jaws are common weapons, but jaws alone are sometimes useful. The toothless jaw of the snapping turtle can cause a bad wound. The beaks of birds serve not only in food-getting but in attacking the enemy. Chickens can strike sharp blows with their beaks. The duck has a broad, soft, shovel-like bill, which is suited for getting plants and insects from the water. He can seize a small foe with it and pinch it hard. The mocking bird will attack enemies much larger than himself and kill them by striking them in the back of the neck.

Clawed limbs make dangerous weapons. Wildcats, lions, tigers, leopards, lynxes, and panthers lie in wait for their prey. They steal up to it quietly. Then, with a sudden leap, they land with their front paws on the back of its neck. In the face of an enemy they strike with their claws in the same way that the house cat does.

Many animals use their limbs to ward off their enemies. The horse and deer and other animals with hard hoofs can give powerful blows with their legs. The kick of the donkey is famous. Jumping animals, which have strong hind limbs, sometimes kick, too. Rabbits have been seen to leap over their enemies, kicking them hard with their hind feet.

There are other kinds of limbs, which are different from those of the four-legged animals. Some of these are dangerous weapons. The eight arms of the octopus, each of which has two rows of suckers, can catch any prey of the deep sea and overcome many of his enemies. The fins of the eagle-ray fish of southern seas are strong and broad. They seem like vast wings as these fishes swoop down on their prey and wrap it in their great fins.

Snakes, which are limbless, have other ways of fighting. Some snakes crush the life out of their prey by winding their strong bodies around it. Such snakes are called constrictors because of this power to crush

Some snakes crush their prey to death

their prey. The pythons of Asia and Africa are the mightiest of all constrictors. They sometimes reach a length of forty feet. They are able to conquer animals many times their own size. The king snake of the southern United States is also a constrictor. He owes his title of "king" to his ability to overcome all other snakes, even the poisonous rattler. The poison does not harm him.

Poison is another deadly weapon with which some snakes are armed. In this country we have four kinds of poisonous snakes: the rattler, the copperhead, the coral, and the water moccasin. In other parts of the world many others are found. The famous cobra of India is the deadliest of all, but even he is not safe from all enemies. The mongoose, a tiny animal sixteen inches

long, can conquer the cobra. It is not because the cobra's
poison cannot harm him that he is able to overcome the
snake. It is because he is too keen and quick. He waits
for a good chance before he attacks. Then, catching
the cobra's head in his mouth, he pins the jaws shut.

The poison of snakes is found in a sac in the roof of
the mouth. This sac is connected with two long, hollow
teeth, called fangs. The snake stabs his victim with the
fangs and thus puts the poison into its body. Only
poisonous snakes have fangs, but all snakes have teeth.
If the teeth are large enough, they are useful to the
snake in killing its prey and in battling with its enemies.
Such teeth are not connected with poison sacs.

Spiders too are armed with poison. They use it to
kill their prey and protect themselves. Only a few, if
any, of the spiders of this country are harmful to men.

Stings are another kind of weapon. With them some
animals can paralyze both prey and enemy. Wasps
sting other insects, which they use as food. Bees sting
merely to protect themselves. Some water animals have
stings, too. The long, slender arms of the jellyfish have
stings. These can cause so much pain that jellyfishes
are avoided. Because of these stings some small sea
animals that are not harmed by the stings remain under
the umbrella of certain jellyfishes and thus are protected.
The beautiful sea anemones seem to be harmless creatures. They grow along the low-tide mark of the sea
like delicately colored orange, pink, and creamy-white
flowers. What appears to be a mass of gracefully wav-
ing petals is a circle of arms placed around a mouth.

The jaws of this rattlesnake can spread, allow-
ing it to swallow animals larger than itself

Courtesy of the United States Bureau of Biological Survey

These arms are covered with stings. Small animals that
swim by are caught, stung, and devoured. Larger animals brushing up against the sea anemones also feel
their stings and move on quickly.

The commonest weapons that animals fight with
are those they use in killing their prey. Teeth, claws,
limbs, poison, and stings are fierce weapons; but they
are needed, for the battle of life in the wilds and in the
sea is a fierce struggle.

Some animals have weapons that are not used in
obtaining food. They are used only to guard against the
enemy. Such weapons are horns and antlers. The
domestic goat butts, as does also the mountain goat.

Goats meet their foes face to face and try to puncture their skins with their horns. The antlers of the deer can cause death. When in battle, the deer approaches with a slow push forward. Then he pushes back and forth several times before dealing the final blow. With head lowered, he rushes forward and thrusts his antlers into his enemy as soon as they touch.

A caribou, a close relative of the reindeer, was seen in Alaska walking around with the dead body of a wolf in his antlers. He had won in the struggle, but was unable to rid himself of his victim. Whenever he passed a tree he would rub against it, trying to remove the wolf from his antlers. He was walking slowly, for he was unable to run because of the weight of his burden. Another caribou that was with him would run ahead and then wait for his slower companion to catch up.

Tails are useful in fighting or holding off the enemy. Horses and cattle use them in brushing away insects. The strong tail of the large monitor lizard of the tropics can give powerful blows. Some fishes also use their tails as weapons. The surgeon fish has a tail that is sharp on each side. With it he can give terrible side blows. The sting ray, a fish of tropic seas, is also armed with a dangerous weapon. His tail has one or more sharp spines on it. These are about eight or nine inches long and may cause severe wounds.

Disagreeable odors are good weapons for making the enemy hurry away. The skunk is famous for this. Mink and weasels, relatives of the skunk, also have bad odors, but they do not depend on them for defense as much as the skunk does. They are quick to run away from their enemies, but the skunk seems to expect other animals to run. He is slow and stupid, depending entirely on his odor for protection. Muskrats and musk turtles also have disagreeable odors.

The porcupine is armed with an excellent weapon. When attacked, he raises his quills and takes every opportunity to brush against his enemy; for the quills come out when touched and cause bad wounds. He does not, however, shoot his quills at his enemy, as some people think.

The electric ray and the electric eel of South America can give heavy shocks. This is their only means of protection, for, unlike other fishes, they have smooth skins without scales or spines.

All sorts of weapons are useful in the battle for life.

3. Some Animals wear Armor

Some animals have no weapons and depend a great deal on their armor-like skins for safety.

The turtle can retreat into his shell when in danger. The oyster, protected by his shell, lies at the bottom of the water, waiting for the tides to bring him food. The snail draws into his shell for safety. So fine a coat of armor is the snail's shell that the hermit crab makes his home in an empty one. The hermit crab, unlike other crabs, has a soft, weak skin covering his body. He uses the snail's shell as armor. Inside this shell he is well protected.

This prehistoric armadillo was well protected by armor

The covering of crabs and lobsters makes a strong coat of armor. This shell does not grow and so must be shed as the animal grows. In this way he rids himself of whatever may have fastened itself to his shell. The skin of insects and spiders must also be shed. The softer body parts that lie underneath are protected by the tough outer skin.

Nearly all animals have a strong outer skin to protect them. The thicker and stronger the skin is, the more protection it offers. The hide of the rhinoceros is a great help to him. Thick fur protects animals, for it is difficult for teeth and claws to cut through it. The scales of fishes are coats of armor.

E

This is an armadillo living today. Like its prehistoric ancestor, it too is protected by armor

The sea urchin is covered with sharp spines, and most
animals avoid him. The skin of the starfish is also spiny.
The sand dollars, relatives of the starfish, are inclosed
in stony coats. The tiny coral animal lives protected in
stone.

There are many kinds of armor on both land and sea.

4. How Animals Escape their Enemies

Few animals fight unless it is necessary. Even the
strongest and fiercest take flight, rather than fight.
Wildcats try to escape from their enemies. Snakes rush
away, rather than strike. Most animals seek safety by
fleeing from their enemies.

Those that are swift of foot run. The muskrat, a poor runner because he has a heavy body and short legs, escapes by swimming. The weasel, mink, and otter are strong swimmers and take to the water if possible. Those animals that can, leap from their enemies. The rabbit can take an eight-foot jump into a brier patch, where few animals can follow. With a single leap the frog is off to safety. Animals that have wings fly. Birds and insects go off into the air.

Many animals retreat to shelters and remain there until danger is over. The raccoon and members of the cat family seek safety in the tree tops, in tall grass, or in underbrush. The chipmunk, the woodchuck, and many others run to their burrows. The spider, which boldly waits to snare his prey, hides as well as he can when disturbed. The larva of the caddis fly carries about with him the shelter that he has made of sticks and pebbles. In the face of an enemy, he retreats into it. Many insects hide in tiny cracks and corners or under leaves or bark.

In escaping from the enemy, it is important to be able to see him first in order to get started first. One reason why we see so few animals is that many of them have sharper, keener senses than we have. The antelope can see for a distance of two or three miles. The sight of deer and horses is very keen, and since their eyes are toward the sides of their heads they can see in many directions. The eye of a fly can discover approaching shadows. Anyone who has tried to swat a fly knows that. The whirligig beetle, which whirls around on the

Squids protect themselves by giving out a smoke
screen. This helps them to escape from their enemies

top of the water, has an eye divided into two parts.
With one it can look up into the air; with the other,
down into the water.

Many animals depend on a keen sense of hearing.
Snakes rely greatly on their sense of smell. Fishes find
their way about by receiving vibrations or movements
of the water. Dogs tell friends from foes by their scent.

When in danger animals give signals to their own
kind, that they too may escape. Deer flash a white patch
on the sides of their bodies and give off a scent that tells
other deer to take flight. Antelopes too flash two white
rump patches when they are excited. These can be
seen by their own kind at long distances. Herds two or
three miles away will see the signal and take alarm.

The beaver warns other beavers by splashing the water with his tail. Many animals have calls that are danger signals. The chipmunks give out a loud, shrill chip, which warns other chipmunks. Many birds have cries that are alarms. These signals are understood by those for whom they are meant, and all that receive and understand them pay attention to them.

Most animals try to avoid their enemies. Because of this, they spend much of their time hiding. Many never come out in the daytime, but wait until darkness comes before going forth for their food.

Some animals spend their lives in places where few others ever find them. The woodchuck stays in his burrow most of the time. Pocket gophers live almost entirely underground, eating the roots of plants. Moles and shrews spend their lives digging away in the dark earth and thus escape much warfare. Clams, which burrow in the mud on the bottom of lakes and in the sand on the seashore, and the many crabs and worms that live in the sand, all escape warfare. The parchment worm, buried in the sand in the tube he has made for himself, leads a sheltered life. Some small crabs share his tube with him, for they have found it a safe place in which to live. Salamanders are common animals, but we usually find them only under logs and stones.

High cliffs that are reached only with difficulty are places where a few animals live. Those which can find food in such places meet few enemies. Many birds, such as eagles, dwell among them. Mountain goats and sheep meet few enemies in the places where they live.

Some animals lead peaceful lives, for they are avoided by other animals. The toad, because of the poison in his skin, is not wanted as food. He is sought only by the snakes, which do not seem to be hurt by his poison. Few animals seek the mink as food, because his flesh tastes bad. Animals with disagreeable qualities are frequently brilliantly colored. They are easily recognized and avoided. Some of the poisonous snakes are brightly colored. They give fair warning to others to get out of their paths. Some animals have bright patches of color which they bring into view when alarmed. The fire-bellied toad of Europe has a brilliant orange patch on the underside of his body. When surprised, this toad will move his hind legs over his back, seeming to make a great effort to show the warning color to the enemy. Many bad-tasting butterflies, such as the monarch, have bright colors, which serve as a warning to their enemies.

5. Some Creatures Deceive their Enemies

So successful are those that keep out of the battle that animals which are avoided are sometimes imitated by others. The viceroy butterfly, though no relative of the monarch, looks a great deal like it. The viceroy is therefore avoided, although birds like it for food. There are some flies that deceive the enemy by resembling bees. They are protected in this way.

The measuring worm and the walking stick look like twigs and so escape notice. There are some crabs on the Pacific coast that resemble pebbles. Many animals of

The viceroy looks very much like the larger butterfly, the monarch, which is avoided by birds.
Notice how the measuring worms look like twigs[1]

the sea, such as some of the jellyfishes, are colorless and
transparent and cannot be told from the sea water.
Many of the fishes and sea horses living among the great
masses of brilliantly colored seaweed of the tropical seas
look just like the plants around them.

There is one kind of crab that covers himself with
seaweed to escape notice. His last two pairs of limbs
point upward and enable him to carry his mask.

[1] From Linville, Kelly, and Van Cleave's "A Textbook in General
Zoology."

When the hognose snake fails to frighten his
enemies by spreading his head, he plays possum

To pretend they are dead is another way that animals have of deceiving the enemy. This is often called playing possum, for the opossum is famous for this trick. Many insects, spiders, and crabs will become stiff and quiet when touched. They appear to be dead. Many reptiles pretend death in face of danger. The horned lizard, sometimes called the horned toad, will shut his eyes and remain perfectly still. The hognose snake will lie on his back with his mouth open and his tongue hanging out. He appears to have died a terrible death. This death-like pose will be kept almost in spite of what one does to him. But if he is turned over, he will give himself away, for he quickly gets on his back again and takes his former pose.

These fish are called puffers because
they puff up when they are attacked

The hognose snake pretends to be dead only as a last possible chance. First he tries to terrify his enemies. He swells his neck three times its usual size and makes a sharp hissing sound. He seems to be more fierce than the angriest of poisonous snakes. As he hisses, he strikes many times, but never bites. If this bluff has not scared away his enemy, the snake suddenly seems to die.

Other animals besides the hognose snake have a way of swelling up to frighten away the enemy. The puffer fish and the porcupine fish of the tropics terrify their foes by suddenly swelling into enormous sizes. The horned lizard will puff up when he is disturbed and look quite dangerous.

Some lizards have another way of deceiving the enemy. When caught in a struggle, they "leave their tails behind them." The tails of these lizards come off easily and often draw the attention of the enemy while the lizard escapes. The story about the glass "snake"—that it is able to collect itself after it has been broken into many pieces — is not entirely false. There is an animal, a legless lizard, commonly known as the glass snake, that is found in the southern United States. It sometimes sheds its tail when frightened by an enemy, and then it is able to grow a new one. The tail of a mouse seems like a very convenient handle for a cat to seize. But it is not, for the skin covering is loosely fastened and slips off easily, permitting the mouse to escape.

Those that can deceive the enemy often go unharmed. In this way some of the smaller animals can live, even though they are hunted by larger and stronger foes.

6. Intelligence: the Mightiest Weapon of All

Animals are not able to think as human beings do. When the hognose snake plays dead, he does not do it because he thought out this plan of deceiving the enemy. He does it because all hognose snakes do it when in danger. He does it without thinking about it. If someone waves an object in front of your eyes, you naturally close them to guard against a possible blow. If you touch something hot, you draw your hand away before you have had time to realize what you are doing. A small baby would behave in the same way. We were born ready to do these things. The hognose snake was born with the readiness to pretend death in the presence of an enemy. To be able to fool the enemy is a good means of protection.

Horses, dogs, elephants, and monkeys are intelligent. Chimpanzees in zoos have been known to open the locks of their cages. They can be taught many amusing and interesting tricks, for they are one of the most intelligent kinds of animals. Horses, dogs, and elephants can be taught to do tricks and work that are helpful to man.

Although some animals are intelligent, there is a big difference between their intelligence and that of man. With his mind as a weapon, man has been able to conquer. He has invented a language with which he is able to pass his ideas along to other people. He has invented houses to shelter himself and guns to protect himself against other animals. Because of his guns, man is the most dangerous enemy of many animals, and because of his intelligence he has become the ruler of the earth. Yet there are many enemies against whom he is always waging war. You remember that man too is taking part in the battle for life.

Because of their great numbers, some harmful insects are among his worst enemies. There are many more insects than men on the earth, but by using his mind, man is discovering ways of controlling the numbers of some of his insect foes.

Not only is man able to control the numbers of his enemies, but he has learned to improve plants and animals; he has learned to use things around him for his own good.

7. The Constant Warfare

The animals that travel in the greatest numbers are often dangerous enemies. "There is strength in numbers" is an old saying. Several animals can fight an enemy better than one can. Some animals, such as wolves, wild dogs, elephants, and deer can live much better in groups than they can alone. They either hunt together in catching their prey or they unite for protection against their enemies.

Animals living in communities are frequently safer than those that live alone, for community life offers great protection. Beavers, ants and bees are among those that protect themselves in this way. They also unite in building homes and gathering food.

In the constant warfare among animals most of them fight alone. In the struggle each animal is fighting not only for his own life, but for the life of his kind. There is war among the different kinds of animals for the right to stay on the earth, for the earth is crowded with living things. The longer an animal lives, the more young there will be and the greater will be the numbers of that kind of animal.

This warfare is a good thing, for only those animals that are strong can live. Those that are unfit for the battle are sifted out. In the long run it is only the fit that live and have young. Those that carry on in the battle are those that are best suited to take part in it. There is no room for the unfit. Those that live are prepared for the battle of life.

Things to Think About

1. Can you imagine what it would be like to live in hot springs or in polar seas? Yet some creatures live in these places.

2. What would the world be like if no sparrow ever died except of old age?

3. Why do animals need weapons of defense?

4. Why must an insect lay many more eggs than a sparrow if its kind is to continue to live upon the earth?

5. How do colors protect animals from their enemies?

Things to Do

1. Name three animals and tell how they are protected.

2. Make a list of five animals. Then see how many creatures you can find that are enemies of these animals. Of how many plants and animals are your five animals enemies?

3. Make a collection of pictures which show the armors of animals. Perhaps you can collect some of the armors.

Problem 3 · Plants and Animals Depend upon Each Other

Most plants and animals could not live without each other. Sometimes plants help animals, and at other times animals aid plants. Often when one of these two things helps the other, it receives something in return.

Plants make almost all the food there is in the world, and animals depend entirely upon these plants for their food. Some animals, such as cows, horses, and sheep, live upon plants. Other animals, such as lions and wolves, eat animals, but many of the animals they eat must live upon plants. We drink milk from cows, but cows could not live without the grass that they eat. We eat the meat of animals that have fed upon grass, or upon grains, which are produced by plants. Even the fishes that we eat live upon plant life in the water or eat other water animals that live by eating plants. Insects usually eat leaves and young shoots of trees or shrubs. Many animals graze upon the grasses and plants of the prairie. Some meat-eating animals live upon rabbits, mice, and birds, which in turn may use plant food. If anything happened to all the plants in the world, it would not be long before all the animals would either be eaten or starved to death.

Plants depend a great deal upon climate. Most kinds of plants can live only in certain climates. A plant must be fitted for living in a hot or a cold country, in a desert or a swamp, or it cannot grow well there.

Some plants and animals need very little water

Climate does not make so much difference to animals, but they cannot live where plants do not grow. Thus, in a desert country, we find animals that are fitted for eating the kind of plants found there. In temperate climates where there is more water, plants grow plentifully, and there will be found animals fitted for eating the tender, juicy leaves and stalks of these plants.

Many plants are entirely destroyed by animals. Many plants are pulled up by the roots when the animal is feeding, or so much of them is eaten that they die. Perennials (plants which live a number of years) are often injured, but are not usually destroyed. There are some plants, such as the grasses, that are actually benefited by grazing. When the tops are eaten, the grass that is left seems to grow more rapidly.

Some plants and animals live where there is plenty of water

Animals do not like the taste of some plants, and they will not eat them. When animals continue to eat certain plants, and keep them eaten short, the less tasty plants grow tall and shade the desirable plants so much that they die. When a pasture is overgrazed, weeds spring up and kill the grass. Weeds, in many places, kill the less hardy plants.

Some plants have different ways of protecting themselves to prevent animals from eating them. Spines or thorns growing on leaves and stems protect plants. Some plants that have a bad taste are not eaten by animals. Other plants are poisonous and cause death to the animals that eat them.

Animals damage plants in other ways. Many of them destroy plants by gnawing. Beavers cut down trees to build their houses and dams, and they use the bark for food. Their dams often cause water to stand around trees, which die because the water keeps air away from their roots. Rabbits chew the bark from small trees and shrubs, which often kills these plants.

Burrowing animals kill the roots of some of the plants through which they dig. Weeds that are not as easily killed grow in place of the plants. Moles and gophers destroy the roots of plants when they dig their burrows, and the plants die.

Plants and animals depend upon each other in another way. When plants are in the sunlight, they manufacture food. You already know that the leaves of plants are little factories, and that they use carbon dioxide to make starch. Plants separate the carbon from the oxygen; they use the carbon in manufacturing the starch and give off the oxygen as a waste product. This oxygen is breathed in by animals. We can say, then, that animals breathe out carbon dioxide, which is used by the plants to make starch, and plants throw off oxygen that they do not need, and this oxygen is used by animals.

Our daily lives are greatly influenced by plants. Some plants are poisonous, and man has had to learn to know the poisonous plants from those that he may use for food. Man has also learned to use some plants for drugs or medicine. Plants form a great part of man's food.

Many animals use plant products for shelter. Some people build houses out of wood from trees; others build shelters of grasses. Birds, squirrels, and some other animals build their nests in trees.

E

Some animals are necessary to the life of certain plants. How often many of you have seen honeybees buzzing around the flowers and flying from one flower to another, pausing just a second at each flower on their way! Each bee is busy gathering the pollen or sucking the nectar which she will take back to the hive and use to make honey. The bee visits only those flowers where she can reach the pollen and nectar. Her one big duty is to gather all that she can and carry it home.

At the same time that the flower was furnishing the bee with sweets, the bee was doing something for the flower in return. Of course the bee did not know that she was doing any good, but she was helping the flower just the same.

Pollen is needed in flowers to help make the seeds. Some flowers can use their own pollen, but the seeds are frequently not so strong as they would be if pollen from other flowers were used. Other flowers do not produce seeds unless pollen is brought to their pistils from another flower. It is better if the pollen is brought from a flower on another plant.

Since the flower cannot move, it must depend upon something to bring the pollen to it. This may sometimes be done by the wind or by humming birds, but insects carry much of it. Bees, butterflies, moths, and bee flies are important carriers of pollen.

The red clover cannot make its seed unless pollen is brought to it from another red-clover flower. The bumblebee usually acts as the carrier for this plant. When people in New Zealand first tried to raise red clover,

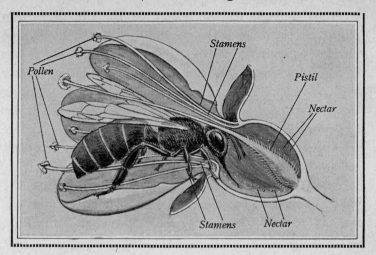

In order to get the nectar, insects must brush against the pollen. They carry this pollen to the next flower they visit

they found that the clover grew beautifully the first year, but it did not produce seed. Later a number of bumblebees were imported, and another crop of clover was planted. This time the bumblebees carried the pollen from one flower to another as they were searching for nectar. With this help from the bumblebees, the clover produced seeds.

Since insects are so necessary to the production of seeds, there are various ways in which the plants attract them. The shape of the flower, its odor, and its nectar attract many insects. Have you ever driven past a field of buckwheat and noticed the sweet odor coming from it? It is said that bees can smell this odor a mile or more away, and that they are attracted by it.

Each time that a bee sticks her head down into a flower, she is helping to carry pollen. The bee usually must reach away down to the bottom of the flower for the nectar. As she pushes down, her body rubs against the parts of the flower containing the pollen, and her body becomes covered with it. She leaves that flower and goes to another, carrying the pollen as she goes. When she reaches into a second flower, some of the pollen that is loosely scattered over her body falls upon the pistil of the second flower. Usually this pollen aids the pistil in making seeds. The bee and the flower depend upon each other.

Up to this time the plants that you have read about in this book have all been plants that have chlorophyll and need sunshine in order to live. You know how plants and animals depend upon each other for many things. There are still other plants that form an important link in this chain of life. These plants do not have flowers or seeds or real roots or green leaves. They do not need sunshine to grow. They have tiny thread-like parts that correspond to the roots of green-leaved plants. They have spores instead of seeds. They do not behave at all as green plants do, except in one way. All plants need a certain amount of moisture and heat in order that they may grow.

This large group of plants do not make their own food. They live on the food that green-leaved plants have made. Some of these plants live on dead plants and animals, and others grow on living plants and animals. They have little threads that reach down into the food

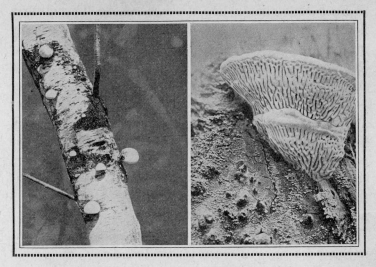

These fungi use food that trees have made

Photograph by T. Howard Hindle

and take it in. They use the food to make cases that contain the spores. When a plant of this kind uses up all the food, it dies. Its spores are carried away by the air to other places where they can grow. These plants are called fungi.

There are many fungi. Mold is one kind. There are other kinds that you know, such as yeast. Have you ever gone out into a field and stepped on a round, brown ball that you found on the ground? Did you squeeze it to see the brown powder that looks like smoke come out? This was a puffball, and the "smoke" consisted of the spores. Puffballs live on the remains of plants and animals that are in the ground.

The mushrooms that you use as food are fungi. They look much like the poisonous toadstools, of which there are many kinds and many colors. Only people who know a great deal about mushrooms should ever pick them to eat.

The shelf fungus which attacks trees or logs is often seen. There are many beautiful sizes, shapes, and colors of this fungus, which grows upon either dead or living trees.

Have you ever looked through a stream of sunlight as it came into a room? Did you notice all the dust in the air? This same air carried millions of spores too tiny to be seen. These spores fall on everything; and if there is food and the right amount of moisture and heat, some of them begin to grow. They may form one of the many kinds of mold or some other fungus.

Bacteria are another form of plant life. They are so tiny that great numbers may stick to a pin point or a particle of dust. They have different shapes. Some are long and slender, others are round, and some have other shapes. They are different from fungi in the way they produce other bacteria. You remember that fungi produce spores, which grow into new plants. The bacteria simply divide into two parts when they have grown to a certain size. Then these two divide, and so on until they are killed. Some bacteria divide quite rapidly, so that there will be a million bacteria in a very short time. Other bacteria divide more slowly.

Bacteria are found almost everywhere. They live in the air, in the water, and in the soil. Many of them

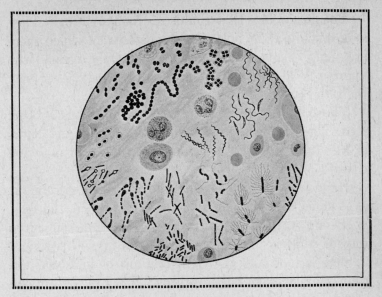

Several kinds of bacteria seen through a microscope

are useful, and some are harmful. Like fungi, they do not make their food, but they take it from other plants and animals. It is because of this fact that fungi and bacteria are so important. By growing upon living plants and animals, bacteria often cause their death. When they grow upon dead plant and animal matter, they cause decay. In this way they help to keep the earth clean. In using plants and animals for food, they use the carbon and give back carbon dioxide to the air. Age after age fungi and bacteria have been at work, returning to the air the carbon dioxide that green plants have taken from it.

Things to Think About

1. How many things can you think of that depend upon some other living object?

2. Try to think of one thing that we eat that does not depend upon plants for food.

Things to Do

1. Find out how to make a culture. Let a fly walk in it and watch for results. Write a story to tell how flies may be harmful.

2. Look at some mold through a microscope. The little white threads secure food for the plant. The little black spheres contain the spores.

3. Think of one plant or animal and write down all the ways in which it depends upon other living things, and all the ways in which other living things depend upon it. Does it eat plants or animals? Is it helpful or harmful to other plants and animals? Is it helpful or harmful to man?

4. See how many kinds of mold you can find. Look on bread, cheese, fruit, and other foods. What do molds do to these foods?

5. Take a walk through the woods and see how many kinds of fungus you can find.

UNIT IX

Men Discover Much about the Earth

1. Scientists Study about the Things which make up the Earth
2. Men learn how to Use the Things which make up the Earth

MEN DISCOVER MUCH ABOUT THE EARTH

Men cannot run so fast as horses. They cannot fly as birds or bats do. They cannot live in water as fishes do. They cannot climb trees so well as squirrels. But men alone of all the living creatures are interested in studying the things about them. They look out into the universe and measure and weigh the stars. They study the earth and the things living on the earth. Discoveries are made of new planets, new stars, cures for diseases, the telegraph, the radio, and many things too numerous to mention. The rest of this book will have to do with what men and women have done, their discoveries and inventions.

Men are interested in the earth and what it is made of. They are interested in ways to use the things they have found in the earth. In Unit IX you will learn of what things the earth is made, and how men have learned to use these things to help themselves.

Man alone of all the living creatures is interested in studying the things about him

Problem 1 · Scientists Study about the Things which make up the Earth

A Greek named Anaximenes, who lived nearly twenty-five hundred years ago, thought that everything in the world was made of air. He thought that when air became thinner, it turned into fire, and that when it became denser, it formed water. He also thought that water could then change into earth. It is not surprising that men thought these things. They knew that water disappeared from the earth and went into the air. They could see this especially when water boiled and changed into steam and vapor; for did not that look like air? Then did not the air change back to water and come raining down from the sky? If a pan of water is set on the stove and boiled away, a small amount of solid material will be left behind. These early Greeks thought that the water had changed to earth. Can you explain what really happened in each case?

Later the Greeks thought that everything in the world was made up of these four things: earth, air, fire, and water. They called them elements because they thought that they were not made of several different things. For a long time these early scientists called all solid materials earth and any sort of gas air. "Water" meant not only that which we drink, or find in rivers and in rain, but anything that looked like liquid.

But you have already learned that air is a mixture of several different gases, including oxygen, nitrogen, and carbon dioxide; so air is not an element. Scientists have learned how to separate water into two gases, oxygen and hydrogen. They also know that earth is made of a number of different kinds of things. You know that many metals, such as iron, gold, and silver, as well as coal and petroleum, are found in the ground. Thus we know that there are more than four kinds of things that make up the earth.

Any substance that cannot be broken up into two or more other substances is called an element.

Scientists have found that everything in the world is made up of one or more of ninety-two elements. Rocks and air contain some of the same things that plants and animals are made of. The coal that supplies us with heat in winter has in it the same element, together with others, as that of which the most expensive diamond is made. Our bodies have this same element in them. Some of the common things that you know a great deal about are elements. Most of the metals are elements; for example, copper, tin, zinc, iron, mercury, gold, silver, lead, and aluminum. A few metals, such as brass, bronze, and so-called German silver, are mixtures of elements and are not just one kind of substance. Brass is a mixture of copper and zinc; bronze is a mixture of copper, zinc, and tin; German silver is a mixture of copper, zinc, and nickel. Such mixtures of metals are called alloys. Other common substances that are elements are sulfur, carbon, oxygen, and phosphorus.

Although there are ninety-two different elements, almost everything in the world is made up of combina-

This is the workshop of a seeker after knowledge who lived several centuries ago. Compare this workshop with the laboratory of a modern scientist, which is shown on the opposite page

tions of only a few of them. Think of it! Everything which is or was alive — all the different kinds of foods, all the different plants and animals — is composed mostly of two or more of twelve elements. These are oxygen, carbon, hydrogen, nitrogen, phosphorus, sulfur, calcium, potassium, sodium, iron, chlorine, and magnesium. The first four of these are the most important ones. The rest occur only in very small amounts.

Over 99 per cent of the earth — the rocks and soil, the water in the oceans, rivers, and lakes, and the air in the earth's atmosphere — is made up of only twelve elements, too. These are almost the same as the twelve

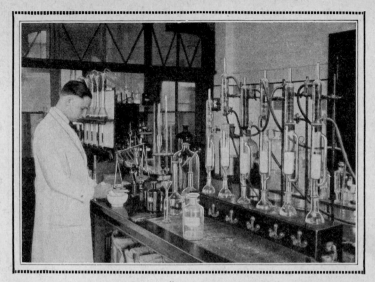

Scientists are constantly at work trying to learn new things

which make up the greater part of living things. Silicon and aluminum are not among those which are found in great quantities in living things, but many rocks are composed largely of these two elements. Silicon makes up over 25 per cent of the earth's crust, and aluminum over 7 per cent. The elements which are found in the greatest quantities in the earth's crust are oxygen, silicon, aluminum, and iron. Together these four make up about 87 per cent of the earth's crust.

Perhaps you would like to know something about some of the important elements.

Oxygen is one of these elements. There is more oxygen in the world than anything else. We know a great deal about oxygen. It is found in all parts of the

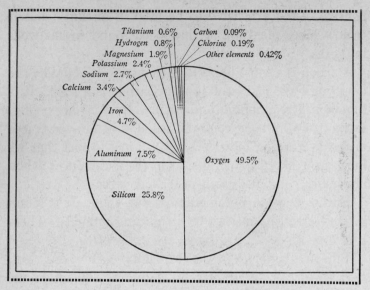

Titanium 0.6%   Carbon 0.09%
Hydrogen 0.8%   Chlorine 0.19%
Magnesium 1.9%   Other elements 0.42%
Potassium 2.4%
Sodium 2.7%
Calcium 3.4%

Iron
4.7%

Aluminum 7.5%

Oxygen 49.5%

Silicon 25.8%

This chart shows the elements that make up the crust of the earth

earth. It is in the food we eat, the water we drink, and
the air we breathe, and in the earth we live upon. The
earth is completely surrounded by it. It is a gas that
we cannot see or smell, but we could not live without
it. Fires cannot burn without it.

Hydrogen is colorless gas. It weighs the least of any
of the elements, and for this reason it has been used in
balloons and airships. But it burns quickly, and therefore it is not now considered safe for use in airships; so
it is being used less in the newer airships.

Helium is not so light as hydrogen. However, it is
used in airships because it will not burn and cause ex-
plosions. Helium has no color. It used to be very ex-

pensive,— too expensive to be used in airships; but it is now more plentiful. It has been found in gas wells in Texas.

Carbon is a most important element. It is unlike the ones you have just read about. Carbon is a solid. It is found in every animal and plant. It is in our bodies, in the trees, in every piece of wood, and in every piece of meat. Carbon may be black, as in the coal that we burn, or it may be colorless, as in the diamond. Carbon is usually combined with other elements.

Sulfur is another element that is a solid. It is found in very small quantities in plants and animals. There is a large amount of sulfur in the yolks of eggs.

Silicon is an element that we seldom hear about; yet, next to oxygen, it is the most common element in the earth. We do not often hear about it because it cannot be found alone. It is always united with some other element. There is silicon in every grain of sand along the seashore. Quartz contains a great amount of silicon. Silicon and oxygen combine to form the compound which makes up quartz rocks. White sand is nearly pure quartz, or silicon and oxygen. Quartz is very hard. As the waves pound the sand against the rocks, the softer rocks are washed away, and the hard quartz is left as a fine white sand.

The elements are somewhat like the letters of our alphabet. We have twenty-six letters in our alphabet. If you look in the dictionary you will see that there are thousands of words. Yet in these thousands of words we use no more than twenty-six letters. They are mixed

E

up in different ways to make words. So it is with all the things in the world. There are only ninety-two elements. Yet there are thousands of different substances in the world.

Elements unite to form the different substances in the earth. These are called compounds. A compound may have two or more than two elements. It never has less than two. Water is a very important compound, which is made up of oxygen and hydrogen. It does not have the same amount of the two gases. There are two parts of hydrogen to every one part of oxygen, which means that there is twice as much hydrogen as oxygen in water. When hydrogen burns it unites with the oxygen in the air, and the two elements form water.

If a current of electricity is passed through water, bubbles of gas will be seen leaving the water at the ends of the wires. If these bubbles are collected, it will be found that at one end twice as many bubbles collect as at the other. If a lighted match is brought near these gases, it will be found that one of them takes fire and burns, while the other causes the match to burn more brilliantly. The gas that burns is hydrogen. The gas that helps the match to burn is oxygen. Where did these gases come from? The water was made of these two gases. The electric current tore the water apart into the two gases of which it was made.

Have you ever noticed what happens to a piece of iron that lies out-of-doors? Does it not turn a reddish color on the outside? Sometimes you can brush a red powder from a piece of iron. You call it rust. But what is rust?

When iron stays out where it is exposed to air and moisture, oxygen very, very slowly unites with the iron, forming rust. Rust is therefore a compound made up of iron and oxygen.

If you look at your silverware at home you may find that part of it looks discolored or stained, and you say that it is tarnished. You have learned that sulfur is an element that is in some of our food. The yolk of an egg has a large amount of sulfur in it. Sulfur is also found in other foods. You eat the food with your silverware. The sulfur of the food touches the silver, and little by little the sulfur and silver unite. They form a thin layer of a compound that must be polished off the silverware.

When two elements unite there is a chemical action. That is, they unite in such a way that they become changed. When anything burns, there is a chemical action. Hydrogen burns with oxygen and forms water. During this chemical action you can see a tiny flame and feel the heat. There was a chemical action between the iron and oxygen when the iron rusted, and another between the silver and sulfur when the silverware became discolored.

Although we cannot see all these chemical actions, they are always taking place. Elements are uniting to form compounds, such as water, rust, or the tarnish on our silverware. These compounds are not like the elements of which they are made. In our bodies, in our homes, in the soil,—in fact, all over the world,—certain elements are uniting, thus forming different substances.

 ### Things to Think About

1. How can there be so many different substances when there are less than a hundred different elements used in these substances?

2. Some of the elements which you may often hear discussed are chlorine, cobalt, copper, gold, iodine, lead, magnesium, mercury, nickel, phosphorus, platinum, potassium, radium, silver, sodium, tin, and zinc. How many of these do you know? How many have you seen mentioned in the newspaper?

3. How are the elements like the letters of the alphabet? How are the compounds like the words that we use?

4. What elements are in carbon dioxide?

 ### Things to Do

1. Wet the inside of a test tube with water by pouring water into the tube and out again. Sprinkle some iron filings or very small tacks into the tube. The water causes them to stick to the sides and bottom. Pour out any loose filings. Now turn the tube upside down and fasten it over a pan of water, with its mouth a little way below the surface of the water. Allow it to stay that way for several days. Why does the water rise in the tube? What happened to the iron? Has it changed?

2. You can see that water is formed when hydrogen is burned. Light a candle and hold a cold bottle just above the flame. When the hydrogen that is in the candle unites with the oxygen of the air they form water. This water collects on the bottle.

3. Scientists have worked out a kind of shorthand to use when they write the names of elements and compounds. They have made a set of symbols for different elements and compounds. "O" stands for an atom of oxygen, "H" stands for an atom of hydrogen, and "Fe" stands for an atom of iron. Look at this list of some of the common elements and their symbols. You need not learn them.

Name	Symbol	Name	Symbol
Oxygen	O	Sodium	Na
Carbon	C	Silicon	Si
Sulfur	S	Phosphorus	P
Nitrogen	N	Chlorine	Cl
Aluminum	Al	Calcium	Ca
Iron	Fe	Zinc	Zn
Copper	Cu	Silver	Ag

4. Examine some iron rust. How does it differ from iron and oxygen, from which it is made?

5. Examine water. How does it differ from hydrogen and oxygen, from which it is made?

6. Examine tarnish on silverware. How does it differ from silver and sulfur, from which it is made?

7. Notice wood that has been burned in a camp fire. Can you find the black substance which is carbon? Heat a little sugar in an old pan and notice that it turns black. What is left? Look at some white sand. This is made of two elements, silicon and oxygen.

Problem 2 · Men learn how to Use the Things which make up the Earth

1. Men learn to Invent

Men, in the early ages, had to go out and gather whatever food they could find. They had to kill with their own hands the animals which they used for their food. This was very dangerous. Since they had no farms, they had to search for berries, fruits, and seeds out of which they could make a meal. At first they did not think of cultivating the soil and raising plants for their food, nor did they know about raising animals for their meat. They traveled from one place to another in search of food. They did all their work by hand. They had no machines to aid them.

We do not know how man first learned to raise his own food. The story of man's farming begins before the beginning of history. As far back as 6000 B. C. the Egyptians knew how to grow barley. The lake dwellers of Switzerland and northern Italy knew how to raise beans, and wheat and other grains that could be used for food. Men of the Stone Age had already learned to tame animals. In many places where remains of early settlements have been found, traces of animals and plants grown by man have been discovered.

We can only guess how man must have first discovered that he could raise his own food to carry him over times when it was scarce. Possibly he noticed that where he had let some seeds fall a plant had grown. Or

This is a way that primitive men had of getting their
food and clothing. This was before there were inventions

possibly he was dragging a stick over the ground, as you sometimes do when you have nothing else to amuse you, and then threw some seeds in the furrow with no particular idea in mind. Imagine his surprise when he found a plant that would give him food growing there! Could he have known then that he had suddenly freed himself from depending on the wild life around him and that from then on he was master of his surroundings?

We know little more about how man first learned to raise animals, except that he made this discovery very long ago. Perhaps on a game hunt one man found an animal that he didn't want to kill because he liked it so much. He may have kept this animal as a pet, but possibly one day, after many unsuccessful hunts, his hunger forced him to kill the animal for food. This may have given him the idea that he could keep animals and use them when he could find nothing on the hunt.

Civilization must have begun with the cultivation of crops. Before man knew how to raise his own food, he wandered about and hunted his prey, as other animals did. When he learned how to raise crops and animals, he was able to settle in one place. He had more time then, because raising his own food was not so difficult as hunting for it from day to day. With his free time he was able to learn other things that gave him greater comfort and happiness.

We can only imagine how man first used machines and discovered that they would make his work easier. The club was probably the first machine. He found that by using it or a bone he could strike an animal with

Man has used levers for thousands of years

greater force than with his arm. Perhaps he used it to defend himself and found later that he could use it in securing food. The club used by the arm makes one kind of simple machine.

Perhaps some cave man thought that the entrance to his cave was too large. He may have decided to put a stone there to fill up the hole. But the stone he wanted was fast in the dirt. Perhaps he pried it loose with a stick. Then, quite by accident, he discovered that he could put one end of a stick under a stone, rest the stick on a log or another stone, then press upon the other end of the stick, and in this way raise the stone much more easily than if he had tried to lift it with his arms.

Little by little man has learned to use more and more objects as tools with which to do work. He has learned

about a few kinds of machines which may be put together, or combined, to make new machines. You have
learned that the whole world is made up of a few elements. Likewise all machines are made up of a few
simple kinds.

When primitive man used a stick to dig out a stone,
or a club or stone with which to strike an animal, he
used the kind of machine which is called a lever. Today
we use machines that work as those early ones did. A
crowbar is used to lift a heavy object; a hammer is
used to pull a nail; a seesaw is used in playing. All
these are kinds of levers. If you have played on a seesaw, you know that if a boy or girl who weighs much
more than you do sits near the rod on which the seesaw
rests and you sit far away from it, you can lift the boy
or girl. We use levers to lift or move heavy objects.

Have you ever used a kind of reel to wind up your
kite string? Have you gone fishing and used a reel to
pull in your fish? You certainly have sharpened a pencil in a sharpener with a crank that you had to turn.
When you did these things, you were using another
kind of machine. This machine is a wheel and axle. If
you use the steering wheel of an automobile, you have
your hand on the outside of the wheel. The axle of the
wheel is the part that causes the automobile to turn one
way or another. In some wells the bucket is fastened to
a rope which passes around an axle, and to pull up the
bucket someone turns a large crank, which is just the
same as turning a wheel. In working with any wheel
and axle you always take hold of the rim of the wheel

How many simple machines can you find here?

or the part of the crank farthest from the axle. The wheel or crank causes the axle to turn and do the work.

Another machine is the pulley. Pulleys are wheels that have ropes which pass around the outside of the wheels. When men move buildings, they use several pulleys which work together. By using a set of a number of pulleys a heavy load can be pulled or lifted fairly easily.

You have all seen a barrel rolled up a board onto a higher level. This board is a machine called an inclined plane. You have all used inclined planes without thinking about it. Have you ever ridden a bicycle from the street up a driveway to get onto the sidewalk? Why didn't you ride over the curb? The driveway was sloped, and this slope was an inclined plane that made it easier to ride your bicycle onto the sidewalk. Roads over a mountain are all inclined planes, but some are easier to travel over than others. A road that slopes gradually is just a longer inclined plane than one that is steep. It is much easier to travel up a gentle slope, even if it is longer, than up a very steep hill.

There are two other simple machines, the screw and the wedge. You have all seen screws used to hold objects together. Jacks having screws are used to raise buildings. Wedges are used very often to split things or push them apart. Knives and axes are very common wedges.

It took years and years for men to learn to use these simple machines. After a still longer time they learned to put them together. In this way they made compound machines, which they used for doing work. Most of the machines we use now are compound machines — that is, two or more simple machines working together.

Since the early people were farmers, farm machines were the first invented. The first plow was probably a forked stick, which was sharpened at the ends and dragged along the ground. Then a handle was put on the plow, and while one man pulled, another man guided it to make it go straight. When two men used the plow, it could be made of a heavier stick than when one man used it. Sometime later when men had learned to use animals to do their work, the plow was pulled by oxen. For centuries the forked stick pulled by oxen was the only kind of plow.

It was not until men learned to use iron and steel

The story of the plow

that the plow was greatly improved. And then men were afraid to use it. Some thought that iron would poison the soil and the crops. Others thought that weeds would grow much faster if iron plows were used. But after a while men gave up those old ideas, and the plow was gradually improved upon, until now plows made mostly of iron and steel are used.

Plows made it possible to prepare a great deal more land for planting and growing crops. But after crops were grown, they needed to be harvested.

At first men cut the grain and grasses with a wide, straight knife that acted as a very sharp wedge. Then they learned that if the blade were bent, it would do better work.

During the Bronze Age the grain was cut by sickles made of bronze. A picture on the walls of a building in ancient Thebes shows two men cutting grain with sickles, while others carry the grain to the place where it was being threshed by oxen.

Early colonists in America used a scythe that had prongs on it, which were called fingers. These fingers were parallel to the blade and caught the grain as it was cut. In this way they helped to leave the grain in bunches. Then men followed behind and tied the bunches together. This scythe was called a cradle and was used until later improvements were added. In 1831 McCormick made a reaper, which cut much more grain than men could cut with scythes or cradles. It did the work of about six men. From that time the reaper and binder has been improved until now, on many large farms, great machines called combines are used, which cut the grain and thresh it. The grain is then loaded into trucks and stored.

2. Machines Change Ways of Living

Farm machines have been only one line of great improvement in machinery. By combining, or putting together, simple machines men have learned to make huge machines for manufacturing clothing, preserving and canning food, lifting great loads, and driving trains and boats all over the world.

During their very early history, men had learned to use the hair of animals and the fibers of plants to make clothing. They spun the wool of sheep or fibers of plants into a thread by twisting small bits of the raw material together. To aid them in spinning this thread the people had a small tool called a spindle. Early people also knew how to weave the thread into cloth. Each tribe had its own kind of loom, which wove the materials for their clothing. But after they had learned to do that much, they made very little progress. For centuries they spun their threads and wove their cloth in much the same way that their grandfathers had done before them.

Just a little more than a century ago most of the clothing was still made in the home. The spinning wheel, which spun only one thread at a time, was used to spin wool into yarn and cotton into thread. Before the wool could be spun, it had to be washed and prepared almost all by hand, with the use only of a small machine. Girls in the family, when very young, were taught to spend their spare time in spinning threads. It took many hours of spinning, by everyone who could, to make thread enough to provide clothing for all the family. When spun, this thread was woven into cloth, or knit into hose, sweaters, or other garments. If materials had to be sewed together, every stitch was made by hand with a needle and thread.

Besides clothing, many other things were made at home or at a neighbor's home. Some neighbors often did one thing, while others did another. Soap was made at home with wood ashes and scraps of fat. Maple sugar was made from the sap of sugar maples. Skins of animals were tanned and made into shoes. Grain was taken to a near-by mill, which was run by water power, and was ground into flour and taken home. Lumber was sawed at mills, and the finest furniture was made by workmen who had small shops. But factories were not known, and they were scarcely needed.

But then changes began to take place as inventions that had just been made gradually came into general use. An Englishman invented the spinning jenny, which was an improvement over the spinning wheel. At first this new machine spun eight threads at a time. The number increased to sixteen, then twenty, then one hundred, as improvements were made. Now a thousand threads may be spun on one machine at one time. The loom was improved and was made large enough to be run by power. First the power was supplied by the ox, then by water wheels, and then by steam engines. With

At one time all the spinning for the family was done at home

the inventions of the spinning jenny and power loom many times the old amount of thread and cloth could be spun and woven in a day.

In America other inventions were being made. Eli Whitney built a cotton gin, which enabled the slaves working in the South to pick the seeds out of much more cotton than they could by hand in the same length of time. Up until this time it took so long to take the seeds from the cotton that it did not pay to raise much. But now the cotton gin made it possible to raise and prepare more cotton for spinning.

Machines had been invented to increase the speed of spinning and weaving, but as yet everything had to be sewed by hand with the needle. In 1845 Elias Howe

E

invented a sewing machine that could sew 250 stitches a minute. This was the invention needed to aid in producing more and better clothing.

However, these new machines were too expensive and too large to be used in the home. It was then that men began to collect spinning machines and looms under one roof, and in this way factories had their beginning. Spinning, weaving, and sewing were taken from the home into factories.

In much the same way that factories for clothing developed, factories developed for making other things. Stockings and sweaters, which had once been knitted at home, now began to be made in factories. Shoe factories took the place of the shoemaker. Furniture factories began to do the work of the furniture makers with small shops. Life began to center about factories and industries instead of the home. More and better clothes and better living conditions have resulted from the invention of machines.

Besides learning how to put simple machines together to make new ones, men have learned to use gas, steam, and electricity to run their machines. Before this they had to use their own strength or that of animals.

The invention of the gas engine has given the power needed to turn great wheels and run man's huge machines. Tractors, trucks, automobiles, and airplanes use gas engines. For a long time steam alone was used to run locomotives and ships, but now electricity is being substituted for steam in some of these engines.

This is not the only part of the book that deals with

machines. You will read more about inventions in later units, especially about those having to do with transportation and communication.

 Things to Think About

1. Can you name any nation which has but few machines?

2. With the invention of modern machines, civilization has advanced more in the last hundred years than in all the centuries before. Can you see why?

3. How do machines help you?

4. Have you anything which has not in some way been prepared by a machine?

5. Why do people not have to work so many hours a day as they did several years ago?

6. What would the world be like without inventions?

 Things to Do

1. Look at your bicycle and see how many kinds of simple machines you can find. How many are there on a coaster wagon?

2. List the machines you can think of which help men to do their work.

3. Collect pictures of machines. See if you can explain them to the class.

4. List some use of each of the following: the lever, the inclined plane, the pulley, and the wheel.

5. Write a story about how a cave man may have made a discovery.

6. Tell how your clothes might have been made a century ago.

7. Lift some object by prying it with a strong stick. Can you lift more or less weight when you take hold at the end of the stick?

8. Bring to school any toy machines you have and explain how they work.

9. Make an excursion to a factory. Ask the men at work to explain how the machinery works.

10. Visit a farm. Watch some of the farm machinery and see what you can explain to the class.

UNIT X

Men have learned Many Things about Electricity

1. What Early Men thought of Electricity
2. How Electricity travels over Wires
3. How Electricity is Made and Used

MEN HAVE LEARNED MANY THINGS
ABOUT ELECTRICITY

When heavy black clouds hung low in the heavens and bright flashes of lightning streaked the sky, lighting it for a moment as light as day, and when deafening noises followed, pounding through the mountains and echoing against the cliffs, primitive people huddled in their caves with fright. This was the only electricity they knew anything about. They could not understand what it was or where it came from. They were frightened.

Today electricity is man's slave. It cooks his food; it lights his house and his streets; it washes and irons his clothes; it runs many of his factories; it does many other things too numerous to mention that make man's work easier.

In Unit XII you will learn how man learned to harness electricity.

Problem 1 · What Early Men thought of Electricity

When people first saw lightning, it was before they had learned to make and use fires. What must they have thought when they saw these great flashes like fire in the sky? Perhaps lightning had struck a tree and caused it to burn. Do you wonder then that they were frightened? Can you see why they might have thought that lightning was fire which was hurled to earth by one of their gods? It is no wonder that they had many strange beliefs, or superstitions, about it. Centuries and centuries passed before people knew that lightning was electricity and knew how it was formed. A long time passed before man realized that electricity was something that could be useful and that could do work for him.

Probably the cave man was the first to learn about electricity and about how to make it. We can only make a guess about how it was discovered. Perhaps a man picked up a piece of amber that looked a little dirty. He rubbed it against his fur clothes to clean it. When he took it away, it pulled the fur toward it. Amazed, he rubbed harder. This time it attracted more fur than before. What fun he must have had! Each time he rubbed the amber, it attracted the fur. He could not understand this strange thing. He ran from one cave man to another and showed this wonderful bit of magic. Others found amber and rubbed it to make it attract certain objects. They wondered about it.

This is a kitchen of colonial days. Can you
tell what the various things were used for?

We do not know whether or not this particular qual-
ity of rubbed amber was discovered in this way. We do
know that the ancient peoples were very fond of amber.
They collected it and made beads and ornaments out of
it. Many of these old beads have been found in some of
the very ancient tombs. The Phœnicians brought amber
all the way from the shores of the Baltic Sea. They
thought they had made a great discovery.

In the seventh century B.C. stories were written about
the strange influence of rubbed amber. People knew
what happened, but they did not know why. Centuries
went by before they knew much more about electricity.

This shows some of the electric inventions
that may be used in a kitchen today

The early Greeks knew the trick of rubbing amber, which seemed to them to be magic. The name the Greeks used for amber was *electron*. It was from *electron* that electricity received its name. This was many years later when men learned more about the "magic" of rubbed amber. They had learned that many objects, when rubbed, would produce an attraction for certain other objects. They knew that, by rubbing certain things, frictional electricity was produced.

The early people collected amber and valued it highly. They rubbed it and saw that it attracted certain objects, but that was all. They had no idea how

great the subject of electricity that they were opening
would become. How little did they dream that in two
thousand years electricity would be doing much of man's
work for him, that electricity would be man's slave.

What would the ancients think if they could suddenly appear on the earth and see us as we live? How
surprised they would be to stand and watch horseless
carts race down the streets! All the electric lights and
signs would fill them with wonder. If they were told
that their clothes could be laundered by machines driven
by electricity, they would be astonished. Imagine one
of our early ancestors, even one from the eighteenth
century, sleeping and waking up after many years, as
Rip Van Winkle did, coming to visit for a day in one of
our homes. How surprised he would be at all the things
that happen during the day! In the early morning a
button is pressed, and the kitchen is flooded with light.
This lamp does not need to be filled with oil, a door does
not need to be closed to keep a draft from putting it out,
and it does not need to be watched. It burns on steadily
as mother puts the bread in the toaster and presses a
button, and the toast comes out when toasted. While
this has been going on, the electric percolator has made
the coffee, and all sit down to a breakfast that was easily
made.

After breakfast father takes the ancestor to work
with him. How frightened he is of the trolley car, electric train, or subway train in which they sit quietly as
they are carried to work. In order that he may miss
nothing, the old gentleman is brought back to the house

to see the washing, ironing, and cleaning done. How easy it is to put the clothes in a machine and watch it as it seems to run by itself, washing the clothes! You know, in his day many women had to wash clothes on a rock in a brook or river.

But how much easier it all is now! Perhaps as mother is doing the laundering, sister uses the vacuum cleaner until everything is clean. Then she makes a pudding or some ice cream, which she places in the electric refrigerator to freeze for dinner. When this work is done, mother orders her groceries by telephone, and then everyone sits down to rest and listen to the radio.

All these machines and devices which are run by electricity are new to the old gentleman. He is amazed. People have learned more about electricity in the last hundred years than they learned in all the years before.

 Things to Think About

1. Why were early people afraid of lightning?

2. Why did ancient people have many strange beliefs and superstitions which we do not believe in now?

 *Things to Do*

1. Ask your grandfather to tell you about his boyhood days. How many inventions have been made since he was a small boy?

2. Write a story to tell how an ancient man might feel today in a big city.

Problem 2 · How Electricity travels over Wires

Electricity that is formed by rubbing amber, a fountain pen, a comb, or a number of other things is called static electricity. Static means that it does not flow. It may jump from one object to another when that object has too much electricity, but it does not flow in a steady stream. Either static electricity remains quiet, or it jumps and forms a spark.

The electricity that we find most useful in doing our work is that which moves along a path and is called an electric current. Currents of electricity flow from one place to another. Electricity travels in a kind of circle from the place where it is made back to the same place. We say it travels in circuits. The electricity used in a doorbell, a toy motor, or a flash light comes from a battery; we can trace the electric circuit from the battery and back to it. The electricity passes through the wires to the bell and causes the bell to ring. When it again reaches the battery, it has made a complete circuit.

Electricity must travel in circuits if it is to serve us. When the circuit is broken by a switch or a push button, electricity will not do these things.

Electricity cannot flow all by itself. There is electric pressure back of it, which pushes it along. This pressure pushes the electricity somewhat as water pressure pushes water through the water pipes. But electricity does not flow as water does; it does not need hollow wires. Electricity travels along solid wires.

Each wire that carries electricity is called a conductor. Some conductors carry electricity better than others. There are good and poor conductors. Copper wire is a very good conductor. Iron wire is not nearly so good a conductor as copper wire.

These wires and every object in all the world are made up of very, very tiny things. These things are so tiny that you cannot see them with a very powerful microscope. We call them atoms.

Everything is made up of atoms. Trees, desks, plants, pencils, wires — everything has atoms. Now each atom has some other tiny things in it that are called electrons. Each electron is a charge of electricity. Usually electrons form little groups in the atom. They may remain in their own little group, or atom, or they may be moving from one atom to another. It is the migration, or traveling, of these little electrons that is what we know as the electric current.

You can play a game that may help you to understand how electricity passes along wires. Each boy or girl will represent an atom. Let each child have a book. The books will represent electrons. The boys and girls form a circle all the way around the room. Each girl or boy should be close enough to the next one to be able to reach him easily. Now remember that these books are electrons and each electron is a tiny charge of electricity. Let one child hand his book to the child next to him in the line. That child passes the book that he already has to the next child, and so on, until the books are moving around the circle, or circuit. This continues until every child is receiving and passing an "electron" on to the next child. As these books are passed from one child to another, so electrons in a wire are passed from one atom to the next atom and so around the circuit. In this way little charges of electricity are carried from one atom to the next. This causes a flow of electricity. You will see that it is not necessary to stand in a circle so long as each child is standing near enough to receive and pass on a book without taking a step.

Of course atoms may have many electrons, just as the boys and girls may have many books. This game shows how electrons may move along.

Now let one boy or girl be the electric switch. This boy or girl can stop or start the electric current by stepping out of the game. When he gets out, the books can no longer move about the circuit. We say he has opened the circuit. When he steps in, he closes it, and the books can again move about. A switch opens and closes the circuit. Push buttons and chains that we use to turn electric lights on and off operate switches. They close and open electric circuits. When we press a button to turn on electric lights, we close the circuit, so that electrons flow from one atom to another.

You can play another game in a gymnasium. The children may again be atoms. They scatter in a long line from end to end of the gymnasium. Then the children pass basket balls as rapidly as possible from one end of the gymnasium to the other. The basket balls are the electrons. This shows something of the way that electricity flows over a wire.

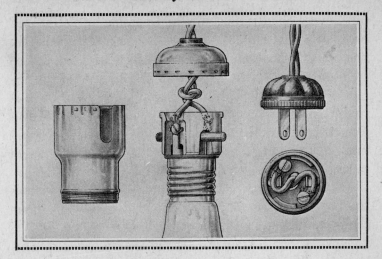

This diagram may help you to wire electric devices at home.
Notice that the insulation should be torn off the ends of
the wire only where they are fastened under the screws

Now we can find out how a doorbell rings when we
press the button. Chemical energy in the battery causes
electrons to move along the wire. The battery is like a
pump; it sends electrons out into the wire, and continues
to send others after them. The electrons pass over the
wire until some of them reach the bell, and the electricity
causes the electromagnet to ring the bell.

You have seen electric wires that are attached to
your electric lamps. Notice the silk threads that are
woven around the wire. If you can, find an old piece of
wire and remove the silk. Usually you will find a layer
of rubber between the wire and the silk. Can you tell
why the wire is covered this way?

Rubber and silk are good insulators. They prevent the escape of electricity. If electric wires are properly insulated, they cannot give you a shock.

You have learned that some conductors carry electricity much better than others. Therefore wires for carrying electricity are usually made of the better conductors. Many are made of copper. The size of the wire is also important. Large wires carry electricity much more easily than small wires which are made of the same material. Some wires resist, or try to prevent, the flow of electricity more than other wires. Some kinds of wires do not conduct electricity easily, and become very hot. The energy of the electricity is changed to heat. You will read about this later when we discuss how electricity is used to make heat.

 Things to Think About

1. It takes only a very short time for electricity to pass along a wire. It travels over miles of wire while you can blink your eye. You push a button, and the doorbell rings almost instantly. The electric lamp is immediately lighted when you press the switch. The street lights all over a city shine out when the current is turned on. What other things happen which make you think that electricity travels rapidly?

2. Why is current electricity more important than static electricity?

3. What are insulators and conductors?

4. What is a complete circuit?

Things to Do

Make an electric questioner. Some boys and girls have made electric map questioners. They mounted a map of the United States or of another country on a board. Then they decided what they wanted to be questioned about: sometimes it was the location of principal cities; at others times it was the capitals of the states.

If you want to learn to locate the principal cities, make a list of them at one side of the map. Put a small brass screw in front of the name of each city. Locate the place on the map where this city is found. Now put another screw at this point. Connect the two screws with an insulated wire on the back of the board. In this same way connect all the names of the cities to their correct locations on the map.

You will need a dry battery and a buzzer or a bell. Connect one end of an insulated wire to the battery and the other end to the buzzer. Now take a long wire that will reach from the buzzer to any of the screws on the map. Attach one end of this to the buzzer. Connect a shorter wire to the other pole of the dry cell. Your electric toy is ready for use. If you want to locate Los Angeles, put the short wire on the screw opposite the name of that city. Then with the long wire touch any of the screws on the map. When you touch the right one, the buzzer will make a sound. When you touch the correct screw, a complete circuit is made. That is why the bell rings.

Other boys and girls have used other ideas. Some have fastened two rows of screws on one side, and two rows on another side, of a board. The two rows on one side had multiplication problems. The other two rows told the

E

answers if the wires were connected correctly. Some children used words and their synonyms. Others used questions in science.

Bird pictures may be used on one side of the questioner and bird names on the other side. This may be used in learning the names of birds.

This electric toy can be used in many other ways. Can you think of a clever, original way to use it?

Perhaps the buzzer or bell makes too much noise. Could you use a small electric bulb that will give a light when you find the right answer?

Problem 3 · How Electricity is Made and Used

1. Generators make Electricity

Although men in very early times made electricity by rubbing amber and other objects, they could not use it in any way. Neither did they learn for a long time how to make electricity that could be used. It was only after men had experimented for several centuries that they discovered how to make electricity do work for them.

One of the early ways of producing electricity that would do work was the use of simple wet cells, which were made of

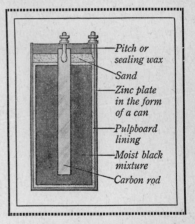

Pitch or sealing wax
Sand
Zinc plate in the form of a can
Pulpboard lining
Moist black mixture
Carbon rod

Cut an old dry cell in two and find these things

liquids and a couple of metal bars. In these cells a chemical action took place which produced electric currents. Later on, dry cells were made which were much like those that are used in flash-light batteries today. They are also sometimes used to ring a doorbell or to drive a toy motor.

If you tear open an old dry cell, you can see what it is like inside. A zinc container holds some sal ammoniac which is mixed with other substances to make a black, moist paste. Above this paste are layers of sand and pitch or sealing wax, which prevent it from leaking out. In the center of the cell is a carbon rod. The carbon rod and zinc container have small posts on the top, which are called binding posts. When a wire connects these posts, or when the cell is in a circuit, the zinc, carbon, and chemicals cause electrons to be pumped out as currents of electricity.

There is no kind of electric cell that can make electricity forever. After the cell has been used a great deal, it sends out only a very weak current or none at all. We say the cell is dead. Can you tell what has happened? As cells are used the flow of electricity grows less until it finally stops. Therefore dry cells are useful in places where they are needed only once in a while. For motors, irons, toasters, and vacuum cleaners, and for lighting our houses, dry cells are not satisfactory.

Electricity for running all kinds of motors and for electrical heating devices, such as toasters, is produced by electric generators, which make, or generate, electricity. These huge machines are made of coils of wire and large magnets.

Do you remember about the lines of force around a magnet? When coils of wire are passed through these lines of force, the electrons in the coils begin to flow, and electricity is generated. Some generators are made so that the magnets turn; others have coils that turn. In either case the lines of force of the magnet are cut by coils of wire, and currents of electricity are produced. By turning the magnet or the coils of wire very rapidly a stronger current is produced.

This boy, in moving the wire back and forth through the
poles of the magnet, causes the magnetic needle to move

But there must be some outside force that turns the
coils of wire or the magnets. The generator cannot furnish force to turn its own coils or magnets. Therefore
generators are run by gas, steam, or water power.
Steam and gas engines are often used. There are great
generators at Niagara Falls run by water power. As the
water there drops many feet, power is obtained to turn
the generators which furnish electricity for many of the
towns around the falls.

Some generators weigh over 100 tons. Can you
imagine how large that would be? A generator of this
size can furnish enough electricity to run 300 street cars.
It would take millions of tons of coal to produce the

they were! This method was far better than using either candles or oil lamps. But a little more than a half-century ago the best method yet found for lighting streets and houses was discovered.

It was Thomas Edison who gave us the electric lamps that we are using today in our houses, streets, and offices. In 1878 he began experimenting with different materials out of which he hoped that a filament could be made to use in an electric bulb. Filaments are the thread-like wires that are inside the bulbs. Edison tried a number of things. He used platinum, and he used paper covered with carbon, but they were not satisfactory. Each time one substance would not work, he tried another.

Finally Edison used a sewing thread that was covered with carbon. He sealed this in a globe out of which most of the air had been pumped, and connected the globe to the electric wires. Imagine the joy when this new bulb remained lighted without stopping for forty hours. This was the beginning of the electric light. Although the carbon threads could be used, Edison continually searched for something that might be better, and he found several things.

After many years an electrical company thought of trying a metal called tungsten. This worked better than anything else that had been tried. Many tungsten lamps are now used. When electricity passes through a fine tungsten filament, the filament immediately becomes white hot. It gives off a light chat may be seen for a greater distance than the light from other fila-

The story of light from the cave man to you

ments. Nowadays in the brightly lighted parts of some cities it seems almost as light as day.

Have you ever known about a football game that was played at night on an electrically lighted field? The lamps give light enough for the players to see almost as well as in the daytime. Certain kinds of electric lights are used in greenhouses to make plants grow all night long. Electric lights have made this quite a different world at night.

3. Why a Fuse "Blows Out"

Have you ever been playing with your electric train in the evening when everything suddenly became dark? Every light had gone out in your house, but when you looked across the street you saw light in other houses. While you were wondering about it, someone said, "The fuse has blown out." Then you asked, "What is a fuse? Why is it used? Why does it go out?"

Fuses are little safety devices which are used to protect buildings against fire. If you remember, many times when a fuse has blown out, something has gone wrong with some electrical device. Often it happened when a lamp was turned on or while an iron was being used. Either too much current was used by too many lights and devices or there was a short circuit.

You have heard people talk about short circuits. They are often formed in cords carrying the current. In each cord that is fastened to an electrical device there are two wires. Each wire is insulated very carefully, but when cords are used a great deal, the insulation may wear off, and the two wires may touch. If they touch, the electricity goes from one wire to the other without going through the electric iron or whatever the device may be. It takes the shortest path back; that is why it is called a short circuit.

When the wire in this fuse becomes too hot, it melts and breaks the circuit

When there is a short circuit, there is a greater current passing over the wires than before, and this makes them hotter than usual. If there is no fuse in the circuit, the wires may become hot enough to start a fire. But if there is a fuse in the circuit, it blows out and shuts off the current.

There is a fuse used for each circuit in the house, and all the current in that circuit goes through the fuse. So long as there is the usual amount of electricity passing through the fuse, everything is all right.

In the fuse is a fuse wire which melts very easily. If there is a short circuit, the fuse wire becomes very hot and melts. It then breaks the connection. It acts as a switch and prevents the electricity from going through the wires in the circuit. Therefore the lights go out until the fuse is replaced with a new one.

When a fuse blows out, you can be sure that there was a reason for it. If there is a short circuit, the cause of it should be repaired before the fuse is replaced. If a cord or some electrical device was the cause of the difficulty, it should be repaired before it is used again.

Some people have been known to place a coin under the old fuse and use it again instead of putting in a new fuse. The coin is a good conductor of electricity and allows a greater current to pass through it than the wires in the house should carry. You can tell why this is very dangerous.

 Things to Think About

1. For what cities do the generators at Niagara Falls furnish electricity? Can you think of another place where great quantities of electricity are generated?

2. Electricity is also used to run many motors. How many motors in the home are driven by electricity? There are sewing machines, vacuum cleaners, and washing machines. Can you think of any others?

3. How many different places can you think of in which electric lamps are used to change night into day?

4. Imagine that there were no electricity for a week. What would happen in our houses in the city and in the country?

5. Why is a fuse like a switch?

6. Why is it dangerous to use anything except a new fuse for one that has been burned out?

7. What are some things that are good to know when one is changing a fuse?

 *Things to Do*

1. Examine a flash light. Explain how it works.

2. Take an electric-light socket to school and tell how it operates.

3. Find out some interesting things about Edison and his inventions. How do his inventions help us?

4. Examine an old fuse, socket, switch, bulb, toaster, and other electrical things.

5. Newspapers and advertisements often have pictures of different electrical devices. Cut these out and paste them on a large piece of cardboard. You can make this chart show the uses of electricity.

6. Cut open a dry cell and find the principal parts.

7. Tell where the electricity used in lighting your home is generated.

8. Find out about the size of the Niagara Falls generators. Tell how they are driven.

9. Make a water wheel that can be used to drive a toy motor.

10. List all the uses of electricity which you can think of.

UNIT XI

Methods of Communication have Changed

1. How Sound is Carried
2. Messages by Dots and Dashes
3. Messages by Telephone
4. Messages by Radio

METHODS OF COMMUNICATION HAVE CHANGED

What a difference there is between using tom-toms, smoke signals, and beacon fires and using the telegraph, telephone, and radio of today! This is the difference between the ways of communication that primitive people had and communication now.

At first men communicated with others only with their voices. One man could not make another understand a message if he were out of reach of hearing. Later, men learned to use signals of various kinds. As tribes and nations were formed, people needed ways other than their voices to send messages. They learned to use other sounds and light. Then it was that they used tom-toms to call their tribes together or signaled from hill to hill with beacon fires or smoke signals.

But our means of communication are quite different. Our newspapers tell about things that happened in Asia, Africa, or Europe a few hours ago. Today we may be in our own home and hear a program from a distant land. We may listen to an explorer in far-away polar regions, to a football game, play by play, in a distant city, or to the president of the United States in Washington. The whole world seems to be at our call by merely pressing a button.

In Unit XI you will learn how this change has been brought about.

An early means of communication

Courtesy of the Detroit Institute of Arts

E

Problem 1 · How Sound is Carried

Sometime when you are walking, stop for a moment and listen. You hear the breeze in the trees, the distant sound of a train, the song of a bird, or the noise of an automobile passing by. The automobile seems to make less noise as it travels down the road, and the sound of the train slowly fades in the distance, as you listen. Have you ever wondered how these sounds come to you? Does something carry them? Why does the sound of the train grow fainter and fainter? Why can you hear better if the wind is blowing from the direction of the sound? Why is it more difficult to hear if the wind is blowing against the sound?

Perhaps you have wondered what sound is. What makes sound? How does the bird sing? What does the engineer do to make the steam engine give a shrill whistle?

Have you ever seen a bell ringing in the distance? The sound of the bell did not come at the same time that you saw the clapper strike the bell. You heard the sound afterwards. Many people ask why they hear thunder after they see the lightning. Why, then, do you not hear the thunder just as the lightning streaks the sky?

Place your hand on your throat and talk. You feel little quivering motions. These little rapid motions back and forth are called vibrations. It is these vibrations that make sound. Watch a bird as it sings. Its little

314

The water was set in vibration by a stone,[1] and air
was set in vibration by plucking the violin string

throat trembles with song. Blow a whistle and you
feel vibrations in the whistle as it cuts the air with a
shrill sound. If you place your hand on a piano or violin
as it is being played, you can feel that instrument vibrate. Sound is made by these vibrating objects. You
can hear a sound only when something vibrates.

Sometimes you can see vibrations. Pluck a violin
string and watch it. The string looks broader as it
moves back and forth. Hold a string or a rubber band
at the ends and pull it tight. Then give it a sudden
jerk. Do you hear a noise? Do you see the trembling
motion of the string? Watch as you play the violin,
beat a drum, or strike two things together. These vibrations that you see produce sound.

At any time that we hear a sound, we know that
something has been set in motion and that it is vibrating.
But sometimes there are vibrations that do not make a

[1] From Caldwell and Curtis's "Introduction to Science."

sound. When an object vibrates too slowly,— that is, when it does not make more than a few vibrations in one second,— you can hear nothing. But when there are many vibrations produced in a second, there is sound.

When sound vibrations strike the air, they make sound waves, which travel in all directions. They travel through the air and carry the sound. It is these waves that bring the sound to your ears. They strike the outside of the ear and are carried inside through the opening, where they beat against the tiny eardrum. This causes the eardrum to vibrate, and as it does so it hits the little bones on the inside of the ear. The bones transfer the tiny wave motions to your nerves, and your nerves carry the message to your brain. All this is done in an instant. It is because of sound waves in the air that beautiful music, the songs of birds, or people's voices are brought to you.

Air, earth, water, and metals carry sound. Sound travels better through some metals, water, and earth than it does through air. Sound cannot travel when there is nothing in which it can form waves. Do you know what a vacuum is? A real vacuum has nothing in it at all. You pick up a bottle, and you say that it is empty; but it really is not empty — it is full of air. Even when a room has no furniture in it or anything else that you can see, it is not empty. It too has air in it. But there are pumps that can take almost all the air out of a bottle or a tank. If they could take all the air out, there would be a vacuum. A vacuum is a place that is really empty; it does not have even air in it.

Air carries sound

If people could fly far up above the earth, far up in space, they could shout, but others would never hear them. There would be no air or other substances to bring the sound to their ears.

Sound travels very rapidly, but not nearly so rapidly as light. While light is traveling 186,000 miles in one second, sound travels about one fifth of a mile. Light travels so swiftly that it could travel a distance equal to seven and one half times around the earth while sound was going about 1000 feet. It takes sound about five seconds to travel one mile.

Light travels so rapidly that you see a flash of lightning immediately, but it is often several seconds before you hear the thunder. Have you ever counted to see how far the lightning was away from you? Since sound travels about one fifth of a mile in one second, it would

take five seconds, or five counts, for each mile. Therefore, if you can count five seconds between the time when
you see the lightning and the time when you hear the
thunder, you will know that the lightning was about a
mile away.

There are two kinds of sound. One kind we enjoy.
We call it music. But one kind makes us want to get
away from it. We do not like it at all, and we call this
sound noise. Music and noise are both made by vibrations. Music is made by smooth, regular vibrations. Vibrations that are jerky make a noise.

Men have learned how to make different instruments for producing sound that is music. The musical
instruments that are used in orchestras or bands produce sound that we enjoy. Some of them have strings
that vibrate. Others have tubes in which one blows,
causing the air to vibrate.

 Things to Think About

1. Have you heard that Indians and early settlers used
to put their ears near the earth to listen for the approach
of the enemy? Do sound waves travel through solid
matter?

2. What are some ways in which we use sound in
communication?

3. What are some ways in which we use light in
communication?

 *Things to Do*

1. Take two very small tin cans and punch a tiny hole through the bottom of each. Pull the end of a long string through the hole of one can from the outside. Tie a big knot in the string on the inside of the can so that the string cannot slip out. Stretch the string the length of the room and put the other end of it through another can, similar to the first one. Have a friend talk softly through the one can, and you listen through the other. Be sure that the string is stretched tight. By using this set you may carry on a conversation. You can do this same thing at home. Stretch a string from your room to the room of a friend next door. Each one has a can. You might use a wire instead of a string. This can be your private telephone.

How can you hear over this small set-up? Do you feel any vibrations in the cans? Why is it better to use a wire than a string? Tell how the vibrations go from your mouth to the friend's ear.

2. Cause a tuning fork to vibrate. Then let the ends of the fork touch the surface of some water in a pan. The fork vibrates and spatters water. Try this with other vibrating objects.

3. Give a show where you make a dummy, or doll, talk. One child holds a conversation with the doll on the stage. Another child, behind a screen, makes the doll talk. He does this with a long rubber or metal tube that goes from behind the screen at the back of the stage up to the doll's mouth. The tube should not be seen. The child behind the screen talks through the tube, and it sounds as if the doll were talking.

4. Sometimes bodies vibrate too rapidly for you to see the vibrations, but they produce sound. Fasten one end of a thin strip of steel about a foot long. Make it vibrate slowly. Does it make a noise? Fasten the same strip of steel at the middle and make one end vibrate. Now do you hear a sound? As the number of vibrations increase, you hear a noise. Many sounds that you hear are made by objects that are vibrating two or three hundred times a second.

5. Sound waves are not the only kind of waves. Throw a pebble in the water. Waves move out away from where the pebble struck. They move in all directions. They are called water waves. Place a cork or stick in the water. Throw a pebble in and watch how the cork moves. How is this like sound?

6. Fasten one end of a rope and raise the other end up and down. When you do this, you send a wave through the rope. The wave passes on and the rope remains where it was.

7. Perhaps you have been in swimming with your head under the water when someone made a loud noise in the water. Did you ever hear the noise? Do sound waves travel through water?

8. Throw a rubber ball against a wall. It bounces back to you. Sometimes sound bounces back. Call down an empty barrel, or call into a large cylinder or tank. Sometimes when you are out in the hills, you call, and the sound of your words strikes a hill and bounces back to you. In the city the sound may strike buildings and bounce back to you. These sounds are called echoes. Thunder sometimes produces echoes in the mountains, and you hear the same noise several times. Can you imagine how primitive man explained echoes?

Problem 2 · Messages by Dots and Dashes

Samuel F. B. Morse was a well-known artist in the United States. He had spent three years studying famous pictures in the art galleries in Europe. It was on a ship returning to America that his mind was turned from art to experiments in electricity.

The electromagnet had only recently been discovered. One of the passengers, Dr. Jackson, had seen several new inventions in Paris, among which was the electromagnet. Dr. Jackson had secured a small electromagnet and had it with him on the boat. Morse was in a group in which Jackson told about the new inventions, and especially about the electromagnet.

Morse had studied a little about magnets and electricity when he was in college. He recalled some of the things he had learned, and with the others Morse asked Dr. Jackson many questions about the new invention. Someone wanted to know how long it took electricity to travel through all the wire of the electromagnet. Dr. Jackson answered that electricity flowed through great lengths of wire almost instantly. This remark made Morse become more interested than ever. It set him to thinking of the possibilities of using the electromagnet in many ways. He wondered why this new invention could not be used for sending messages. Dr. Jackson had said that electricity traveled almost instantly. Then why could it not be made to send messages almost instantly?

A	•—	J	—•—•	S	•••
B	—•••	K	—•—	T	—
C	•••	L	——	U	••—
D	—••	M	——	V	•••—
E	•	N	—•	W	•——
F	•—••	O	••	X	•—••
G	—— •	P	•••••	Y	•• ••
H	••••	Q	••—•	Z	•••• •
I	••	R	• ••		

The Morse code of dots and dashes for the telegraph

Morse worked on his new idea all the rest of the trip. When he left the ship, he had plans worked out by which he could send messages by a series of dots and dashes. He had also made a code. He had the idea, but to construct an instrument that would make the dots and dashes could not be done in a day. It could not be done without expense, and Morse had very little money.

The telegraph was not invented in a day, or in a month or in a year. It took years of work to make an instrument that would carry out his idea. It took thousands and thousands of dollars.

For several years Morse continued his painting to make a living. In every spare minute he worked on his new idea. Electromagnets could not be bought because there were none being made for sale. They had to be made by the person who wanted them. Morse had a blacksmith bend a piece of iron into the shape of a horseshoe. You remember that the wire that is wound around

Samuel F. B. Morse at work on his inventions

the iron in an electromagnet must be insulated. But Morse could not go to a store and buy insulated wire, as you can. Insulated wire was not on sale. He had to buy the thread and wind it around the wire by hand. These were only a few of Morse's difficulties.

Morse secured help from Alfred Vail, who had become interested in Morse's plans. Vail furnished money for the experiment. He also aided by working along with Morse. In 1838, about six years after Morse's return from Europe, he and Vail had a telegraph that would work. But there was still much to do. Morse had to secure a patent. Then he had to prove to the public that this invention would do what he said it would.

After many difficulties the men secured $30,000 from Congress to help them build a telegraph line between Baltimore and Washington. In 1844 the line was completed, and the first message was sent over wires by dots and dashes. The sending of that message, though it is not far from Washington to Baltimore, was a wonderful event. Today telegraph messages are sent all over the world many times a day.

What could we do without the telegraph? How could trains run? How would the newspaper get news?

 Things to Think About

1. What is it that carries the message over a telegraph wire?

2. How do newspapers secure their news from distant places?

Things to Do

1. Read more about the life of Samuel F. B. Morse.

2. Find out in how many ways the telegraph is used.

3. You can make a very simple sending and receiving set. Secure a thin strip of iron. You may use the iron strips from around fruit crates, or a steel spring. Strips from a toy mechanical set may be used. Put a short screw in a small block. To this screw attach a small insulated wire. The insulation should be scraped from the end of the wire so that the bare wire touches the screw. Remember to do this whenever you connect an insulated wire. The other end of the wire is attached to a battery. Nail the end of a short strip of iron *a* to the block. The strip should be long enough to reach the screw. Bend the strip so that it does not touch the screw except when you press down on the strip. This makes the sender.

On another block, nail a longer strip *b* and bend it. Under the end of this strip put a long screw *c*. Wind an insulated wire (No. 24) around the screw. Make the turns of wire very close together. Connect one end of this wire to the battery, and the other end to strip *a*.

Now press on the sender *a*. If everything is all right, *c* becomes an electromagnet and pulls the strip *b*. Take your finger off the sender, and the receiving strip *b* should fly back into place. Why? If you bend a nail so that *b* touches it when it is released by the electromagnet, it will make another click. Can you cause the receiving strip to sound out dots and dashes?

4. Compare means of communication between New York City and California before and after the invention of the telegraph.

Problem 3 · Messages by Telephone

Professor Alexander Graham Bell made one of the most important inventions that has ever been made. Bell was a professor of speech. He had studied the human voice and was very much interested in it. He first lived in Scotland, and while he was there he had the opportunity to examine an early telegraph set. He wanted to learn more about it.

' In his voice-training Bell had noticed that, as he sang a certain note near a piano, that same note on the piano answered back. The string on the piano had picked up the vibration from the note that Bell sang, and produced the same tone. As Bell looked at the telegraph set, he probably thought of this. He wondered if the human voice could be carried over wires as well as dots and dashes. He imagined a flat, circular plate of iron that would pick up sound and send it over wires by electricity. He thought of another flat, circular iron plate on the other end of the wire that would change the electrical vibrations back into sound. He set to work to make what he first called a "singing telegraph."

Bell came to Boston as a professor of speech. This teaching position gave him money and time to work on the singing telegraph. At first he worked in the basement of the house in which he was staying. He worked hard and long with little success. Later he and his assistant, Thomas A. Watson, toiled for months in an attic. During months of need the two inventors worked to make an instrument that would talk. They made many devices and many attempts, but time after time these experiments failed to work. They had scarcely any money now, but they did not give up easily. They believed in what they were doing and continued to work. Each possessed an instrument, and the two instruments were connected to each other.

The first telephone

Then, quite by accident, they discovered the way that would lead to the invention. While they were experimenting one day, Watson plucked a wire that had stuck. It caused a sound in the instrument that Bell was working on and gave Bell an idea to follow up. In 1875, with a clock spring, they made a transmitter and a receiver. One day, as they were working, Bell said into his instrument, "Mr. Watson, come here, I want you." Watson heard him over his instrument and rushed in excitedly. This was the beginning. It took ten more months of hard work before they had completed an instrument that would connect people, some distance apart, by speech.

Bell called his invention a telephone. The Greek word for "far" is *tele*, and the Greek word for "sound" is *phonos*. What better name could he have given it

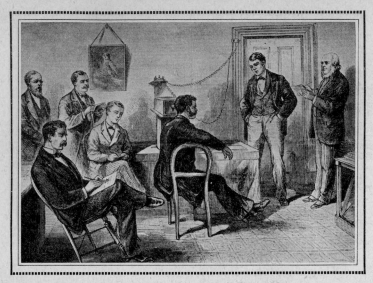

Bell demonstrating the telephone. It seemed almost a
miracle to hear a person's voice coming out of a box[1]

than *telephone*, "far sound"? At that time he did not
realize through what great distances this invention
would carry the sound of the human voice. We know
that now telephones connect almost all parts of the
world.

Do you have a telephone receiver in school that you
can take apart? Unscrew the top part and find the
thin, round sheet of iron. If you do not have a receiver,
look at the illustration and see if you can find this piece.
It is called the diaphragm. The diaphragm is the part
that sends out into the air waves which make us hear
over the telephone. As you take it off, do you notice

[1] From Leslie's newspaper, 1877.

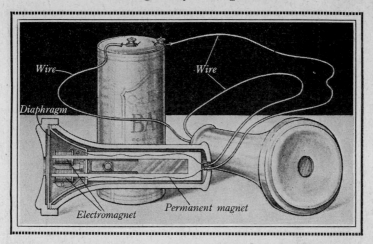

Two receivers may be used as a telephone. One person talks
into one receiver, and another listens over the other receiver

that it is pulled by something underneath? Below the
diaphragm there is a permanent magnet, which pulls it.
There are also several other important things. There is
an electromagnet, and two wires leading out from it.

Connect two receivers and a dry cell, as in the illustration. Have another child talk into one receiver as
you listen in the other. Can you hear him? You can
answer back, and he can hear you. It was with two
receivers that Bell and Watson first talked. That was
the first telephone. Later Bell made the transmitter.

Look at the drawing of the transmitter. This is the
part of the telephone into which we talk. Notice that
it also has a diaphragm. Back of the diaphragm is a little
chamber, or box, of very tiny pieces of carbon. Then
there are two wires leading out from the transmitter.

E

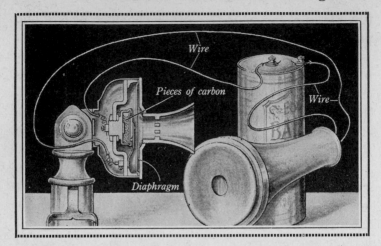

How to wire a one-way telephone

Connect one wire of the receiver and one wire of the transmitter. Take off some of the insulation and be sure that the two bare wires are connected. Connect the other two wires to the battery. This allows an electric current to pass through. Have your friend talk into the transmitter. Can you hear what your friend says? You have set up a tiny telephone system. In this set-up you cannot answer. If you had two transmitters and two receivers, could you set them up so that you could talk to each other?

Should you like to know how the words come to you from your friend? You remember that we talked about sound vibrations in the air? These vibrations in the air made by your friend's voice strike the diaphragm of the transmitter. As they do so they bend the diaphragm just a little. The diaphragm presses on the tiny pieces of carbon in the carbon chamber, or box, and presses them close together.

There is an electric current passing through the carbon and on out through the wires. There are no wires going through the carbon; so the only way that electricity can pass through is for the carbon to let the electrons pass. They can go through only by going through the carbon pieces.

Have you, with a group of friends, ever crossed a small stream of water on stones? You stepped from one stone to another. If there were many stones above the water, all of you went across at the same time. But if there was only one line of stones, you had to go across in single file.

In the carbon box the electrons, or bits of electricity, go through one little piece of carbon to another, but not in just the same way that you stepped on the stones. These little pieces of carbon must be touching each other before the electrons can go through. If many pieces are touching, many electrons run through, and the current of electricity is strong. If there are only a few pieces touching, just a few electrons can pass, and the current of electricity is weak.

When the diaphragm presses against the carbon chamber, it pushes the pieces of carbon very close together. How many electrons can hurry through? Then, as the air motion on the outside grows less, it lets the diaphragm spring back, and it does not press close to the carbon pieces. They spread apart and are not so crowded. Can more or fewer electrons pass? Since only

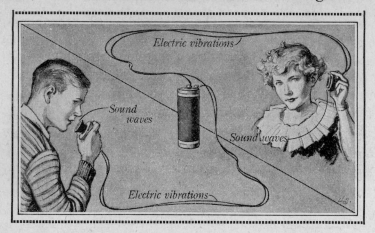

Electric vibrations

Sound waves

Sound waves

Electric vibrations

Sound waves changing to electrical waves, and electrical waves being changed back to sound waves

a few can pass, there is only a small amount of electricity passing through the wires to the receiver.

But let us see what is happening at the receiver. Take an electromagnet and attach it to one cell; count how many thumb tacks it will pick up. Then attach it to two cells. How many does it pick up now? As more electricity passes through the wires, the electromagnet is made stronger, and it picks up more tacks. The current coming over the wires to the receiver becomes stronger as more electrons pass through the transmitter. This makes the electromagnet in the receiver stronger, and it pulls the diaphragm, bending it in farther. As the diaphragm moves back and forth with the increase and decrease of the number of electrons, waves of air are sent out from the receiver. These waves are like the ones that struck the transmitter. These puffs of air strike the eardrum. The vibrations strike the bones, and the nerves carry the message to the brain. In this way messages are carried all over the world by this wonderful machine, over highways of wire.

Sound waves do not travel over the telephone wires. The sound waves are changed into electrical vibrations in the transmitter, into which you speak. These electrical vibrations are turned back into sound waves in the receiver.

 ### Things to Think About

1. How have the telegraph and the telephone helped the development of our country?

2. What is it that carries the message over a telephone wire?

3. Why was it important to know about the electromagnet before the telegraph could be invented?

 ### Things to Do

1. Find out more about Alexander Graham Bell.

2. Connect two telephone receivers to a battery and use as a telephone. Connect a receiver and a transmitter to a battery, and use as a one-way telephone.

3. Take apart an old telephone receiver and transmitter, and find the most important parts.

Problem 4 · Messages by Radio

You have heard of waves which carry light from the sun to the earth every day. You know that heat waves carry heat to the earth from the sun and to different parts of a room from a radiator. There is yet another kind of waves. These are electrical waves. It is these waves which are used in radio work.

Electrical waves are traveling about us all the time. They are ever present, but we do not know it unless we have a device to find them.

A program is given in front of a microphone in a broadcasting station. The sound of the program is changed into electrical waves at the station and broadcast. These waves are changed back into sound by your own radio. We hear the program just as it was broadcast.

Every day radio messages are sent to all parts of the world in a few seconds. Radio has done much to unite the different parts of the world.

Radio waves travel very rapidly. They travel so rapidly that they cross the ocean in a fraction of a second. Radio programs have been broadcast and listened to by many nations at the same time. It is possible for us to listen to a speaker as he talks in a large auditorium in a distant land and hear each word as soon as — in fact, a little before — people in the back part of the auditorium hear him. Radio waves are like light waves; they travel very rapidly.

Things to Think About

1. What travels from the broadcasting station to your radio?

2. In what ways is the radio more useful than the telephone and telegraph?

3. In what ways are the telephone and telegraph more useful than the radio?

4. Who are some of the men who have made the radio possible?

 **_Things to Do_**

1. Visit a radio broadcasting station.

2. Find out what a patent is. Why do people secure patents?

UNIT XII

Men Improve Transportation

1. Early Transportation
2. The Invention of the Steam and Gas Engines

MEN IMPROVE TRANSPORTATION

Do you like to travel? How far away from your home have you been? How did you travel? Do you know how you would have traveled three, four, or five thousand years ago? In the early ages men had to depend upon their own feet and legs for traveling about. During a man's entire life he could see only that part of the world that was close to him.

You have learned how men have improved methods of communication. They have also improved their ways of travel. Instead of walking or swimming to every place we want to go to, we ride quickly and comfortably. Today we can travel across the ocean in a few days by ship or across the continent by train or airplane. Man has become a great traveler. In Unit XII you will learn of some of the inventions that have brought about this change.

Problem 1 · Early Transportation

Methods of travel have changed greatly since men first started to go from one place to another. We do not know how they first discovered new ways of traveling, but we do know what methods they used.

One of the first things that men discovered to help them cross a lake or stream was a log. Can you imagine what may have caused them to begin using a log? Perhaps one man saw a log with a bird or other animal on it floating down a stream. That may have given him the idea that he too might float on a log. He tried it by sitting or lying on top of a log. He paddled with his hands and feet, and this carried him where he wanted to go. Then others began to use logs. Perhaps later a man found that a stick helped him to paddle. The use of a stick led men to make and use oars. The log was the first boat; this was the beginning of travel by water.

The log was only a beginning. Many changes took place, and many years passed, before boats became the modern floating palaces that we find on the oceans today.

There were many difficulties connected with using the log as a boat. Since logs are round, they turned over quickly in the water. If you have tried to sit on a log in the water, you know how difficult it is to stay on top. Early men were often tipped over in the water. To prevent the logs from tipping so easily, men learned to flatten them on top. Then they turned over less often.

After fire was discovered, men gradually learned that they could hollow out their logs by the use of fire and a few implements. This made a much better boat. Men could sit down in these boats and not get wet while traveling. This was a great improvement. Step by step, the log was becoming an important means of travel.

Another improvement was made when men learned to fasten a number of logs together in the form of a raft. This raft was much more useful than a one-log boat. Heavier loads could be carried on a raft. A man could put his family and all his belongings on it and cross a stream. This was one way by which families moved from one place to another. Even during the early history of America, pioneers, when moving west with their families, crossed the rivers on rafts which were made of logs. That was the best, and sometimes the only, way of crossing.

As years passed, men learned to fasten their logs together in different shapes. They were not fastened together in a flat mass, but those on the outside were built up so that they made a raft that was rounded on the sides in a kind of boat shape. This was the beginning of the growth of the real boat.

As boats were gradually improved, men learned to use a number of oars for rowing the boat. The boats became larger and larger. It took more and more men to row them. When Rome was at the height of her power, she had great boats that were rowed by many slaves. Rowing was slaves' work in many of the coun-

Early transportation

An early Egyptian boat rowed by slaves
From a model in the Metropolitan Museum of Art

tries of that time. Sometimes there was more than one row of oars, and the slaves sat on benches one above the other. The old Roman galley was one of this type.

After a number of years someone discovered that if a sail was set up, the wind could help to drive the boat. At first only small sails were used, and they were not very successful. Then larger sails were put up, and men learned to depend more and more upon the wind to drive their boats. But even so, they continued to use oars, as well as sails.

It was a long time before men learned to depend entirely upon sails. It was not until the sixteenth century that boats were made without oars.

By this time the compass had come into use in Europe, and, with their sails driven by wind power, men began to travel all around the world. The ships in

Animals are used to carry burdens in some places today

which they traveled were now much larger than the early ones, and they had many sails.

The boat had developed from one small log, through the raft and the galley, to the large sailing ship. But sailing vessels offered one great difficulty. They could not move if the wind were not blowing. They were often delayed in their travels because of unfavorable winds. But for years men knew no better power than wind.

However, men did not limit themselves to travel by water. They were improving the methods of land transportation at the same time that they were developing water travel.

At the very first men had to depend upon their own feet to carry them to different places on land. If a cave man wanted to move his family to a cave where food could be found more easily, the family had to walk and carry their belongings in their arms or on their backs. When men returned from the hunt, they carried what they had killed on their shoulders or backs. Sometimes two men carried a load hung from the middle of a stick, each end of which rested on a man's shoulder. But carrying burdens in this way was difficult and awkward.

As men learned to tame wild animals, they began to use the animals to carry their loads. In some countries men learned to use dogs; in desert countries they used camels; and in some countries they used horses.

At first the loads were placed on the animals' backs. Later, men made frameworks of poles that were pulled by some of the animals. Two poles were fastened to a horse, one on each side, and a framework was built on them on which burdens were laid; the free ends of the poles rested upon the ground. The horse dragged this drag cart and its load. Part of the family sometimes rode on the horse, and others rode on the drag cart. For a long time this was the principal method of travel on land in some countries.

At other times a framework was fastened to a log and the log was dragged. After many years men learned that a log would roll more easily than it could be dragged. They made a framework above a log and cut the ends of the log in the form of axles, which turned in the frame on which the load rested. When the framework was pulled, the log rolled along the ground.

Then men learned to use wheels. At first wheels were solid, but men found that solid wheels were awkward

© The Science Museum, London

Logs here are used as rollers. As the image is rolled
off the logs they are carried forward to be used again.
Compare this with the way we move heavy objects today

and heavy, and to make them lighter men began to cut
out parts of them. Later this developed into the wheel
with spokes, which we use in transportation today.

During the centuries that followed, men made many
improvements upon the inventions that had been made
before. About three thousand years ago two-wheeled
carts called chariots were used in Egypt, Greece, and
Rome. In the thirteenth and fourteenth centuries much
of the travel in Europe was done on horseback and in
two-wheeled carts. Then the four-wheeled carriage came
into use, which, some people think, was first made by
putting the backs of two two-wheeled carts together,

E

© The Science Museum, London

Transportation improves

and taking out the tongue of one of them. At first they were used only by kings and other rulers. Later they were used by all people.

In the early part of the eighteenth century the four-wheeled carriage was used a great deal. In America, at the time of the Revolutionary War, the roads were poor, and there were few carriages. The first carriages in America were two-wheeled. Later the four-wheeled carriage, or coach, was introduced. In the middle of the eighteenth century, stages, which were large four-wheeled coaches for carrying passengers, traveled between Philadelphia and New York. It required three days to travel that distance, which is now covered by train in about two hours. By this time, speed and comfort in traveling were slowly developing. You will read later about how the speed has been increased many times.

 Things to Think About

1. What ways of travel did the early Indians have?

2. How do Eskimos go from one place to another?

3. Why do logs float?

4. How did the discovery of fire and the invention of certain tools aid transportation?

5. During the gold rush in California, how long did it take people from the East to get out there? How does this compare with the length of time that it now takes to go to California?

6. Some people travel more in one summer than most people did in their entire lives a few years ago. Have you traveled more than your parents and your grandparents had at your age? Why is this?

 *Things to Do*

1. Name some of the peoples that have migrated in the past.

2. Name some of the animals that were first used for transportation.

3. Secure some information from encyclopedias and other books about some of our common domestic animals.

4. Write a story that tells how you think early men started to domesticate animals.

Problem 2 · The Invention of the Steam and Gas Engines

1. Steam can do Work

The invention of the steam engine changed man's ways of travel and his ideas of speed. Certain facts had been known about steam for centuries. A man in Egypt named Hero, who had studied mathematics and physics, knew these facts about two thousand years ago. He had even made use of this knowledge and made a steam engine. This was the first steam engine about which we know. But you could never guess how he used this engine. You know that we use engines to give power to our boats and trains. But Hero did not use his engine for anything like that. He used it only as a toy. Should you like to know how it worked?

© The Science Museum

This was the first steam engine. It was made by Hero about two thousand years ago and was used only as a toy

You have seen a toy balloon that was filled with air and then turned loose. As the air came out, the balloon whirled about the room. It moved because of the air

348

which was coming out. It came out with such force that it pushed the balloon one way while it went the other. Certain lawn-sprinklers turn around for the same reason. The water comes out in one direction and forces the sprinkler to turn in the other direction. Hero's engine worked in much the same manner. The engine was a big globe. As the steam came out, it caused the globe to turn around. No doubt Hero was very proud of his engine and showed it to many of his friends. But it was hundreds of years before men used steam to do much work. They probably never even thought that there was any work that such a toy could do.

Do you know why steam works for us? Do you know some of the things that Hero knew? How many times have you watched steam as it came out of the teakettle? A small pan of water changes into great quantities of steam. You have already learned that it changes into about 1700 times as much steam as there was water. That is, one gallon of water, when boiled, makes about 1700 gallons of steam. When water turns into steam it expands. You have seen an example of this when a flask or can of water was closed with a stopper and heated. You know that the pressure of the steam blew out the cork. Men knew these things about steam, but they did not think of using steam to do work. After Hero it was about eighteen hundred years before anyone, again, did much about steam.

During the seventeenth century the mines in England were being sunk deep into the ground. As they were sunk deeper and deeper, water began to collect in them. Miners began to need a machine that would pump out the water. At this time people were interested in steam, and many men tried to invent a steam engine that would do the necessary work at the mines. Many men tried many experiments. Several men made engines, some of which were used, but they did not prove entirely satisfactory. Having learned from the failures of others, Thomas Newcomen invented a steam engine that proved successful and was used for many years.

An important early improvement in the steam engine was made by a small boy who had to tend an engine. The steam engine made by Thomas Newcomen in England in 1705 had two taps, or valves, which had to be turned on and off by hand. This work was usually done by boys, a task which they found tiresome and which gave them little chance to play.

A young boy named Humphrey Potter had this job. One day he thought of something about the engine that had not occurred to him before. One tap had to be turned off as one part, called the beam of the engine, rose to its highest point, and one had to be turned on as the beam sank to its lowest point. He got the idea of tying strings from the beam to the tap handles and letting the motion of the beam turn the taps on and off. The story goes that when he had tied the strings so that the beam would close and open the taps, he left his engine, to play with a group of boys.

We do not know what was said when it was discovered that the steam engine was working without

Humphrey Potter's care, but it was realized that a great discovery had been made. Iron rods were later used instead of strings, and this idea was used on all steam engines of that time. After that the engine worked about three times as fast as it did before, and it could do just that many times the amount of work.

This machine, as it was now improved, was used for about seventy-five years. In 1764 James Watt, an instrument-maker in the University of Glasgow, was given a school model of the Newcomen engine to repair. He was not satisfied with the way it worked, and tried to figure out a way to improve it. In this engine much of the steam was wasted. In 1765 Watt invented a way to prevent the waste of steam. At the same time he made improvements which cut the cost of running the machine. Modern steam engines are built on much the same design as the engine which Watt made.

In many cases inventions have been made because there was a great need for them. Near the close of the eighteenth century people needed a boat that did not depend upon the wind, and one that would move a little faster than the old boats were able to do. People both in Europe and America felt the need. At that time the United States had millions of acres of fertile land that could not be easily reached. Roads were very poor. It was impossible to travel on them at some times of the year. Pioneers moving westward often had to carry their goods on pack horses, so narrow and steep were the paths over the mountains. In some cases they followed a newly made road, driving a yoke of oxen hitched to an

At one time people traveled in canal boats pulled by horses

awkward, heavy wagon. Had these people been able to travel by boats, their traveling would have been very much easier.

Perhaps there was a greater demand for a steamboat in the United States than anywhere else. Many people laughed at the idea. Among the many men who became discouraged was John Fitch. In 1787 he made a trip on the Delaware River at Philadelphia in a steamboat which he had made. He traveled at the rate of three or four miles an hour. But few people had faith in steamboats, and Fitch failed to get enough money to continue with his boat, and he became discouraged. However, Fitch taught the world a great deal about steamboats, and from his experiences other men profited.

It was Robert Fulton who received the honor of having the first successful steamboat, one that would travel in service and would pay the builder for building it. When a boy, Fulton had been interested in boats. He and a friend used to fish from a flatboat. They rigged up a pair of paddle wheels, one on each side of the boat, which were connected by a rod. The boys were able to turn the paddle wheels with the rod and make going by boat easier.

In 1807 Fulton's boat the *Clermont*, with a paddle wheel on each side as in his childhood boat, but this time turned by steam, made a round trip between New York and Albany. People gathered along the banks of the Hudson ready to laugh at Fulton's failure. They did not believe such a boat could ever move, and they called it "Fulton's Folly." At first the boat began to move, and then it stopped. People were all convinced now that it could not go. But the *Clermont* again moved, and this time it steamed up the river, making 150 miles in thirty-two hours. When men farther up the river saw the clouds of steam and smoke, they became frightened and called it a monster. To be sure, 150 miles in thirty-two hours seems a very slow speed to us now, but for the first boat it proved that it was a useful and possible means of travel.

Fulton used the steam of the engine to turn a paddle wheel. It was in these paddle wheels that improvement was needed. They were fastened to the sides of the boat. Later, men showed that some kind of wheel at the back of the boat was better. The kind that is used today is called a screw propeller. Nowadays nearly all steam-boats use these propellers.

Some of the large new steamers now use steam tur-bines. In a turbine the steam is forced against a wheel with many blades, somewhat like a windmill wheel. The force of the steam against these blades drives the wheel around, and this motion is used to turn the pro-pellers. Steam turbines take less space than the older kind of engine and run more smoothly.

Since the day that the *Clermont* steamed its way against the current of the Hudson, steam has made a big step forward. Where once it took ships six weeks to cross the ocean, it is done now in five days. Steamships have aided men in their travels for over a century.

Some of the big ships now are beginning to use elec-tricity, and some day electric ships may take the place of steamships.

2. The First Locomotives

You have just learned how men traveled on the water and how they improved their methods of water travel. But the water routes did not carry them everywhere they wanted to go. They must at times travel on land; and as civilization advanced, faster means of travel were needed. Stagecoaches were not fast enough.

It was in 1680 that Sir Isaac Newton, who had dis-covered a number of facts in science, first tried to make a steam carriage which he hoped would go thirty miles an hour.

The *Clermont*, the first successful steamboat, as it steamed up the Hudson

Cugnot's steam engine turning over while
taking a corner at three miles an hour

Newton used the same principle that Hero had used
in his steam engine about eighteen hundred years before.
He reasoned that if steam were forced out of the back
of the engine, the force would cause the engine to move
forward. Although Newton did not carry out his idea
successfully, it made a few other men think that such a
thing as a steam carriage might be possible.

In 1769 Cugnot, a French army officer, made a three-
wheeled steam engine that could travel three or four
miles an hour. But this engine could not make enough
steam to keep going for long at a time. It had to stop
every ten minutes to get up more steam.

In 1772, in the United States, Oliver Evans, a wagon-
maker's apprentice, tried to use steam to make a wagon
go. But people in the United States were not ready to

believe that such a thing could be done. Evans wrote to Congress to secure aid, and he took his ideas to some of the greatest engineers, but they only laughed at the idea of using steam to run a wagon.

In 1804 Evans proved that such a thing could be done. He made a scow, or flat-bottomed boat, with a paddle wheel at the back, and with wheels so that it could be used on land too; both on land and in the water it was steam that made it go. Evans tried to form a company to build a railroad, but he failed. Although he could not get money to build his railroad, he still had faith in it and foretold that at some time people would travel on railroads at fifteen miles an hour and that "passengers will sleep in the stage." Today we travel much faster than fifteen miles an hour and sleep on trains in comfort. Yet people only laughed at Evans's ideas.

Trevithick in England, in 1804, made a steam engine which was used in mines for hauling coal. It carried a heavy load for nine and one half miles at the rate of five miles an hour. But his engine was not practical.

It was Stephenson, who had been a fireman, brakeman, and an engineer in the Newcastle mines in England, who worked out a coal tramway in 1814. This engine drew eight wagons at the rate of four miles an hour and was cheap enough to be practical. The first locomotives had cogged wheels, but Stephenson's engine had smooth wheels.

In 1825 the first general railroad opened in England, with Stephenson as engineer. He gave a public demonstration of an engine that pulled several wagons at eight miles an hour. Although few people had faith in his engine, many rode on the wagons. A man on horseback rode ahead of the engine to clear the track of cows, chickens, and people. Sometimes the horse had difficulty in keeping ahead of the train. This was the beginning of railroads.

In 1829 the Baltimore and Ohio began to build its line in this country. In 1831 an engine called the *De Witt Clinton*, on the Mohawk and Hudson line, pulling the first train built only for passengers, started traveling between Albany and Schenectady. On its first trip it carried three cars, which looked like stagecoaches. The engine weighed scarcely seven thousand pounds, was eleven and one-half feet long, and had four wheels which looked like wagon wheels (see picture on page 360). The coaches were filled with passengers, and away they went, at a speed of from fifteen to thirty miles an hour. The age of speedy travel had begun.

All the difficulties had not been overcome, even when the steam locomotive was invented. Certain companies had been permitted to collect toll on certain roads, or turnpikes. These turnpike companies now felt that the railroads would ruin their trade; so two of them forbade the railroads to cross their territory. Therefore it was sometimes necessary for the railroads to unite with the turnpike and canal companies.

At first railroad companies did not use the same width of track; so a locomotive and cars from one road could not travel over the track of another road. In some

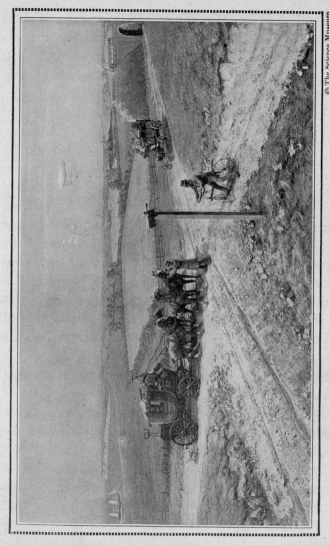

This shows that in the nineteenth century people were using several ways of traveling about

One locomotive today is as large as the *De Witt Clinton* and its coaches

towns, where there was more than one railroad, the passengers had to change roads. In some of these towns the railroads were not permitted to travel inside the towns. Therefore it was necessary for passengers to hire a teamster to cross the town to the other railroad, thus providing trade for the teamsters. In other places there were laws which said that engines should not go faster through the towns than a horse walks. The engines had to slow down to a speed of about two and one-half miles an hour.

At first, in winter the engines got so cold that it was difficult to keep up enough steam. In some places horses were kept, to be used in case the engines failed. When companies used horses to haul the carriages, it gave farmers an idea. The roads over which they hauled their produce were in poor condition. Therefore some of the farmers drove their horses and wagons on the railroad tracks. That worked all right until the farmer met a train coming around a curve or down a steep

Early street cars were pulled by horses

grade when neither could turn out. Such happenings often resulted in serious accidents and many lawsuits.

Smokestacks on the engines were huge and had to be pulled down when trains went under bridges. Engines were run by wood and water. At first there were no stations along the road, and conductors had heavy cardboard tickets which they sold to the passengers. They kept the money they received in a strong tin box. The engines had no whistles, and the conductors had to blow big tin whistles. When a conductor wanted to give a message to the engineer, he had to wave or shout. There was no bell for him to ring.

The coaches were very cold and uncomfortable. There were no wash rooms or water, and the cars were not heated. On the cold, wintry days children along the

E

One of the early street cars

tracks sold hot stones and bricks to passengers to use as foot-warmers. Traveling then was not like traveling now.

Many improvements have been made on our railroads. Today trains carry comfortable sleeping and dining coaches. All passenger coaches are heated in winter, and on some railroads they are cooled in summer.

Railroads gave people the idea of running cars along city streets. At first horses were used to pull cars along rails, but soon electricity came into use. By the beginning of the twentieth century electric cars were traveling along elevated lines and through underground tunnels in large cities.

Lately electric locomotives have been made, and many railroad companies are beginning to use them instead of steam locomotives. Some day all our trains may be run by electricity.

The first American automobile. How does
it compare with automobiles of today?

3. The Gas Engine and the Automobile

The invention of the gas engine around 1876 gave
man another kind of power. Instead of steam to push
the piston, the gas engine uses exploding gas. Gasoline
is used as fuel. It is changed to a gas and mixed with
air. This mixture can easily be exploded. Electric
sparks are used to explode it. The exploding mixture
has pushing power, and a piston and rod in the same
chamber with it are pushed into motion. A shaft connected with the rod sends this motion to a wheel.

Several men tried using the gas engine to turn wheels for "horseless buggies," as the first automobiles were called. When people first saw automobiles on the street, they would often cry out, "Get a horse!" These early automobiles did not look as though they could move along with their own motor. In 1895 there were only four automobiles in this country.

The automobile has changed the life of modern man. At low cost and high speed he can get about from place to place. Farmers in country districts are no longer cut off from cities, and city people can easily get into the country. Distance no longer shuts people off from one another.

Man developed transportation very rapidly once he had invented the steam and the gas engine and learned the use of electricity. He can now speed over the land, the water, and through the air.

4. Good Roads are Necessary for Good Transportation

Science has given us many wonderful inventions. It has quickened our speed of travel from that of walking — about four or five miles an hour — to that of an airplane, 150 miles or more an hour; on the ground we can go sixty miles or more an hour in an automobile. But this speed on the ground would not be possible without good roads.

If you were to go to China today, you would find some of the farmers bringing produce or goods to market on wheelbarrows. There is a framework on both sides of the wheel on which the produce or even people can be carried. There are automobiles in China, but many of the roads are so poor that in some places automobiles cannot possibly travel. Some of the roads are soft earth, with a narrow paving about a foot wide. Only a wheelbarrow can travel on such a road.

The first steam automobile was made in England in 1801 by Trevithick, but roads were so bad at that time that he turned his attention to a locomotive that would travel on rails.

In parts of Africa it is still necessary for people to travel on camels because there are no roads on which automobiles can travel. It is only with good roads that rapid travel by automobiles has developed.

A few years ago there were few good roads in the United States. Today we find paved roads in almost all parts of the country.

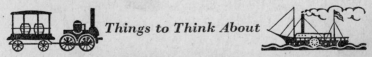 *Things to Think About*

1. Why does steam have so much power?

2. How does the speed of Fulton's boat compare with the speed of modern boats?

3. Why are steam locomotives successful, while steam automobiles proved unsuccessful?

4. Why did the discovery of America encourage the improvement of transportation?

5. What can we do to prevent accidents?

6. How can roads be improved to prevent accidents?

7. Why did automobiles encourage people to build better roads?

8. Why do you think that we have gas engines in automobiles instead of steam engines?

 Things to Do

1. With your teacher's help put some water in a test tube. Place a stopper very gently in the test tube. Heat the water to boiling, and watch the steam blow out the stopper.

2. If you have a toy steam engine, see if you can tell just how the steam makes the piston move. How does the piston move the flywheel? Explain to the class how it works.

3. Make a collection of pictures of locomotives. Compare some of the older ones with the new ones.

4. Make a scrapbook of "The Story of Boats." Tell how some of the boats are better than others.

5. Make a scrapbook called "The Story of Transportation."

6. Name new industries which have come as a result of our new ways of transportation.

7. Explain how the gas engine works. Show in what ways it is different from the steam engine.

UNIT XIII

Men Fly

1. Air has Weight
2. How we Fly

MEN FLY

You have read about how man learned to travel over the solid and liquid parts of the earth. For centuries man watched the birds, the bats, and the insects as they gracefully traveled through the air, and wished he could fly. At first he knew so little about the air or about machines that he did not succeed. In Unit XIII you will read how man invented flying machines which were heavier than air and also those which were lighter than air.

Problem 1 · Air has Weight

Look around the room. What is everywhere around you? Can you see it? Can you take any of it in your hand to feel it? Wave your hand, and you feel a gentle breeze. Air is all around, but you cannot see it. You cannot feel it except when it is moving. Can you tell if it weighs anything?

Tie an empty balloon to one side of a set of scales. Place just enough weight on the other side to make the two sides exactly even. Now they are balanced. Blow up the balloon until it is full of air and twist it so that the air cannot come out. Are the scales balanced now? The side that has the balloon full of air hangs down below the other side. Does this show that air has weight? It does not weigh a great deal. It would take about two barrels of air to weigh one pound. Two barrels of air would be as much as all the air in a column that is one foot square and thirteen feet high. That would make thirteen cubic feet of air.

When you think of thirteen cubic feet of air weighing only one pound, it seems like very little weight. But now think of how high a column of air there is above you. Air extends 200 miles or more above the earth. It gets lighter as one goes up into the atmosphere. Most of the air is within three or four miles of the earth.

If you placed twenty bundles of cotton on top of one another, what would happen to the bundle at the bottom? It would be pressed into a smaller space.

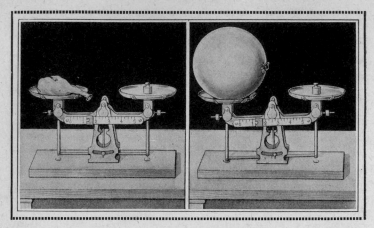

Air has weight

That bundle of cotton would weigh just as much as it did before, but it would be crowded together. It would be more dense. Cotton is very light; but when twenty bundles are piled on top of one another, they press down on the lowest bundle with considerable weight.

Air does not weigh much. It is very light. It weighs much less than cotton. Like cotton, the upper layers of air are less dense than the layers of air on the bottom. The layers of air that are near the earth are heavier than layers of air fifty miles above the earth. The layers at 100 or 150 miles above the earth weigh very little. But when you add together the weights of all the layers from the ground up to 200 miles, air weighs a good deal. All this air is pressing upon the earth and upon objects on the earth. Do you know how great this force of air is?

Men have measured the weight of the air. They have found that it is about fifteen pounds to the square inch. That means that on every square inch of your table, your desk, your book, and your body, there are almost fifteen pounds pressing down. We call this pressure. We say that there are fifteen pounds of air pressure pushing on every square inch of surface.

15 pounds air pressure on this square inch

How many square inches are there on your desk top? Can you find out how many pounds of pressure there are on your desk? This is an enormous force. It seems at first that this amount would surely break the table and force it against the floor. Can you understand why it does not? There is air underneath the table and on all sides of it. The air is pressing up underneath the table with as much force as it is pressing down on top. The air pressure pushing up is equal to the air pressure pushing down. They balance each other. The table is neither pushed up or down.

How many square inches are there on your hand? Suppose there are about five square inches. If there are fifteen pounds of pressure pushing down on each square inch, how many pounds of pressure are there on the back of your hand? How can you hold up so great a pressure? How many pounds are pushing upward on the bottom of your hand?

There are several experiments which show that air has pressure. Take a piece of glass tubing and heat it in the middle over a flame until it begins to get soft. Keep turning the tube in your fingers so that it will be heated evenly all around. Pull the two ends of the glass very slowly. Do not pull hard. As the glass softens, it gets thinner and thinner in the middle. It thins out into a fine thread and breaks in two. When the glass has cooled, break the tip of one piece so that there is a very tiny hole. Now take a one-hole rubber stopper that fits a bottle or flask. If you cannot find one, make a hole in a cork that fits the bottle. You can make the hole by burning it with a hot nail. Make the hole large enough to twist the piece of glass tubing through. If the glass does not fit the cork tightly, you can later melt paraffin and pour it around the glass. Now fill the bottle about one third full of water. Fit the cork into the bottle, with the small end of the glass tube on the outside. Be sure that the other end of the tube is below the water and near the bottom of the bottle. Take a deep breath and blow into the tube. Take your mouth from the tube and move your head away quickly. What happens? How long does the fountain flow? Why do you need to blow into the bottle each time you want the water to squirt out as a fountain? Sometimes to make a higher stream you can hold your finger over the tube in between deep breaths and blow in several times.

When you blow air into the bottle, it goes through the water. You can see it bubble through. It is trapped above the water. There is no extra space for the air; so it is crowded into the same space as the air that is already inside. It tries to expand. The crowded air has an increased pressure. As soon as you stop blowing, the air on the inside of the bottle pushes with greater force than the air outside of the tube. The air inside forces

Read how this boy causes the egg to go into the bottle
without pushing it in, and then how he gets it out again

the water out of the tube until the air has all the space
it needs; then the pressure is the same as it was before
you blew into the bottle. The fountain ceases to flow.

Experiment: Peel a hard-boiled egg. Twist a small
piece of paper, set fire to it, and drop it into a dry milk
bottle. Place the egg quickly in the neck of the bottle. Why is the egg pressed into the bottle? What
happened to the air inside the bottle? Where was there
the greatest pressure?

How can you get the egg out of the bottle? Turn
the bottle upside down and shake the egg until it is
partly in the neck of the bottle. Place the mouth of the
bottle over your mouth and blow hard. If you blow
hard enough the egg will be shot out. Why?

Experiment: ‹Fill a very small bottle about half full of water. A small perfume bottle works very well. Place your finger over the mouth of the bottle and lower it, bottom up, into a large bottle that is almost full of water. Now take your finger away from the bottle. The bottom of the small bottle should be level with the top of the water in the large bottle. If your little bottle is not level, it may have a little too much water or too little water in it. You will have to experiment until you get the right amount of water in the small bottle. Now place the cork in the large bottle and press on it. If your experiment is set up correctly, the little bottle sinks. As you loosen the cork, the little bottle rises. If the large bottle is shaped so that it has two flat sides, you can make the little bottle go down by pressing on the sides of the large bottle.

Can you explain what caused the little bottle to go down? Notice the water in the little bottle. When you press on the cork, the air under the cork is pressed, and it in turn presses on the water. The water is forced into the little bottle, which makes it heavy enough to sink.

We make use of our knowledge of air pressure in many different ways. For example, the Weather Bureau uses it to forecast the weather. It has instruments, called barometers, that tell what the air pressure is. If the barometer reading is high or is becoming higher, it indicates fair weather. But if the barometer shows low pressure, or if it is a "falling barometer," it shows that there will be rain or storm. A "falling barometer" means that a period of low pressure is coming.

Things to Think About

1. Why is it that for centuries men knew so little about air?

2. Why can we fly kites?

3. Why is air lighter at the top than at the foot of a mountain?

 **Things to Do**

1. What other air experiments can you find out about? Try these and then show them to the class.

2. Learn how to make a barometer. Can you forecast the weather by using this barometer?

3. Keep the barometer readings and a record of the weather for a month. See if the barometer has indicated the weather.

Problem 2 · How we Fly

1. The First Attempts at Flying

From very early times we hear stories about men who watched the birds and wished to fly as they did. We hear tales of men who tried to fly or who made wooden birds that flew. One story is told of a man who made a wooden pigeon that flew. There is another story of a man who made an eagle that went out to meet the emperor on his victorious return. These stories are only imaginary, but they show us that men have always been interested in trying to fly. What would these men say if they could see our airplanes and airships flying in great formations?

Men watched birds that were many times heavier than air, and yet they soared through the air with scarcely a movement of a muscle. Why couldn't men do the same thing? Kites were made that could be flown for hours by the air that was pressing from beneath the kite. It was pressure that lifted the kite and kept it flying. Surely men could make a large machine that would travel through the air!

Neither gasoline engines nor steam engines had been invented when men first began trying to fly. They had to depend upon some kind of wings that would hold them up without a motor or engine. The first experimenters used gliders. They made large wings of different shapes and sizes that they fastened to their bodies. With

An old myth tells how a father and son tried to fly with feathers fastened to them with wax. But the son went too close to the sun, which melted the wax and caused him to fall

these they climbed to the second story of a house or to the top of a hill and glided from there.

One young German boy named Otto Lilienthal experimented for many years. He succeeded in making a device with which he glided many feet down a hill. He made hundreds of flights and made a study of flying. By this time the steam engine and other power machines had been invented. After gliding without power, Lilienthal decided to put an engine on his glider. Everything was ready for trying out his power machine, but he wished to make one more trial flight in the glider. He had recently added another part to the glider, which made flying a little different from what it had been before. During this trip the wind suddenly became very

E

Lilienthal's glider

calm. The German inventor became excited because of the new method in guiding the machine. He could not gain control, and the glider fell. Lilienthal was seriously injured and his power machine was never put into use.

2. The Wright Brothers Fly

Two brothers in Dayton, Ohio, had always been interested in trying to fly. When they were very small boys, their father brought home a toy flying machine. The toy was soon broken, but the boys had got an idea; they wanted to make more flying machines.

Wilbur and Orville Wright experimented for years. They built and flew kites in order to learn more about the air. They read the things that Lilienthal had written

The Wrights' flying machine

about flying. They compared what he said with the ideas that Langley, another American inventor, gave.

The brothers worked very quietly and said very little about what they were trying to do. They set up a bicycle shop at which they made their living. They made their gliders during spare time at the shop.

From the United States Weather Bureau they learned that at Kitty Hawk, North Carolina, the winds were best for flying. Therefore the Wright brothers, for several years, took their gliders to Kitty Hawk for trials in gliding. They studied how to balance their machine. They worked quietly and made many flights. Only a few people knew about their experiments.

Later these brothers decided to try to make a flying machine. During the winter of 1902 they had made a small gasoline engine. This they fitted into the machine. In December, 1903, they made their first successful flight at Kitty Hawk. It was the first successful flight in a heavier-than-air machine that had ever been made. But very few people knew that the Wright brothers had worked with flying machines at all. They made two more machines, and after many trials one of the brothers flew twenty-four miles in thirty-eight minutes.

It was not until 1908 that Orville Wright made a trial flight before a small audience. People watched him breathlessly. Much to his surprise, and more to the surprise of the people below him, he remained circling above the crowd for an hour and fifteen minutes. This wonderful news was telephoned to Washington, D. C., and from there it quickly spread all over the world.

The United States government asked the Wright brothers to give another trial flight. This was given, as thousands of people watched. These men continued flying and made many wonderful flights. They received many prizes for the work they did to advance aviation.

At last man had learned to fly, yet a great deal remained to be learned about flying. We do not know all about flying now, but in the last twenty-five years we have learned much.

Airplanes have been used so successfully that Admiral Richard E. Byrd has flown about the north and south poles in them.

Colonel Charles Lindbergh thrilled the world when he faced the dangers of the Atlantic Ocean in his transatlantic air flight in 1927. Orville Wright had stirred

Admiral Byrd's airplane at Little America in the Antarctic continent. This is the airplane in which he flew over the south pole

the world with his successful flight of one hour and fifteen minutes less than twenty-five years before. From a nonstop flight of one hour and fifteen minutes, airplanes had developed so that Lindbergh had now made a nonstop flight of thirty-three hours and thirty-two minutes. He had flown 3610 miles at 107 miles an hour. Several others have crossed the Atlantic Ocean since then. In May, 1932, just five years to the day after Colonel Lindbergh made his solo flight to Paris, Mrs. Amelia Earhart Putnam made a record in her flight to Ireland. She was the first woman to fly alone across the Atlantic. How much better will the airplanes be that are made twenty-five years from now?

If you wish to send a letter from New York to California as rapidly as possible, you place an air-mail stamp on it and drop it in a box with other letters. This letter will be taken to a plane that carries air mail, and in thirty hours the plane will carry it to California. It takes the plane only thirty hours to carry a letter the same distance that it would have taken a stagecoach many days to carry it.

There are passenger planes now that carry people safely across the United States in a few hours, and it costs only a very small amount more to travel by plane than it does by train.

Airplanes are used in many other ways. Their use in spraying large fields is a great help in a very important fight against insects. They are useful, too, in providing speedy relief for people in trouble and in watching for forest fires.

3. Airplanes

What a noise you hear as the motor spins the propeller of an airplane at the rate of 2000 revolutions a minute! You sit at ease in your comfortable chair as the pilot moves the controls and you take off. You gaze out of the window as the rudder of the plane becomes level with the nose. It leaves the ground and goes higher and higher, climbing at the rate of one thousand feet a minute. This is almost as fast as the swiftest elevator can rise. You rise far above the city, up among little white skiffs of clouds that float about and below you. But this is not all that you see.

As you look down upon your city, it looks like a little toy village. The houses look the size of doll houses, and automobiles run along the roads like ants dodging in and out. A square mile looks the size of a city block, and it seems that you are merely floating in the air as the plane races along at 150 miles an hour. How fast that speed would be on earth! How swiftly you would pass the trees and houses down there! It would seem faster in the air if you were passing any objects. But up here there is nothing but air near you, and you can only hear it whistling as it strikes the plane.

Have you wondered how it is possible to be gliding through the air like this? Perhaps when you land the pilot will tell you what holds the plane in the air, and how all the instruments around him help him to guide the plane.

The body part of the plane is called the fuselage. The plane that you are riding in probably has a fuselage with a cabin in which ten passengers can ride. The fuselage may be made of a metal called duralumin. This metal is almost as light as aluminum, and it is much stronger. Why should the metal be as light and as strong as possible? The duralumin is covered with linen that is painted with a substance that makes linen air-tight. In the fuselage you will see the controls and the instruments. The landing gears underneath have shock absorbers. Perhaps you notice when you land that you do not feel many hard bumps.

A plane may have one wing or two wings. If it has two wings, it is called a biplane. Biplanes were the first airplanes that were developed, and they are still in general use. If the plane has one wing, it is a monoplane.

The inside of a passenger airplane

The larger planes are now almost all monoplanes. What kinds of monoplanes and biplanes do you know?

At the tail of the fuselage there is a wing-like device that is called a horizontal stabilizer. Another device is hinged to the rear end of this stabilizer. This is the elevator, which helps to make the airplane go up or down. The vertical fin keeps it straight; it helps the aviator to pilot the plane in a straight path. The rudder is hinged to the back of the vertical fin. The rudder helps to turn the plane. When the rudder is moved to the right, the plane turns right, or if it is moved to the left, the plane turns left. The rudder steers the plane.

On each wing there is a little hinged part that is called an aileron. These help to bank the plane, that is, to tip the plane when it is turning. When the aileron,

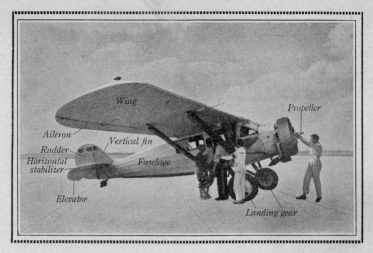

Parts of an airplane

on the left wing is up, that on the right wing is down, and the plane banks to the left. This is because the air pushes down on the wing of which the aileron is up. That wing is pushed down as the other wing is lifted. These ailerons are also used to help balance the plane when it is going straight.

The airplane propeller is the part that really causes the plane to go forward. The propeller is like a screw. You have seen metal screws bore into wood. In much the same way the propeller bores into the air and pulls the plane with it. The propeller is not straight, but it is twisted so that it will screw its way through the air.

But you do not know yet how the airplane stays up in the air. Look at the wings. They are set at an angle. The propeller throws the wind back over and under the

One of the United States navy airships

wings; when the plane is moving, the wings are moving into the wind. The air on top rushes over the wings so rapidly that it partly forms a vacuum. There is very little pressure pushing down on the wings. But the wind underneath the wings pushes up with great force. When all the force pushing up is greater than the weight of the airplane, it rises.

4. Airships

We hear the humming of motors and look up to see a bright silvery gleaming mass floating like a cloud through the sky.

Airships are lighter than air. They are made in such a way that they weigh less than that same amount of air. The framework may be made of duralumin. Duralumin is composed mostly of aluminum, with some copper and smaller amounts of manganese, magnesium, silicon, and iron.

The covering of the airship is painted with four coats of a nonburning material. The outer coats contain aluminum. It keeps the rain out and reflects the rays of the sun. Since the rays of the sun are reflected, they heat the ship very little.

Helium is being used to float the newer types of airships. It is not quite so light as hydrogen, but it does not burn, as hydrogen does. The helium is not contained in one large bag. Inside the large bag of the airship are a number of smaller ones. These small bags, or balloons, are each full of helium. If one bag is punctured, the others are saved.

Airships will probably be used a great deal in the future for passengers and for light freight.

 Things to Think About

1. What is the difference between gliders and airplanes?

2. What gave men the idea that they might be able to fly?

3. Why did man not invent the airplane a long time ago?

4. What kind of information does an aviator need about the air?

5. Why is the fuselage of some airplanes made of duralumin?

6. What is the latest great event in flying? Who last crossed the Atlantic Ocean by airplane?

7. What is the biggest airship?

 *Things to Do*

1. Learn more about the invention of the airplane.

2. Make a small airplane. Name and explain the uses of the parts of an airplane.

3. Name all the different kinds of airplanes that you can. Tell how they differ.

4. If you have ridden in a plane, tell of your experience. Write a story about how the trees, buildings, automobiles, and people looked.

5. Tell what the *Graf Zeppelin* did. What is the *Macon*? the *Do-X*?

UNIT XIV

Men make the World a more Healthful Place

How many days did you have to spend in bed last year because you were sick? If the number was less than fourteen, you spent less time than the average for everyone in the United States. Do you like to have to spend your time in this way? Of course not. What can be done to prevent it?

All through the early ages in the history of the earth, animals were unable to cure or prevent their own diseases. Even early men did not know what caused diseases or how to cure them. It has only been through many years of study that scientists have learned not only how diseases are caused, but how many may be cured or even prevented. Now they know how to cure many ills of plants and animals. In Unit XIV you will read about some of the things that scientists have done to enable us to have a more healthful place in which to live.

Problem 1 · Ideas about Disease have Changed

People have not always known as much about disease and ways of keeping their bodies healthy as they do now.

Many ancient people believed that sickness was caused by demons or evil spirits which came to live in the body. Had you been a sick boy or girl then, you probably would have thought that an evil spirit made you sick. Your friends would have felt sorry for you and have tried to cure you. Do you know what they might have done? They probably would have put on hideous masks and have danced about you, making loud and terrifying noises to frighten away the evil spirits. Or they might have called their medicine man, who would have used charms and magic to make you well. Sometimes people kept horrible images in their homes to frighten away the evil spirits. Even now there are people who believe that a rabbit's foot or some such charm can keep bad luck away. Of course nearly everyone knows now that a charm cannot cure or prevent a disease.

Even at the time that the ancient Greeks reached their greatest knowledge of medicine, there were many people who used magic in order to please their angry god of healing. These people thought that their illness was a punishment for having displeased this god. Often they made offerings and sacrifices to please him. Some even said that it was wrong to prevent illness, because

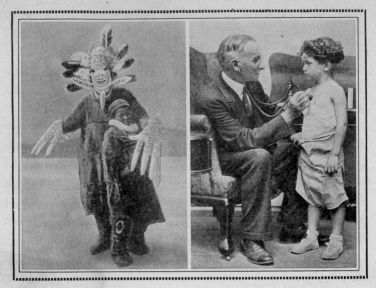

An Eskimo medicine man tries to cure the child by frightening away the evil spirits. The physician examines his patient to find the cause of the illness

illness was a punishment for doing wrong and men should not interfere with the will of their gods.

Hippocrates, a great Greek physician, who lived about four hundred years before Christ, thought that we had four different kinds of liquids, or humors, in our bodies, and that when there was too much of one or too little of another, illness resulted. We still speak of being in a good humor or in a bad humor, even though we know that Hippocrates' explanation of the cause of illness was wrong.

At other times people thought that something came from the ground which caused illness. It was noticed that fever occurred more often among people living in swampy places, and it was thought that a "bad air" rose from the swamp, which caused the disease. Now we know that this disease attacks people near swamps because mosquitoes, that increase, or breed, in the swamps carry the germs which cause malaria. When a mosquito carrying malaria germs bites a man, some of the germs get into the man's blood, and he is almost certain to become ill with malaria. Another mosquito may bite the man who is ill and take some of the germs from the blood of the sick man into its stomach. Then this mosquito may give the disease to someone else by biting him and leaving the germs in his blood.

When it was thought that diseases were caused by the night air, naturally everyone closed all the windows at night. Some people still do this, even though scientists have shown us not only that diseases are caused in other ways but also that plenty of fresh air at night is healthful.

When a few men no longer believed that diseases were caused by spirits, they tried to find out what might cause them. They learned that certain plants sometimes helped to cure certain diseases.

It was only a little less than seventy-five years ago that men learned how some diseases are caused by extremely small plants and animals. Now we know that probably more than three fourths of our illness is caused by them. These small plants are called bacteria, and the tiny animals are called protozoa. They are so small that you cannot see them without a very powerful

E

microscope, and thousands of them can live in a drop of water. Many of these tiny forms of life are helpful. Only a few are harmful. Bacteria and protozoa sometimes cause plant and animal diseases, as well as those which attack man.

Scientists have studied about the cause and cure of diseases and the best way of preventing them. These men have had many adventures and have fought many battles against the enemies of health. Some of them have given their lives in order that we may know how to save the lives of others. Doctors spend many years learning about the human body so that we may all know how to be healthy. We all know that it is much better to prevent illness than to have to cure it.

We now depend so much on other people in our daily living that we cannot ourselves see to everything that concerns our health. If you live on a farm, you may take care to locate your well in a proper place so that the water may not be spoiled by drainage from toilets and farmyard manure piles. But if you live in a city or town, the water is brought to your house through pipes, and you must depend on the department of health to see that you get pure water to drink. Likewise in a city there must be a sewer system to carry away the waste.

In ancient Rome, which was a very large city, all the waste ran into the middle of the streets. Clear, pure water for drinking did not run into any of the houses except those of the very rich. For the rest of the people there were fountains along the sidewalks. The overflow of water from the fountains washed away the filth in the streets. Raised stones were set at the crossings so that people could cross without having to walk through the sewage. Surely this must have been unhealthful, and, indeed, Rome had many epidemics, or plagues, in which thousands of people died. But at least the Romans tried to keep their city clean, for it is said that great pipes carried the waste from every street. Conditions would have been worse if it had not been for the plentiful supply of water brought many miles from the hills to help keep the streets clean.

When nearly all a family's food was raised on its own farm, each housewife could be sure that it was clean and wholesome. In these days, however, when even farmers eat food from cans, bottles, packages, and jars, we must depend on the manufacturers to give us pure food.

So cities and towns have departments of health and other special departments to see that we get clean water and that our sewage and garbage are properly cared for. The Federal government makes pure-food laws and appoints inspectors to see that they are obeyed. It is most important to us that these departments of the government be run carefully and honestly.

 Things to Think About

1. What are the duties of the board of health in your town or city?

2. Why must we depend upon other people to help us keep healthy?

 *Things to Do*

1. Ask your teacher to help you make some cultures of bacteria. Look at the bacteria through a microscope. Perhaps your class can visit the laboratories of your board of health and learn more about bacteria.

2. Find out how scientists learned that malaria was caused by a mosquito.

3. Tell why you should wash your hands before you eat.

4. Tell how science has caused people to be cleaner than they were a long time ago.

Problem 2 · How we are Supplied with Pure Water

Everyone must drink water in order to live. Yet water, which is so necessary to life, has been one of the most common ways in which disease germs have spread. Millions of bacteria can live in the water we drink. They can be carried by the water for miles and miles, thus carrying disease from one place to another. When you look at a tumbler of clear, sparkling water, you cannot tell whether it is pure or not. Bacteria have no color and are too small to be seen. People cannot tell by looking at or by tasting or smelling water whether or not it is pure enough to drink. Water may have a disagreeable odor or taste and yet be perfectly harmless, or it may look clear and be tasteless and without an odor, and yet carry the dangerous germs of typhoid fever.

From the earliest times wells have been one of the chief sources of drinking water. Nearly all farmhouses and small towns still get their water from wells. Some of these wells are owned by individuals; others are owned by towns, and from these water is pumped into large reservoirs. From the reservoirs water is supplied to the houses through pipes. Some fairly large cities still depend upon wells to fill their reservoirs and furnish a large part of their water supply. Some wells may contain water that is good to drink. Others may contain water that is filled with harmful bacteria. This depends on where the water which flows into the wells comes from.

You have studied about the cycle of water. It is part of this cycle that helps to supply the wells with water. The sun causes the water to evaporate from oceans, lakes, seas, and rivers into the air. During rainstorms this water falls again to the earth. Usually rain water, before it reaches the ground, is quite pure, but it does not remain so for long. After heavy rains great quantities of water collect in streams and are carried off to rivers and then to seas, lakes, and oceans, where it may again evaporate. But other quantities of water go down through the soil. Sometimes, before it seeps into the earth, it passes over manure piles or through sewage or waste lying about. As the water washes over these, it dissolves some of the impurities and then carries them down into the soil. Sometimes this water flows into shallow wells or into wells that are located in low ground, carrying disease germs along with it.

Some of the water continues to seep down through the layers of soil until it reaches a layer of rock, through which it cannot pass. More water moves downward until the layer of soil above the rock is as full of water as it can be. We call this underground water.

Usually this underground water is several feet below the surface. While it was soaking down through many feet of soil, sand, and gravel, some of its impurities and disease germs were left behind. Therefore wells which are supplied from a pipe driven deep down into the ground are much safer. Any drainage from yards which empties into this water will have soaked through many feet of soil, which helps to cleanse it.

Hillside cut away

Soil filled with water

Rock

Is this a good location for a well?

Sometimes the hard-rock layer reaches the surface on the side of a hill or mountain. The water flows along above it until it also reaches the surface. When water runs out of the ground in this way, it is called a spring. Such spring water is often pure because it has been filtered through soil.

When people began to live near one another in towns and cities, it became difficult to supply enough water by means of separate wells. It was possible, however, to pipe water into the houses. Of course this was an advantage. People did not then have to carry water from an outside well or from the kitchen pump to upstairs rooms. If a water company supplies the water, it is required to make sure that it is supplying water fit to drink. Therefore the water company filters the water and sometimes adds chemicals to it to kill any germs that may be present. The reservoirs where the water is stored are carefully guarded to prevent waste from being dumped into them. Very often the city or town government takes over the task of supplying the water and collects taxes in order to pay for the cost of this service.

You have already read how in ancient Rome a great deal of water was used to wash the dirty streets. People did not know how to make iron pipes large enough to carry much water in those days; so they dug tunnels in the ground and lined them with cement. Sometimes they had to tunnel through solid rock. Imagine how much work that must have been before modern rock drills had been invented! Sometimes these cement pipes were carried over flat places for many miles on high arches. We still call the pipes which carry water from reservoirs to cities by the same name that the Romans used, that is, aqueducts. The Latin name for water is *aqua*. An aqueduct is a pipe for carrying water.

Some cities located on rivers draw their drinking water from them. River water is likely to be most dangerous since people often empty sewage into rivers. Thus the sewage from one city is carried down the river and is mixed with water drawn for drinking purposes by another city farther down. Therefore care must be taken to make this water safe for use.

Much of the water that supplies New York City falls as rain 150 miles away from the city. Reservoirs to

An old Roman aqueduct

catch rain water are often formed by building a huge dam across a small stream. The water collects behind the dam until finally it makes a large artificial lake, sometimes covering acres of land. Other cities pipe their water from lakes that are found up in the hills and mountains.

In any case the water goes through several processes to make sure that it is fit to drink. First, the water is allowed to stand until the sediment settles to the bottom. If you put a handful of dirt in a large jar or milk bottle about half full of water, you can see how this takes place. Shake the bottle until the water is very muddy. Set it aside and see what happens. The particles of dirt begin to settle to the bottom, and after some time the water is quite clear. When water is used from rivers, this process is especially important.

A plant where the water supply for one of our large cities is filtered

After the sediment has collected at the bottom of the settling tank, the water passes through layers of sand and gravel where the finer particles of dirt are strained out. After the water has been filtered, it is often shot up into the air in fine sprays. This helps to purify it because sunlight and air help to kill disease germs. Many cities add chlorine to the water to kill any germs that may continue to live after it has been filtered and exposed to the sun by spraying.

If you go camping and have to use water from a lake or river, it is always best to boil the water before you drink it. Boiling is the surest way of killing all bacteria. However, it drives out the air, and then the water tastes flat. The water may be mixed with air by shaking it in a bottle.

Things to Think About

1. Why is it important to drink pure water?

2. Why is it sometimes dangerous to drink from a spring?

3. What happens to bacteria when water is boiled?

 *Things to Do*

1. Draw a picture of a farmhouse, with its farmyard, barn, cattle pen, and so on. Put the barn on a small hill and the house on the slope of the hill. Where should you locate a well in order that it might be safest?

2. Find out where the water comes from that supplies the following places: New York City; Chicago; San Francisco; Long Island; San Antonio, Texas; Roanoke, Virginia; Des Moines, Iowa; and your own town or city.

3. Visit a filtration or aëration plant and describe it to the class.

Problem 3 · How Waste Materials are Removed

If you are a good camper, you always have a clean camp. Papers are burned, garbage is buried, and all other waste is put out of the way underground. On many farms there is a heap far enough from the house not to be annoying. All kinds of waste materials, such as manure and garbage, may be added to this pile. This material gradually decays and may be used for fertilizer. When a number of people live together in larger towns and cities, such primitive methods of taking care of waste will not do. Sewage is now usually carried from houses through closed pipes. Sometimes it is run into a river or lake. This is very likely to spread disease. To prevent this, chemicals are sometimes added to the sewage in order to kill disease germs.

Getting rid of kitchen garbage is another big problem in large cities. Some cities carry much of their garbage out to sea in large, flat-bottomed boats and dump it. This is sometimes carried back by the waves and washed upon the shores and beaches. The modern way of getting rid of such refuse is to burn it in large incinerators, or furnaces. Incinerators are heated by flames so hot that even the black smoke, which usually forms when garbage-like material is burned, is destroyed also.

Another important part of city housekeeping is keeping the streets clean. In many large cities of Germany special devices are used to keep the streets clean, such as rubbish cans and collecting trucks which make it possible for the cans to be picked up and emptied into the trucks without scattering odors or refuse. The people are proud of their clean streets and do not throw old newspapers and candy wrappers about. Some nations have strict laws against throwing things in the street, and people are fined if they disobey.

But we should find it very difficult to keep this world clean from garbage, decaying plants and animals, and other refuse if it were not for certain very great help we get. What do you suppose gives us this help? Little plants so small that you have to magnify them hundreds of times to see them. These plants are bacteria, which you have already read about. The plant-disease germs are bacteria, too. Some bacteria are harmful and cause disease, while others are useful in keeping the earth clean. Many bacteria live on decaying plant and animal material. As they live on this material, they use it up and change it into forms which go into the soil to serve as food for other plants. Molds and such plants as mushrooms and toadstools also help the bacteria in this process.

Suppose a tree falls in the forest. What happens to it? We say that it decays. Bacteria help it to decay. Suppose an animal dies in the field. It decomposes, or decays, and goes into the soil. In the same way the leaves that fall to the ground each autumn gradually become soil. Bacteria also help to destroy the sewage after it has been dumped into the river. In some modern sewage plants the bacteria are allowed to destroy the harmful germs in the sewage before it is run into the river. Then the bacteria are killed with chemicals. Thus the rivers are kept more nearly free from disease bacteria.

 Things to Think About

1. How do bacteria help to keep the world clean?

2. How are toadstools and mushrooms useful?

3. What should we do if there were no bacteria to cause the decay of plants and animals which have died?

4. Are you a good camper? Do you throw papers in the streets?

 **Things to Do**

1. If you live in a city, find out how the garbage is taken care of. Does it seem to you to be a healthful way? a scientific way? Are any scientific inventions used in keeping your city clean and free from garbage and sewage?

2. Find out how diseases spread from one city to another by sewage that is emptied into a river.

Problem 4 · How Food is kept from Spoiling

You have learned that the small plants which cause things to decay do us a great service in helping to keep the earth clean. But when things decay which we wish to use for food we are not so pleased.

What are the most common ways in which food spoils? What happens to bread and some other foods when they are left closed up in the bread box for some time? The food may become covered with gray, blue,

Spores from mold fell
upon this bread and grew

or yellow spots. These spots are really gardens of very tiny plants growing on the food, just as the plants in the garden grow from the soil. These plants are called molds.

If you look at a piece of moldy bread under a magnifying glass, you will see that there are little fine stalks growing out of a crisscross of white thread-like structures. On top of each stalk there is a little round knob. These knobs are white at first, but as the mold grows they turn a darker color. Then they burst open and scatter a fine powder all around. One of these specks of powder may fall on another piece of bread and grow

407

into more mold. They act somewhat like seeds, for other plants may grow from them. They are not real seeds, such as we find in the flowers of green-leaved plants; they are called spores.

Why does the bread begin to mold? Where do these spores come from? They are very small and light and are floating about in the air. If they fall on something they can use for food, and if it is in a place that is moist and warm and dark, they grow rapidly. Different kinds of molds have different-colored spores, just as different kinds of plants have different-colored blossoms. Some molds live better on one kind of food than another. They attack bread, jellies, lemons, oranges, leather, and many other substances. A little mold on food may not make it harmful, but it gives the food an unpleasant odor and taste; so we do not wish to eat moldy food. If the mold on top of a jar of jelly is removed, the rest of the jelly is good to eat.

But there are other ways in which food may spoil. What happens to apples or potatoes when they are kept a long time? Brown places appear, the fruit or vegetable becomes soft and has a disagreeable odor. We say it is rotting. This is just the same kind of decay that you learned about in Problem 3. It is caused by bacteria and fungi. Some bacteria and fungi cause things to rot. Other kinds of bacteria and fungi cause disease. Still other kinds give flavors to foods, such as cheese. Remember that bacteria are small plants, and molds are small plants. But these plants do not have green leaves. You also learned that mushrooms and toadstools helped to decay things on the surface of the earth. They are not green either. Do you know why plants are green? The green substance in plants helps them to make their own food from water and gases in the air. Plants that do not have any green cannot make their own food. Therefore they must live on dead plants and animals. Some of these forms of bacteria and fungi even attack living plants and animals.

Are there any other ways in which food spoils? Sometimes we say that catchup "works." Do you know what that means? When catchup has spoiled, it has a sharp, sour taste. When things spoil in this way we say they ferment. Things which have sugar in them often spoil if left too long in a warm place, because they ferment. Still a third kind of plants cause things to ferment. They are called yeasts. Again, these plants are not always harmful, because yeast is used in making bread. The yeast acts on the sugar and starch in the flour of the bread and gives off bubbles of a gas called carbon dioxide. This gas blows the bread full of holes and makes it light.

Now that we know what causes our food to spoil, we should be able to find out how to keep it from spoiling. When bacteria were first discovered in decaying matter, people did not know where they came from and thought they made themselves. About eighty years ago scientists found that if they boiled meat broth, then put it into clean glass tubes, and then closed the tubes with cotton, the broth kept for long periods of time without decay. The boiling killed all the bacteria in the broth and on

E

the tubes, and the cotton prevented any bacteria from getting into the tubes to spoil the broth. The bacteria were filtered out by the cotton, just as they are filtered out of underground water by the soil and sand. This proved that bacteria came from the air.

In order to prevent food from spoiling, we must first be sure that all bacteria in it are killed, and then we must keep it away from the air until we are ready to use it. That is why food is kept in jars and tin cans. The food will keep without spoiling until after the can has been opened. We also try to keep food covered and wrapped as much as possible in order to keep bacteria and mold spores from getting into it. Bread wrapped in wax paper and milk in covered bottles are more likely to be clean than unwrapped bread and milk dipped from a pail or can.

There is one other way in which we might prevent food from spoiling. If we could prevent the plants from growing, even if they did get into the food, that would help. Where does your mother put the milk and butter to keep them? In the ice box, of course. You know that most plants do not grow well in cold places. Neither do bacteria, yeasts, or molds. So we put food in the ice box. The plants will grow much more slowly, and the food will not spoil so quickly.

Another way to prevent bacteria and yeasts from growing is to put a chemical in the food which will kill them. The only difficulty is that chemicals which will kill bacteria will also, unless care is taken, be harmful to people who eat the food. So just enough must be put in to preserve the food, but not enough to harm the people who eat it. The law forbids the use of some of these chemicals. Others may be used in only very small amounts, and the label on the bottle must tell how much is used. See if you can find a catchup bottle that tells what chemical and how much of it is used.

There are a number of different kinds of bacteria which produce poisons in food. Some of them do not even change the odor of the food. Sometimes the bacteria are in the food because the animal had a disease. Therefore it is important that animals used for food be inspected. To cook food thoroughly is the surest way of guarding against these bacteria, since cooking kills most of them. Food having any disagreeable odor (which usually means decay) should not be used. Such decay is most likely to occur during hot summer weather. Once in a while you may see in a store a can of food the end of which bulges outward. Never buy such a can. This means that the food has begun to decay. This decay forms gases, which press on the can and make the ends bulge outward.

One of the hardest foods to keep is milk. Bacteria cause milk to sour. Louis Pasteur, a great French scientist who found out a great deal about bacteria, worked out a way of preserving wine from spoiling. Pasteur found that moderate heating for about half an hour would kill most of the bacteria. This method is now used to keep milk from souring. In machinery made for the purpose, milk is held at a temperature between 142° and 145° F. for thirty minutes, then rapidly cooled

How milk is bottled after it has been pasteurized

to a temperature of 45° to 50° F. Such milk is said to be pasteurized and is usually free from disease bacteria.

We all know that milk is a good food; but, unfortunately, it can carry disease bacteria either from the cows or from the people who handle it. Some bacteria may even get into it while it is being carried from the cow to the place where it is used. Therefore great care must be taken to see that milk comes from healthy cows that are kept in clean barns. All pans, cans, and bottles used should be heated very hot to kill all bacteria. Then the milk should always be kept covered to prevent the entrance of more bacteria; and it should be kept cool to prevent the rapid growth of any bacteria that may be present. Whenever possible, one should avoid buying milk from open containers.

Things to Think About

1. What should you do to prevent food from spoiling?

2. Why should vegetables and fruits be washed before they are used?

3. How can you prove that air carries bacteria?

4. What do we mean by pasteurized milk?

5. In some states cattle are tested for tuberculosis. Why is this important?

6. Why is food heated before it is canned?

Things to Do

1. Should you like to make some mold gardens? Place a slice of bread on a plate, moisten it slightly, and let it stay exposed to the air for half an hour or so. Then cover the bread with a glass baking dish so that you can see what happens without disturbing it. Set it away in a warm, dark place. After a few days you will have a fine growth of mold. You may put small squares of bread into glass jars and treat them the same way. Try exposing them to the air at different places. If you find mold of several colors on one piece of bread, you may want to make "pure cultures"; that is, you may want to grow mold of only one kind. To do this, prepare a fresh piece of bread. With a needle or pin transfer some of the colored mold which you wish to grow to the prepared slice of bread. Then, if you keep it covered from the air all the time, only this one kind of mold spore will be on the bread, and you will have a growth of this one kind of mold.

2. Find out what part of the ice box is the coldest; the warmest. What is the best way to arrange different foods, such as milk, butter, eggs, vegetables, in the ice box?

3. Read the life of Louis Pasteur. How many things did he do that help us to fight disease?

4. Look at the labels on such food as catchup, preserved cherries, vinegar, and so on. Has any chemical, or preservative, been used? How much? Is the food artificially colored or flavored? Why are these things stated on the labels?

Problem 5 · How Diseases are kept from Spreading

Bacteria which cause diseases may spread in many ways if they are not checked. They are not often carried in the air or on clothing and books, as many people think, for most bacteria are destroyed by sunlight and dryness. However, if people cough or sneeze, they often spray droplets of moisture containing disease germs into the air, and these may be breathed into the nose, throat, and lungs of other people near them. Here there are favorable conditions of darkness, moisture, and warmth, and they will begin to grow, thus giving those people the disease.

Certain diseases, such as typhoid fever and tuberculosis, are sometimes carried by milk and water. Sometimes a cow has the disease; at other times the germs get into the milk in other ways. Some people, after having typhoid fever, do not again get the disease themselves, but they carry the germs around with them. Such a person is called a carrier. If he is working in a restaurant or a dairy, he may cause hundreds of cases of the disease, or a typhoid epidemic.

Many diseases are carried by insects. The fly has hairy, sticky pads on its feet. If it lights on a place where there are disease germs, it may carry them to some other place and transfer them to food which is eaten, thus starting the disease. Since flies increase, or breed, in decaying matter, they usually carry bacteria

415

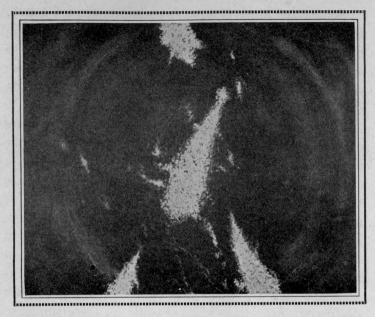

These bacteria grew from those carried by a fly
on its feet. They are seen through a microscope

with them. One kind of mosquito carries malaria; another kind carries yellow fever. In these cases the germs are not bacteria but protozoa, that is, small animals instead of small plants. These little animal germs live part of their lives inside the mosquito and part inside the blood of the person bitten by the mosquito.

The tsetse fly carries the germ which causes sleeping sickness, a disease which is greatly dreaded in Africa. Other insects besides the fly which carry germs stuck to their hair and feet are fleas, bedbugs, lice, and cockroaches.

Some other kinds of animals may carry disease germs. Rats have been especially troublesome. They go on board ships and thus carry disease from one country to another. Special rat guards are often attached to the mooring lines of a ship so that the rats cannot go on or off the ship.

You have learned that scientists and departments of health are taking every possible care to make our world a more healthful place in which to live. City water supplies are well cared for, and we can be almost sure that the water we drink is pure. Cows are tested for diseases, and only the milk from well cows is used. Most of the milk in the cities is pasteurized, so that good milk is provided. We are protected from diseases when the garbage and sewage are properly disposed of. Insects and rats are killed, and their breeding places are destroyed. Men have learned to do all these things to prevent the spreading of disease. But they have done more.

Scientists have learned another way to insure us of good health. You know that they first found out what causes diseases. Then they learned how to cure most diseases, and now they know actually how to prevent certain diseases from spreading and also how to prevent the disease itself.

Have you ever seen a small card on a house with the word *Measles* on it? If you read the card, you learned that someone in that house had measles. This card was a warning to you so that you would not expose yourself to the disease, that is, go near the person who had it. When people have certain diseases which you could "catch" from them, they are kept at home, and other people are kept away from them. We say that they are quarantined. This is to prevent disease from spreading to other homes. Sometimes, if people have been exposed to a disease, they too are quarantined to see if they have it. People are usually quarantined for smallpox, measles, scarlet fever, and diphtheria. By keeping such people at home, others are not exposed to the disease, and it does not spread from the people that have it.

Care is taken that diseases shall not spread from one country to another. Years ago, when ships entered certain seaports, they had to stay in the harbor for forty days to see if any diseases developed, before anyone was allowed to come ashore. Now, when a ship enters New York Harbor, it must stop awhile and take aboard inspectors, who examine the passengers before they are allowed to land. In these days, however, the delay is usually only a few hours. If persons are found to have a contagious disease,— that is, one that is "catching,"— they are taken off the boat and held in quarantine at Ellis Island.

These are some of the ways in which disease bacteria and protozoa are kept from spreading. But there are other things that doctors can do to prevent a person from catching a disease, even if he is exposed to it. Some people already have tiny things in their blood which kill the bacteria and prevent them from causing a disease. These tiny things in the blood are called

© Ewing Galloway

Ellis Island. People who have a contagious disease when they enter New York Harbor on a ship are kept in quarantine here

antibodies. If a person has these antibodies, he is said to be immune, which means that he will not take the disease. Some people are not naturally immune, and they are the ones the doctors can help. Doctors can cause antibodies to form in their blood.

Diphtheria is one disease which may be prevented in this way. First, doctors test you to see if you have the tiny antibodies in your blood. This is called the Schick test. Diphtheria bacteria give off a poison that is called a toxin. The doctor puts a small amount of pure toxin in your skin. If you have the antibodies, nothing happens. That means that you probably would not take the disease if you were exposed to it. In this case you do not need to take any further treatment. But if the place in your skin gets red after the toxin is put in, that means that you do not have antibodies in your blood and that you would probably take the disease if exposed. If the Schick test shows that you would take diphtheria, the doctor treats you to make you immune to it. He has a substance called toxin-antitoxin which he puts into your blood. This causes the antibodies to form, and this makes you immune to diphtheria. The treatment is very simple and is a protection against that disease.

However, a diphtheria toxin-antitoxin treatment does not make you immune to other diseases. Every disease that can be prevented has a method of its own for its prevention. You can be vaccinated against smallpox, or you can have treatments to prevent typhoid fever. These are the treatments which make you immune. Since scientists have learned how to inject substances into the blood of people and make them immune to smallpox, typhoid, and diphtheria, the number of cases of these diseases has decreased greatly.

Scientists are always working to find new or better ways of curing and preventing illness. If we take their advice, it will help us to keep well and strong. Science has freed us from the fear of many diseases.

We have seen in this book that man has changed his earth a great deal. He has improved it by means of inventions and discoveries; but perhaps the most important of all are his discoveries about how to make the world a more healthful place in which to live.

Things to Think About

1. Why was it so difficult to find out what caused diseases?

2. What can be done to prevent flies and other insects from carrying bacteria to our food?

3. How did mosquitoes affect the building of the Panama Canal?

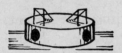 **Things to Do**

1. Look up the life of Dr. Jenner, and tell what he did to help to prevent disease.

2. Make a list of things that you can do to help make this world a more healthful place.

3. Do you stick pencils in your mouth, or do you bite your finger nails? Tell why this is not a good thing to do. Can you break this habit?

UNIT XV

The Future of the Earth and of Man

What will Man make of his Future?

THE FUTURE OF THE EARTH AND OF MAN

The record of the rocks tells you that during millions of years the earth and life on the earth have been changing. Do you suppose these changes have now come to an end? Or are the winds and waves still tearing down the hills and mountains? Is the frost splitting the rocks just as it did ages ago? Are continents rising and falling now just as they did when the reptiles covered the land? Do the seas creep in and recede even as they did when the earth was young?

All these changes are still taking place before our very eyes. Indeed, they are taking place more rapidly than ever before. This is because man has added his efforts to the forces of nature. He turns rivers from their courses. He irrigates the desert and clothes it with life. He chops down forests and builds great cities. He carries plants and animals from one country to another. He kills off whole species of animals. Such things as these have completely changed the conditions under which many plants and animals must live. It has been estimated that man is causing life on the earth to change ten thousand times as fast as it did before he came upon the scene.

What do these changes mean for the future? What is the world going to be like in time to come? What will become of man? Will he go on making new discoveries and inventions? What will he do with these discoveries and inventions? Will he conquer more diseases? Will he live longer? Will he be happier? Perhaps you have already thought about these and similar questions. We invite you to think about them now.

Problem · What will Man make of his Future?

The earth is old, and yet it is young. It is old, for it has existed for millions of years. It is young, for it will continue to exist for millions of years yet to come. During all these years to come astronomers believe that the sun will continue to give enough warmth to the earth for plants and animals to live upon it. They believe, too, that no disaster, such as a collision with a heavenly body, will happen to the earth for ages and ages.

Night will follow day, and season will follow season, as our planet continues to turn on its axis and to swing around the sun. It seems, therefore, that the future of the world is a long one. There will be plenty of time for all living things to change enormously. Our first thought is about the future of man. Will man improve, or will he sink back to where he was in the beginning?

Man himself has not existed very long as time is reckoned in the life of the world. If the entire history of the earth is thought of as being twenty-four hours long, man appeared only five or ten minutes ago.

Yet in this short time he has come out of the darkness of the caves and has become a questioner, or seeker after truth. We might call him the discoverer, because he alone of all living things on the earth can discover new things. He can do this because he can think. Man has learned that there are reasons for the darkness and the storms that frightened him. He learned to change

E   425

his ideas when he found that his old ideas were no longer true. He discovered fire and invented numbers and languages, learning to speak and write them. He made weapons and became a hunter instead of the hunted. He domesticated animals and plants and became a herdsman and a farmer. Each change added to his security and comfort. May we not expect future changes to do the same?

Through this ability to think, man has discovered new substances, such as iron, coal, petroleum, and rubber, and has made important uses of them. He has invented machines, by means of which he has developed power beyond anything known before. There is no reason to suppose that his ability to think will forsake him or that he will no longer discover and invent.

By constructing the microscope and the telescope, man has improved his sight. He has improved his hearing by the invention of instruments so delicate that he can hear the sap rising in the trees. In a way he has improved his hands by putting tools into them or by using machines instead of them. In the same way he has improved his legs by constructing new means of travel — means by which he exceeds the speed of any other creature. He has added to the power of his voice until it can be heard by thousands through the loud-speaker and by millions through the radio. Should man continue to discover and invent, what will be his future? Will he use these new discoveries and inventions for the good of mankind, or will he use them to make war and to destroy civilization?

Not all the changes which are now taking place are to the advantage of the human race. Some of them may even threaten man's continued life. It is certain that he is wasting his natural resources. For example, he is using the coal and oil of the earth thousands of times faster than nature can make it. He is destroying forests without replacing them. His food supply is threatened because in his crops he is taking from the soil certain substances needed for plant life. One of man's chief problems is to look ahead, to see that natural resources are not used up faster than they can be replaced; to keep the soil fertile; to invent new sources of power when those which cannot be replaced have been used. But the greatest problem of all is for man to learn how to use these natural resources and to preserve the beauty of the earth so that there will be food and happiness for everyone.

Thus you can see that there are many, many ways in which changes are going to take place in the life of human beings. Just what these changes will be, we cannot say, although we know that they will be very great. In a way, therefore, the authors cannot write this last unit. You must write it yourselves. The future is going to be what you and other boys and girls make it. If you do not write "The Future of the Earth and of Man" with your pens, you will at least take your part in it.

The problems which you face will be many and interesting. You will be able to face them with satisfaction and success only if you understand the great principles of science. You have just finished studying the last book in the series called Pathways in Science. When we gave the books that name we thought of science as a great region across which there were many paths. No doubt you will study science next year and very likely for a number of years after that. You will make more difficult journeys in the land of science — journeys where the paths are not so well trodden or perhaps where you have to make your own paths.

The present age is often called the Age of Science. The future in which you will live may be even more scientific. People are going to think more about science than ever before. You will want to take your part in the thought of the world by which you are surrounded. You will do your part by the things you do and think. Your part is important. As you study more about science, you and those of your time will be able to answer more wisely the problem of "The Future of the Earth and of Man."

Science Words

This list of science words and explanations may be used as a dictionary to help you in studying the problems suggested in this book. When you come to a new word, find the explanation of the word. It will help you to understand what you are reading.

The explanation for the words, given in this book, will not tell everything about the words that might be told. The authors have tried to give the kind of information that they thought will be most helpful to you now. In your later science work you will learn a great deal more about some of these words.

Some of these words you will find are very useful. You will want to learn to use them. See how many of these words you can use at home and at school.

Following the explanation, you will find the number of the page where the word is first used in the book. In the index you may find the numbers of other pages on which the word is used. You will also find following some of the words Roman numerals, such as III, IV, V. These numbers refer to other books of "Pathways in Science" in which these terms have been used.

Adapted. Plants and animals are more or less adapted to live in their natural homes. Fish live in water because of the way their bodies are made. Birds are able to fly (p. 139)

Adult. An animal is an adult when it is full-grown. A butterfly is an adult insect (p. 140; also in V)

Agate. A quartz rock which has its colors arranged in stripes, or bands (p. 101)

Aileron. The hinged part of the wing of an airplane which helps to turn and balance it (p. 384)

Air pressure. The pressure of the air. The usual air pressure is about fifteen pounds on each square inch at the surface of the earth (p. 371; also in III, IV, V)

Alkali. A very active chemical substance which is used with fat in the making of soap (p. 75)

Allosaurus. A kind of flesh-eating dinosaur (p. 151)

Alloy. Certain metals may form a close mixture called an alloy (p. 261)

Aluminum. One of the elements. A light, silvery-colored metal. Often used in kitchen utensils (p. 264; also in V)

Amber. Some trees give a sticky material, called resin. Amber is a fossilized resin (p. 287; also in V)

Amethyst. Purple quartz (p. 101)

Amphibia. A class of animals. Toads, frogs, salamanders, mud puppies, and newts are amphibians (p. 139; also in V)

Amphibian. An animal which belongs to the class of Amphibia (p. 139)

Ancestor. A forefather. Your grandparents and great-grandparents are your ancestors (p. 140)

Annual rings of growth. The circles, or rings, which mark the growth made by a tree every year. They may be easily seen on stumps (p. 172)

Anteater. A mammal which lives on ants (p. 162)

Anthracite. A kind of coal. Sometimes called hard coal (p. 137)

Antibodies. Substances in the blood which prevent the taking of certain diseases (p. 419)

Aquarium. A tank in which water and plants are kept (p. 209; also in IV, V)

Archæopteryx. An extinct bird (p. 156)

Armadillo. A burrowing animal whose head and body are protected by bony plates (p. 190)

Arthrodira. A kind of extinct fish (p. 125)

Asphalt lake. A large deposit of asphalt (p. 103)

Astronomer. A scientist who studies the stars and other heavenly bodies (p. 20; also in V)

Atmosphere. The gaseous part of the earth (p. 73; also in IV, V)

Atom. The smallest part of an element that takes part in a chemical change (p. 293)

Axis. A straight line around which a body may turn, or rotate. Both spinning tops and planets have an axis (p. 31)

Bacteria. Bacteria are tiny plants. They are so small that we need a microscope to study them (p. 114)

Barometer. An instrument which measures the pressure of the air (p. 374; also in IV, V)

Basalt. Rock made from lava which has cooled slowly on the surface of the earth (p. 98)

Battery. Two or more electrical cells connected together so as to operate some electrical device such as an electrical bell (p. 295)

Beetle. Some insects are beetles. A lady bug is a beetle (p. 218; also IV)

Binder. A machine for cutting and tying grain (p. 278)

Bituminous coal. A kind of coal, often called soft coal (p. 136)

Boll weevil. An insect whose larvæ destroy the cotton in the pod, or boll (p. 215)

Boric acid. A small white crystal. Sometimes a solution of it is used in the treatment of eye injuries (p. 102)

Breed. To raise living things, or to cause them to grow and develop (p. 393)

Brontosaurus. A kind of plant-eating dinosaur (p. 149)

Buoy. Things floating in water or other liquid are buoyed up by it (p. 150)

Caddis fly. An insect whose larvæ live in water and are protected by a case (p. 235)

Calcium. One of the elements. A soft, grayish metal. A large portion of our skeleton is calcium (p. 262; also in V)

Carbon. One of the elements. A black solid. Coal is largely carbon (p. 136; also in V)

Carbon dioxide. A colorless gas, a compound of carbon and oxygen. Soda water is carbon dioxide dissolved in water (p. 209; also in IV, V)

Caterpillar. *See* Larva.

Cell. Every living thing is made of cells as some houses are made of many bricks. These cells are too small to be seen without the help of a microscope (p. 108; also in V). The word is also used in reference to certain electrical devices, such as dry cells.

Cement. To bind particles of a substance together (p. 90)

Chemical action. The action which takes place when elements or compounds unite or separate. Rusting of iron and burning of wood are examples of chemical action (p. 267)

Chemicals. Substances. Often refers to the materials used to find out what things are made of. Limewater is a chemical which may be used to show that the breath contains carbon dioxide (p. 300)

Chlorine. One of the elements. A greenish-yellow gas. Salt is the compound formed when sodium burns in chlorine (p. 262; also in V)

Chlorophyll. The green coloring matter in plants (p. 252; also in V)

Circuit. Electricity flows in a circuit. In ringing a doorbell, electricity flows from the battery to the bell and back to the battery (p. 292)

Citrus-fruit fly. An insect whose larvæ destroy citrus fruit (p. 215)

Clay. Certain soil composed of very fine particles (p. 92)

Climate. We say that the climate is the kind of weather we have day after day and season after season. We live in a temperate climate (p. 128; also in V)

Club moss. A kind of plant. It is not a true moss (p. 131)

Cluster of stars. A group of stars so close together that they often seem to be one star unless seen through a telescope (p. 23)

Coal Age. An age of the earth in which dense vegetation covered much of its surface (p. 121)

Cobalt. One of the elements. Cobalt is used in making certain steels (p. 49; also in V)

Cobra. A poisonous snake of Asia (p. 228)

Cocoon. The silky shell, or case, spun by a larva (p. 218; also in II, III, IV, V)

Coil. A coil consists of several turns of wire (p. 300)

Cold-blooded. Animals whose bodies are of about the same temperature as the place they are in are said to be cold-blooded (p. 156; also in III, V)

Colony. A group of the same kind of plants or animals living together is called a colony of plants and animals (p. 126)

Combine. A machine which may cut, thresh, and sack grain (p. 279)

Comet. A body which travels around the sun. Comets have "tails," and their paths are somewhat egg-shaped (p. 40; also in V)

Compass. An instrument used to tell directions (p. 342; also in III, V)

Compound. A substance composed of two or more elements in definite proportions (p. 266)

Compound machine. A machine made of two or more simple machines. Bicycles and gasoline engines are compound machines (p. 276)

Condense. When small particles of a gas, as water vapor, gather together into larger particles, as fog or clouds, we say that the gas has condensed (p. 73; also in IV, V)

Conductor. A material along which electricity will flow is called a conductor (p. 293; also in IV, V)

Cone. The fruit of certain trees (p. 131; also in II)

Cone-bearing tree. A tree whose seeds are borne in cones (p. 131)

Conglomerate rock. A sedimentary rock made of sand and pebbles cemented together (p. 91)

Constellation. A group of stars. The ancients divided the sky into constellations (p. 23; also in V)

Constrictor snakes. Snakes which wind around their prey and crush them to death (p. 227)

Contagious disease. A disease which may be transferred by touching (p. 418)

Copper. One of the elements. One of the few metals found free in nature. This was the first metal used by primitive man (p. 261)

Copper sulfate. A solution of blue vitriol (often called blue stone) used in the manufacture of powders and solutions for killing insects (p. 102)

Copperhead snake. A poisonous American snake (p. 228; also in V)

Coral. Coral is formed out of the hard parts, or skeletons, of certain animals. Many islands are made largely of coral (p. 126)

Coral snake. A poisonous snake (p. 228; also in V)

Cordaites. A kind of tree, living in the Coal Age, now extinct (p. 131)

Cottony-cushion scale insect. An insect which destroys certain fruit trees (p. 211)

Cradle. A scythe with a wooden frame, used in harvesting grain (p. 278)

Crater. The opening, or mouth, of a volcano (p. 53)

Crystal. A small particle formed by very small particles joining and hardening together in regular order (p. 80)

Cultivation. The proper care of land so that crops may be grown (p. 214)

Culture. Scientists often grow bacteria in order to learn more about them. Such a growth is called a culture (p. 256)

Cycads. Certain kinds of plants are cycads (p. 169)

Cycle of water. Water evaporates from the surface of the earth, becoming water vapor in the atmosphere. Later the water vapor condenses. This constant evaporation and condensation that goes on all the time is called the water cycle (p. 398)

Deposit of minerals. A collection, or gathering, of minerals found in the earth (p. 66)

Descendant. You are the descendant of your grandparents and great-grandparents (p. 131)

Diabase. An igneous rock which has cooled below the surface of the earth (p. 99)

Diamond. Crystallized carbon. The hardest mineral known (p. 100)

Diaphragm. A thin, round piece of steel, in a telephone receiver, which can vibrate back and forth (p. 328)

Dinosaur. A group of reptiles that are now extinct. There were many kinds of dinosaurs during the Age of Reptiles (p. 147; also in III)

Diplodocus. A kind of plant-eating dinosaur (p. 148)

Dissolve. When a substance dissolves, it separates into such fine particles that each piece is between particles of the liquid. Salt dissolves in water (p. 75; also in III, IV, V)

Dry cell. One source of electrical energy (p. 297; also in IV, V)

Duralumin. An alloy of aluminum, copper, and other metals. It is light and almost as strong as steel (p. 383)

Earthquake. A sudden movement, or shaking, of the rocks of the earth (p. 68; also in IV)

Echo. Sometimes, when one shouts, one hears the sound come back after a few seconds. The return of a sound is called the echo. It is caused by sound waves being reflected back by a hill, building, or some other object (p. 320)

Eclipse. There are solar and lunar eclipses. During a solar eclipse the moon gets between the sun and the earth, and the moon throws a shadow on the earth. During a lunar eclipse the earth gets between the sun and the moon and throws a shadow on the moon (p. 27)

Eel. A kind of fish that is shaped somewhat like a snake (p. 123)

Elastic. Able to bend or stretch. A rubber band is elastic (p. 55; also in V)

Electric eel. A fish with an eel-like body that can give an electric shock (p. 232)

Electric generator. A machine which causes electricity to flow (p. 300)

Electric ray. A fish with a broad, flat body which can give an electric shock (p. 232)

Electrons. Tiny bits of electricity (p. 293)

Element. A substance which cannot be broken up into other kinds of substances (p. 261)

Eohippus. The name given to the first horse. *Eohippus* was the ancestor of the horse we know today (p. 183)

Epidemic. When many people in a certain region suffer from a certain disease, there is said to be an epidemic of the disease (p. 395)

Erosion. The carrying away, by wind or water, of soil and rocks (p. 67; also in IV, V)·

Eruption. The breaking out from a volcano of gases, water, vapor, dust, ashes, and lava (p. 60)

European corn-borer. A kind of insect whose larvæ destroy corn plants (p. 215)

Evaporate. When a liquid changes into a gas and passes into the atmosphere, as when water slowly disappears from a pan, we say the liquid has evaporated (p. 75; also in III, IV, V)

Exist. To live (p. 81)

Experiment. A way to discover new facts about the things about us (p. 10; also in V)

Expose. To display. Rocks that are covered by dirt are exposed if the dirt is taken away (p. 67)

Extinct. Anything which lived or was active at some time in the past but now is quiet or no longer exists is said to be extinct. Some volcanoes are extinct. They have not erupted in hundreds of years (p. 59; also in III)

Extinction. Becoming extinct (p. 128)

Fahrenheit (F.). Most of the thermometers in our homes and at school have the Fahrenheit scale. Water freezes at 32° and boils at 212° on the Fahrenheit scale. F. stands for Fahrenheit (p. 35; also in IV, V)

Fang. A hollow tooth, found in poisonous snakes, through which poison is forced into the victim (p. 229)

Feldspar. A mineral with a pearly appearance (p. 99)

Fern. A plant with broad, feather-like leaves, but no flower (p. 128)

Fertile. A fertile soil has plenty of material for plants to use in making food (p. 87)

Fiber. Material which can be made into threads (p. 279)

Filament. A fine wire inside electric-light bulbs (p. 304)

Filter. To purify by passing through a strainer, or filter. Water may be filtered through sand (p. 399)

Filtration plant. A number of tanks filled with layers of sand through which water is filtered (p. 403)

Fin. A thin part of the body of a fish which extends out into the water and which helps the fish to swim (p. 123)

Flowering plant. A plant which produces flowers. Many plants do not have flowers (p. 143)

Force of gravitation. A force or pull which two objects have for each other. If one object is large, as in the case of the earth, this pull is very strong (p. 31; also in IV, V)

Forecast. To predict, or tell, what is going to happen before it does happen (p. 374)

Formation. (1) An arrangement of rocks (p. 102). (2) A large group of moving objects acting together. Soldiers usually march in formation (p. 376)

Fossils. Any remains left by plants or animals long ago. They may be footprints or skeletons. From them can be learned many things about life long ago (p. 81; also in III)

Freeze. To change from liquid to solid. Water freezes at 32 F. (p. 67; also in II, III, IV, V)

Frictional electricity. A form of electricity made by rubbing two things together (p. 289; also in V)

Fungus. A plant which is not green. Fungus plants cannot make their food, but live on other plants or animals. Mushrooms are fungus plants (p. 253; also in IV, V)

Fuse. An electrical device inside of which there is a wire called a fuse wire, which melts easily. In case of a short circuit the heated fuse wire melts, thus preventing the electricity from flowing through the circuit (p. 306; also in IV)

Fuselage. The body of an airplane (p. 383)

Fuse wire. A wire which melts very easily and therefore may be used in fuses (p. 307)

Galaxy. A vast system of stars. Our sun is a star in a very large galaxy (p. 22)

Gas. A substance which spreads out, filling as much space as it can. Steam is a gas (p. 31; also in III, IV, V)

Gas engine. An engine driven by the energy of exploding gas. Usually this gas is a mixture of gasoline vapor and air (p. 282)

Germ. A living thing so small that it can be seen only with a microscope (p. 393)

Geyser. A sudden spurting or throwing of water into the air from a deep hole in the earth (p. 63; also in IV)

Gill. Oysters, fish, and tadpoles breathe the air in the water through their gills as many land animals breathe through lungs (p. 140; also in III, IV)

Ginkgo tree. A kind of tree, a descendant of trees of ancient ages (p. 174)

Glacial border. The edge of the glaciers during the Ice Age (p. 195)

Glacier. A mass of ice and snow which has collected in cold regions or high places. As more snow piles on top, it slowly moves forward, either melting in lower places or breaking off into the sea (p. 194; also in IV)

Glass snake. A kind of lizard with no legs whose tail comes off easily (p. 242)

Glider. A flying machine something like an airplane, but with no motor (p. 376)

Gnat. A small kind of mosquito (p. 218)

Gneiss. An igneous rock which usually contains mica, feldspar, and quartz minerals, in bands (p. 100)

Gold. One of the elements. A heavy metal, used for making jewelry because it does not combine readily with any elements (p. 261)

Gopher. A burrowing animal (p. 237)

Granite. An igneous rock which usually contains quartz, feldspar, and mica minerals (p. 91)

Helium. One of the elements. A light, colorless gas used in airships. It is called helium because it was first found in the sun (p. 264)

Hermit crab. A kind of crab which lives in empty shells (p. 232)

Horizontal stabilizer. An instrument for balancing the airplane. It is located at the tail (p. 384)

Horseshoe crab. A kind of animal with a turtle-like shell and a long tail which is found along the shores (p. 126)

Horsetail. A kind of plant (p. 130)

Hydrogen. One of the elements. A colorless, odorless gas. The lightest element known and for that reason the first gas to be used in airships. Because it easily takes fire many airships are now filled with helium (p. 264)

Ice Ages. At several times in the past large areas of the earth have been covered with thousands of feet of snow and ice. Such periods are known as ice ages (p. 194; also in IV, V)

Ichthyosaurus. A kind of flesh-eating dinosaur living in water (p. 153)

Identify. To recognize. One can identify rocks, plants, and animals if one knows them when one sees them and can tell what kind of rock, plant, or animal they are (p. 108)

Igneous rock. One of the three great classes of rocks. Igneous rocks were formed by heat. They were melted at one time, then cooled (p. 97)

Immune. To be immune is to be protected against a disease by a substance within the body (p. 419)

Incinerator. A furnace for burning garbage (p. 404)

Inclined plane. A kind of simple machine. Sloping roads are inclined planes (p. 275)

Inhabit. Certain animals live in certain regions, as kangaroos inhabit Australia (p. 123)

Insect. An animal whose body is divided into three parts. All insects have six legs. Houseflies are insects. There are thousands of different kinds of insects (p. 142; also in II, III, IV, V)

Insulator. A substance which does not carry electricity is an insulator (p. 296; also in IV, V)

Intelligence. Ability to learn (p. 242)

Invertebrates. Animals with no backbones, as jellyfish and insects (p. 123)

Iodine. One of the elements. A dark-gray solid, used chiefly in making iodine solution (p. 268)

Iron. One of the elements. A heavy metal. So many things are made of iron today that this is sometimes called the "Age of Iron" (p. 54)

Jellyfish. A soft-bodied, boneless animal living in sea water (p. 117)

Joint. The place where two bones of the body of an animal are joined (p. 127)

Kangaroo. A marsupial found in Australia, with long and strong hind legs and a long tail (p. 163)

King snake. A kind of constrictor snake (p. 228)

Laboratory. A room in which demonstrations or experiments may be made (p. 262)

La Brea Pits. Asphalt pits near Los Angeles in which bones of animals now extinct have been found (p. 191)

Larva (*plural*, **larvæ**). At one time, or stage, in the life of certain insects they look something like worms. Some larvæ are called caterpillars (p. 218; also in IV, V)

Lava. Molten rock which flows out of volcanoes or cracks in the earth's surface (p. 60; also in IV)

Lead. A metal; one of the elements (p. 261)

Lever. A kind of simple machine. The handle of a pump is a lever. A crowbar may be used as a lever (p. 273; also in I)

Light year. The distance light can travel in a year. Light travels 186,000 miles in one second. Astronomers sometimes speak of stars as being so many light years away (p. 18; also in V)

Lightning. An electrical discharge between clouds and the earth, between cloud and cloud, or between different parts of the same cloud (p. 287; also in V)

Limb. A leg, arm, or wing (p. 153)

Lime. A white or gray substance used with sand to make mortar and plaster. Sometimes it is used on gardens to improve the soil (p. 92; also in IV)

Limestone. A kind of sedimentary rock. Many times it is formed by the skeletons of animals that have died in the oceans (p. 92; also in II)

Lizard. Some reptiles are lizards. Most lizards have four legs and a long tail (p. 156)

Llama. A South American animal related to the camel (p. 188)

Loom. A machine for weaving cloth (p. 279)

Lunar eclipse. An eclipse of the moon. *See* Eclipse (p. 27)

Magnesium. One of the elements. A light, silvery metal used in some medicines and in making fireworks and flashlight powder (p. 262)

Magnet. That thing which has power to attract. There are several kinds of magnets: artificial, magnets made by man; bar, magnets shaped like a bar; electromagnets, magnets which owe their attractive power to the flow of electricity around them; horseshoe, magnets shaped like a horseshoe; natural, made from a certain kind of iron ore which has power to attract (p. 300; also in I, III, IV, V)

Magnetic lines of force. A magnet is often described as being surrounded by magnetic lines of force (p. 300)

Magnifying glass. Objects seen through a magnifying glass appear larger than they are (p. 99; also in II, IV)

Malaria. A disease caused by the bite of a certain kind of mosquito (p. 393; also in V)

Mammals. Animals whose young are fed on milk (p. 146; also in III, IV, V).

Mammoth. A large animal which lived a long time ago but is now extinct. A mammoth was something like an elephant (p. 185; also in III)

E

Many-celled. Made of many cells. Most living plants and animals that we know are made of many cells (p. 116)

Marble. A metamorphic rock made from limestone (p. 91)

Marsupial. A mammal whose young are carried about in a pouch by the mother. A kangaroo is a marsupial (p. 163)

Mastodon. A kind of animal related to the elephant. It is now extinct (p. 185)

Mediterranean fruit fly. A fly which has done much damage to fruit (p. 211)

Membrane. The skin stretched across a drum is a membrane. Many parts of our bodies are protected by coverings, or membranes (p. 153)

Mercury. A shiny metal which is a liquid at ordinary temperatures. It is an element (p. 261; also in II, V)

Metamorphic rock. One of the three great classes of rocks. A metamorphic rock has been changed by heat and pressure until it is no longer the same kind of rock that it was before the heat and pressure affected it (p. 95)

Metamorphosed. Changed (p. 96)

Meteor. A small object traveling in space. If it reaches the earth's atmosphere, the friction of the air makes it glow as a streak in the sky (p. 45; also in V)

Meteorite. A meteor which has fallen to the earth's surface (p. 47; also in V)

Mica. A flaky mineral with a shiny appearance (p. 96)

Mica schist. A schist which contains many flakes of mica (p. 96)

Microscope. An instrument which helps us to see very small objects (p. 108; also in III, IV)

Midge. A very small fly (p. 218)

Migration. Many animals, such as birds, migrate south in the autumn and north in the spring (p. 208; also in IV, V)

Mineral. A substance which is found in the earth (p. 99; also in IV, V)

Mold. A kind of fungus plant (p. 253; also in IV)

Molten rock. Rock which is melted and become a liquid (p. 55; also in IV)

Mongoose. An animal found in Asia (p. 228)

Moon. Some planets have more than one moon. The earth has but one (p. 5; also in II). *See* Satellite

Muck. Decayed material (p. 136)

Mushroom. A kind of fungus plant (p. 254; also in II)

Musk ox. A hoofed Arctic animal (p. 195)

Nectar. A sweet liquid formed in flowers. Bees make honey from nectar, and some other insects use nectar for food (p. 250; also in IV, V)

Newt. An animal much like a salamander (p. 140; also in V)

Nichrome. An alloy used in toasters and other electrical heating devices (p. 303)

Nickel. One of the elements. A hard, silvery metal. Used in plating other metals and, mixed with other metals, to make some of our coins (p. 261)

Nitrogen. One of the elements. A colorless, odorless, tasteless gas found in the air. It does not combine at ordinary temperatures with other elements. Nitrogen is one of the necessary plant foods (p. 260; also in IV)

Obsidian. A volcanic rock which has a smooth, glassy surface (p. 98)

Octopus. A sea animal with eight arms (p. 227)

One-celled. Made of one cell only. A number of simple plants and animals are only one-celled. They are so small that they cannot be seen without the help of a microscope (p. 113)

Orbit. The path, in the heavens, of a revolving body like a planet or comet (p. 46; also in V)

Oxygen. One of the elements. A colorless, odorless, tasteless gas found in the air. Oxygen combines readily with most elements to form many compounds (p. 209; also in IV, V)

Parasite. A plant or animal which lives on some other plant or animal (p. 209; also in V)

Particle. A very small piece of anything (p. 38; also in V)

Pasteurized milk. Milk which has been heated to about 145° F. for thirty minutes, then cooled rapidly (p. 412)

Peat. Decayed material which will burn (p. 136)

Petrify. To change into stone (p. 106)

Phosphorus. One of the elements. A poisonous substance. It burns readily. Used in making matches (p. 261)

Pistil. A part of a flower (p. 250)

Piston. Pistons are used in gas engines and in steam engines. They are the sliding parts which are pushed by the exploding gas in gas engines and the expanding steam in steam engines (p. 363 ; also in IV)

Piston rod. The rod, fastened to the piston, which moves the piston back and forth (p. 363 ; also in IV)

Pitch. A thick, sticky material found in some trees (p. 172)

Plague. A deadly disease (p. 395)

Planet. A large body revolving around the sun. Venus and the earth are planets (p. 20 ; also in V)

Platinum. One of the elements. A heavy, silvery metal used for making jewelry because it does not combine readily with other elements (p. 268)

Platypus. An egg-laying mammal (p. 160)

Poison sac. A holder, or sack, in the roof of the mouth of poisonous snakes (p. 229)

Polestar. A star in the northern sky toward which the axis of the earth seems to point (p. 24)

Pollen. The yellow dust found in flowers (p. 250; also in IV, V)

Pore. A small opening. Animal and plant skins have many pores which can be seen only with a microscope (p. 86)

Potassium. One of the elements. A very light metal. Used in making some medicines. Potassium is a necessary plant food (p. 262)

Pressure. A heavy or strong pushing against something (p. 59)

Prey. Certain animals are the prey, or food, of other animals (p. 225)

Primitive. Simple, crude. Early. The first plants and animals were primitive ones. They lived in the very early times (p. 131)

Primitive man. The ancient people, living thousands of years ago, had few tools and lived in a simple way. We say that that long-ago time was the time of primitive man (p. 271)

Protozoa. One-cell animals. Protozoa are the most simple animals (p. 393)

Pterodactyl. A kind of flesh-eating flying dinosaur (p. 153)

Pudding stone. A conglomerate rock (p. 92)

Puff ball. A kind of fungus plant (p. 253)

Pulley. A kind of simple machine. Pulleys are frequently used to lift heavy objects (p. 275)

Pupa (*plural*, **pupæ**). At one time, or stage, in the life of an insect it rests in a shell or skin. This stage is known as the pupal stage, and the insect is called a pupa (p. 218; also in V)

Python. A constrictor snake (p. 228)

Quarantine. To place or keep a person suffering from a contagious disease in a separate building or district so that the disease may not be caught by others (p. 418)

Quartz. A very hard, glassy mineral (p. 98; also in II, V)

Quartzite. A metamorphic rock made of sandstone (p. 96)

Radio. A means of sending messages by electrical waves without connecting wires (p. 334)

Radioactive. Some substances such as radium give off light and heat and are called radioactive (p. 66)

Radium. One of the elements. A rare metal used in the treatment of diseases (p. 59)

Rattlesnake. A poisonous snake with rattles attached to its tail (p. 228)

Reaper. A machine for cutting grain (p. 278)

Receiver. The part of the telephone which changes the electrical energy to sound waves, so that they may be heard by the ear (p. 327)

Reflect. To turn back. A mirror reflects light (p. 21; also in III, V)

Regulator. Something which regulates, or controls. A heat regulator regulates the temperature (p. 16; also in V)

Reproduce. To have young. If living things did not reproduce, there would be no more life on earth (p. 214)

Reptile. A cold-blooded crawling animal (p. 147; also in III, V)

Revolve. To turn around an object, as the earth revolves around the sun (p. 13)

Rivals. Animals which want the same food are rivals of each other (p. 225)

Rock drill. A machine which can drill holes in rock or concrete (p. 400)

Rotate. To turn or spin around an axis. A spinning top and the earth rotate (p. 31; also in IV, V)

Rudder. The device by which ships or airplanes are steered (p. 384)

Rust. A compound of iron and oxygen (p. 267)

Sago. A kind of starch (p. 170)

Salamander. A small kind of amphibian (p. 140; also in V)

Satellite. An object revolving around a planet. Our moon is a satellite of the earth (p. 35)

Schist. A metamorphic rock made from shale or slate (p. 96)

Scientist. A person who studies plants, animals, rocks, the earth, or the stars and finds out things that no one knew before (p. 12; also in III, IV, V)

Scorpion. A kind of invertebrate animal (p. 126).

Screw. A kind of simple machine. Wood screws are examples (p. 276)

Screw propeller. A device with blades which can be used to drive a ship or airplane (p. 354)

Scythe. A tool for cutting grain or hay (p. 278)

Sea anemone. An invertebrate sea animal whose mouth is surrounded by arms for getting food (p. 229)

Sea lion. A kind of large seal (p. 190)

Sea urchin. A small sea animal protected by a shell and spines (p. 234)

Sediment. When a swift-moving stream flows along, it usually picks up small rocks, sand, and dirt. Later the stream may deposit it somewhere. All this material is called sediment (p. 89)

Sedimentary rock. One of the three classes of rocks. Sedimentary rocks are made from sediment which has been pressed and hardened and cemented together (p. 89)

Seismograph. An instrument which makes a record of earthquakes (p. 70)

Sequoia. A kind of evergreen tree (p. 172)

Sewage. The waste material carried in sewer pipes (p. 395)

Shale. A sedimentary rock formed out of clay (p. 92)

Shooting star. *See* Meteor

Short circuit. When the insulation is worn off of electric wires, the electricity does not complete its circuit through the electric iron or other electric device but makes a short circuit by taking the shortest path back (p. 306)

Shrew. A mouselike animal which lives in the earth, feeding on worms and insects (p. 237)

Sickle. A tool for cutting grain or grass (p. 278)

Silicon. The second most abundant element, found chiefly in the earth's crust (p. 265)

Silver. One of the elements. A heavy, whitish metal, used for coins, jewelry, and photographic films (p. 261)

Sloth. A mammal living in the forests of South and Central America which hangs upside down by its feet while feeding on tree leaves (p. 186)

Sodium. One of the elements. A soft, silvery metal. It is found chiefly in salt (p. 262)

Solar eclipse. An eclipse of the sun (p. 27). *See* Eclipse

Solar system. The sun and all the bodies and their satellites which revolve about it form the solar system (p. 15; also in V)

Sound waves. The vibrations which can be heard (p. 316)

Space. The earth and the stars are traveling in space (p. 16)

Species. When a number of plants or animals are of the same kind, they are said to belong to the same species (p. 174)

Spider. An eight-legged animal with two main body parts (p. 229)

Spore. Some plants do not have seeds but grow from spores. Spores are very small (p. 129; also in IV, V)

Stamen. A part of a flower which produces the pollen (p. 251)

Star. A glowing mass of gas. Every star is a sun (p. 5; also in II, III, IV, V)

Static electricity. *See* Frictional electricity

Steam. Water vapor produced by boiling water. Steam is invisible (p. 64; also in II, IV)

Steam turbine. A kind of steam engine in which the steam is forced against a wheel with many blades (p. 354)

Stegosaurus. A kind of plant-eating dinosaur (p. 151)

Sulfur. One of the elements. A yellow substance used in making matches and in medicine, and in making sulfuric acid,—the acid used in automobile batteries (p. 261)

Sun. A glowing mass of gas, around which the earth and the other planets revolve. We receive light and heat from our sun. Stars are suns (p. 16; also in II, III, IV, V)

Tapir. A hoofed animal with short legs and long snout, found in South and Central America (p. 192)

Tarnish. A compound formed by chemical action. Silver often becomes tarnished by uniting with sulfur (p. 267)

Telescope. A tube containing lenses which is used to view distant objects (p. 12; also in III, V)

Tide. The regular rise and fall of the water along the shores of the ocean (p. 31; also in V)

Tin. One of the elements. A silvery metal which is frequently used as a protective coating for other metals (p. 261)

Toadstool. A kind of fungus plant (p. 254)

Toxin. A kind of poison which is formed in animals when they are sick with certain diseases (p. 419)

Toxin-antitoxin. A substance put in the blood which causes antibodies to form in the blood (p. 420)

Transmitter. The mouthpiece of the telephone, into which we talk (p. 327)

Triceratops. A kind of plant-eating dinosaur (p. 151)

Trilobite. An extinct sea animal (p. 118)

Tungsten. A hard, heavy, gray metal element used for making electric-light filaments (p. 304)

Tuning fork. A piece of steel shaped something like a fork. It vibrates when struck, giving a certain tone (p. 319)

Tyrannosaurus. A kind of flesh-eating dinosaur (p. 153)

Underground water. Water which flows in layers of soil or porous rock below the surface of the earth (p. 398; also in IV, V)

Universe. This world, our sun, and the farthest star are all part of the universe. Sometimes used to include only one system, or galaxy, of stars (p. 10)

Vaccinate. People can be made to be immune against some disease by vaccinating them (p. 420)

Vacuum. Space with nothing in it (p. 291; also in V)

Valve. A sort of door in a tube which opens and closes readily. Valves are used in steam and gas engines (p. 350)

Vent. An opening (p. 64)

Vertebrates. Animals with backbones. Horses, fish, and man are vertebrates (p. 123)

Vertical fin. An instrument to help keep an airplane in a straight path (p. 384)

Vibration. A rapid movement back and forth. Violin strings vibrate, and so do drums when they are beaten. All sound is caused by vibration of the air (p. 54). *See also* Sound waves

Volcanic action. The work of volcanoes (p. 63)

Volcanic glass. *See* Obsidian

Volcano. A mountain from which gas, ashes, and molten rock are erupted (p. 41; also in IV, V)

Walrus. A kind of sea animal something like the seal (p. 190)

Warm-blooded. Animals whose bodies remain at the same temperature all the year are said to be warm-blooded (p. 156; also in III, V)

Water moccasin. A poisonous water snake (p. 228)

Wedge. One of the simple machines (p. 276)

Wheel and axle. A kind of simple machine. Egg-beaters and pencil-sharpeners are examples of the wheel-and-axle machine (p. 274)

Yeast. A kind of fungus plant (p. 253)

Zinc. One of the elements. A bluish metal which is used as a protective coating for iron. Such iron is known as galvanized iron (p. 261)

Index

Key to the Sounds

ă *as in* at
ā *as in* ate
ä *as in* arm
ĕ *as in* bet
ē *as in* be
ē̇ *as in* her

ĭ *as in* bit
ī *as in* bite
ŏ *as in* got
ō *as in* go
ô *as in* horse
oi *as in* oil

o͞o *as in* food
ŭ *as in* us
ū *as in* use
ŋ *as in* ink
th *as in* bathe
zh *like the* s *in* pleasure

451